The Essential
AENEID

Virgil

The Essential
AENEID

Translated and Edited by
Stanley Lombardo

Introduction by
W. R. Johnson

Hackett Publishing Company, Inc.
Indianapolis/Cambridge

11 10 09 08   2 3 4 5 6 7

For further information, please address:

Hackett Publishing Company, Inc.
P. O. Box 44937
Indianapolis, IN 46244-0937

www.hackettpublishing.com

Cover design by Abigail Coyle and Brian Rak

Interior design by Meera Dash and Elizabeth L. Wilson

Composition by William Hartman

Printed at RR Donnelley

Library of Congress Cataloging-in-Publication Data

Virgil.
    [Aeneis. English. Selections]
    The essential Aeneid / Virgil ; translated and edited by
Stanley Lombardo ; introduction by W.R. Johnson.
        p. cm.
    Abridged edition of Lombardo's translation of the
Aeneid, published in 2005.
    Includes bibliographical references.
    ISBN 0-87220-791-9 — ISBN 0-87220-790-0 (pbk.)
    1. Aeneas (Legendary character)—Poetry. 2. Epic poetry,
Latin—Translations into English. I. Lombardo, Stanley, 1943-
II. Title.
    PA6807.A5L583 2006
    873'.01—dc22
                                                    2005022889

    ISBN-13: 978-0-87220-791-2 (cloth)
    ISBN-13: 978-0-87220-790-5 (pbk.)

Contents

BLACK SEA

THRACE

Aeneadae

MACEDONIA

roceraunia

Troy (Ilium)
▲ *Mt. Ida*

Tenedos

PHRYGIA

THESSALY

ASIA MINOR

E P I R U S
(CHAONIA)

*AEGEAN
SEA*

MAEONIA

throtum

LYDIA

Actium
odona

EUBOEA

Leucas

BOEOTIA

Delos

Zacynthus

ARCADIA

Strophades

Cyclades

Cythera

Mt. Ida ▲ Pergamum

CRETE

0   100   200 mi

0   100   200   300 km

Note on the Latin Text

This translation is based on the Oxford text of R. A. B. Mynors. I have consulted the commentaries of T. E. Page and R. D. Williams, and occasionally I have adopted their readings. It was once the custom to begin the *Aeneid* with four introductory lines (first quoted by Suetonius, now rejected by most editors), placing the *Aeneid* in the context of Virgil's earlier works, the *Eclogues* and *Georgics*, so that the poem opened as follows:

I am the poet who once tuned his song
On a slender reed and then leaving the woods
Compelled the fields to obey the hungry farmer,
A pleasing work. But now War's grim and savage
Arms I sing. . . .

Introduction*

The *Aeneid* is an epic poem about the destruction of civilizations and their resurrections. Its insistence on the human capacity to hope, even when—especially when—that hope is tested on the brink of ruin, lends the poem what many have felt to be its universality and has enabled it to exercise its hold on the imagination of the West for just over twenty centuries. Yet Virgil's epic is no simple tale of hope and triumph. Most epics concern themselves with celebrating the defeat of the enemies who had threatened doom to the community for which the epic poet composes his victory poem, and the *Aeneid,* in this regard, resembles other specimens of its genre. But in constructing his celebration of Rome's empire, Virgil never loses sight of the huge costs of the victory he is praising and never forgets that most winners were once losers. Impressed by this steady emphasis on suffering and loss, some readers of the poem feel that its representations of imperial glory tend to be overshadowed by an opposing tragic vision. What fuels the poem, however, is neither triumphalism nor defeatism but its pervasive tension between exaltation and lament. This severe dialect—a counterpoint of defeat and triumph, abjection and salvation, death and rebirth—is the *Aeneid*'s mainspring. The steady equipoise of this double vision arms the *Aeneid* with its unique power to comfort as well as disturb readers even today.

The enduring appeal of this epic over the past two millennia is easy to appreciate. Spend an hour or so leafing through the pages of *The Times Atlas of World History* and you will quickly be reminded of how, from the earliest days to the present, the boundaries of the tribes and nations of Europe (and elsewhere) are continually and sometimes radically erased, renegotiated, redrawn—by invasion, by civil war, by "barbaric" incursions. The peoples of Europe have always understood what it means to be displaced and exiled, to be conquered, to be an immigrant or an émigré, to lose one's homeland and to search, desperately, for a new one. To such readers down the centuries, the closing verses of Book 2—where Aeneas, the epic's hero, prepares to lead the survivors of burning Troy to safety—have always spoken with an incomparable and poignant clarity:

---

*An expanded version of this Introduction first appeared in Virgil, *Aeneid* (Hackett Publishing Company, 2005).

I was surprised by the great number
Of new arrivals I found, women and men,
Youth gathered for exile, a wretched band
Of refugees who had poured in from all over,
Prepared to journey across the sea
To whatever lands I might lead them. . . .
There was no hope of help. I yielded
And, lifting up my father, sought the mountains.
                              (2.942–47, 951–52)

Yet it is not for the dispossessed alone that this passage has extraordinary resonance; any student of human history knows that Aeneas' speech represents an event all too familiar in human experience and captures an unhappy truth of the human condition: however secure the present may seem, our deepest intuitions— from ancestral memories to the collective consciousness—recognize our communities to be fragile, vulnerable, contingent.

Aeneas is, to be sure, a quintessentially Roman hero in a Roman epic that glorifies the rebirth of a new and better Rome. But if his being a Roman hero were more important than his being a human being, he and his poem would never have managed to transcend the collapse of the Roman Empire and then find a steady welcome in civilizations that replaced it. For diverse readers in very different times, Aeneas has functioned as a sort of epic Everyman, one who escapes by the skin of his teeth from being dispatched on what Hegel would call "the slaughter bench of history" and thereby comes to incarnate the capacity of human beings to endure existence on the brink of ruin—and then to begin again and to flourish. If the tribes and nations of Europe had not kept discovering their need for his story and its message, Aeneas and his poem would long since have joined the many other texts from ancient Rome (and Greece) that have vanished into oblivion or, even if extant, have gone from being revered to ignored—and then all but forgotten.

But for all its appeal to diverse individuals, tribes, and nations over the past two thousand years, it is no accident that the *Aeneid* had its origins in a very particular set of circumstances at a very special moment. As he set about composing his epic, Virgil seized upon a specific cluster of thoughts and feelings about triumph, salvation, and thanksgiving shared by his first readers. This shared outlook had its roots, in turn, in a series of momentous events that took place throughout the century preceding the decade Virgil devoted to writing the *Aeneid* (29–19 B.C.E.). The stability of Rome and of its empire had been shaken by a steady series of civil wars and by the increasingly violent erosion of its political and social institutions. For many observers, eloquently spoken for by the historians Sallust and Livy, a prime cause of this incremental deterioration was the very success that crowned Rome's imperial expansions in the two centuries before the birth of Christ. From this perspective, Rome's blessings were its curse, and its prosperity seemed to generate irreparable damage to its values and its ideals by prompting, particularly among its leaders, a culture of greed and harmful competition—one that left its political, military, economic, and social traditions in shreds. These vicious tendencies spiraled to what seemed their final implosion when Julius Caesar fought his civil war with Pompey and his allies (49–45 B.C.E.); yet they degenerated even further when, after a decade of turbulence and confusion, Marc Antony (Caesar's second-in-command) and Octavian (his grandnephew) fought their own civil war (32–30 B.C.E.); they were finally extinguished only when Octavian, soon to become Augustus, vanquished his adversary and thereafter gradually constructed a throne for himself out of the ruins of what had once been a republic. As monarch of Rome and its empire, Octavian-Augustus was able to impose on his vast realm a stability that was as secure as it was welcome. The Romans and the nations they had conquered sighed with relief. The time was ripe for a monumental epic poem that memorialized their deliverance and gratitude.

Beyond any claims to universality—and centuries after the passing of the historical conditions that gave rise to the epic that celebrates him—Aeneas still enjoys his original renown as the ideal Roman hero. As such he symbolizes (scandalously to some, among them that great reader of the *Iliad,* Simone Weil) the might and right of the Roman Empire just as it was nearing its zenith around the time of Christ's birth. Not surprisingly then, in periods when rulers feel called on to assert their kinship with the Roman Empire and its divinely chosen emperors, this purely Roman Aeneas, rather than his Everyman twin, seems to offer them a powerfully iconic validation. But the figure of Aeneas finds its essential poetic truth not in its value as political propaganda but in the man's capacity to survive, to endure, to cherish good hope. His particular greatness is rooted in his ferocious resolve to win salvation for his people, in the selfless determination that no obstacle thrown in its way can undo. Nevertheless, for all his heroism, he isn't too good to be true. What finally wins him our trust is his troubled humanity. Aeneas is no bloodless, self-righteous automaton. We see him in moments of brooding self-doubt and even near despair. Like Moses, another hero who leads his people to a promised land whose blessings he will not live to enjoy, Aeneas has enough in the way of human error to lend him a surprising verisimilitude. More so than with most epic heroes, his story of escape and struggle, of a fearsome journey's good end rings true; despite his larger-than-life virtues and all the divine guidance he receives, he is sufficiently vulnerable, sufficiently (to paraphrase Housman) "a stranger and alone in a world he never made" that we can see something of him in us and of us in him.

The Legend of Aeneas in Homer's *Iliad*

According to the legends that grew up about the Trojan War (which took place roughly twelve centuries before the birth of Christ), a great army of Greeks laid siege to the city of Troy, determined to avenge the abduction (or seduction) of Helen, Queen of Sparta, and to restore her to her husband. Homer's *Iliad*, his monumental epic treatment of these legends, takes place toward the end of the war's tenth and final year, but it ends before the Greeks take and burn the city to the ground, slaying all but a few of its males and making slaves of most of its women. Aeneas is one warrior who survives this catastrophe, preserved by fate for a high, mysterious calling.

But despite his being thus singled out, and although in the catalog of Trojan forces in Book 2 of the *Iliad* he is listed second only after Hector, the city's greatest champion, Aeneas plays a relatively small and somewhat ambiguous role in the epic. Aeneas makes a memorable appearance in Book 5, where, having encountered Diomedes in battle and having been wounded by him, he is rescued by his mother, the goddess Aphrodite (Virgil's Venus), and then, when she fails in her efforts to rescue him, by the god Apollo, who pronounces him "a man . . . honored as much as Hector" (*Iliad* 5.505),** an estimate of his value we find echoed when he next appears, in Book 13. There, when Deïphobus, seeking to take vengeance on the killer of a comrade, goes looking for Aeneas to help him, he finds him "in the rear, the last man there, / Angry as always at Priam, / Who utterly failed to honor his worth" (*Iliad* 13.477–79). When Aeneas moves against him, Idomeneus asks his comrades

---

**Quotations from the *Iliad* and the *Odyssey* are from the translations of Stanley Lombardo.

for help, describing Aeneas as "a hell of a fighter / And in his prime" (*Iliad* 13.505–6). Soon after this, though Aeneas fights for a while with genuinely Homeric gusto, he fades into the blur of the carnage. Finally, in Book 20, Aeneas briefly shares the full spotlight with the Greek's fiercest warrior, Achilles himself, whom he challenges to single combat. Undeterred by Achilles' stinging insult ("Even if you kill me / Priam's not going to hand his kingship to you. / He has sons of his own, and he's not senile yet," *Iliad* 20.188–90), Aeneas answers him with a long piece of bravado, but his spear fails to pierce Achilles' shield, and he is about to suffer a fatal retaliation by Achilles when he is spirited away from death by Poseidon (Virgil's Neptune), who justifies his intervention to other gods by describing Aeneas as "a guiltless man" who "has always / Pleased the gods in heaven with his offerings," and who, further, is destined to get out of Troy alive in order to build a new Troy elsewhere, over which he and his progeny will rule (*Iliad* 20.302–14). These verses explain why Aeneas, almost alone of the Trojan heroes, escapes Troy's doom, and they define the qualities that will henceforth define his character: he is innocent (that is, not guilty of crimes in the eyes of the gods) and he is pious (that is, unlike most men, who sometimes forget or botch their devotion to the gods, Aeneas offers his sacrifices to them with scrupulous reverence). That such a paragon is marked for a special destiny is hardly surprising.

Juno, Jupiter, Fate, and Fortune

In the *Iliad*, Juno's Greek counterpart Hera hates the Trojans as much as she loves the Greeks, so it is only to be expected that she will continue persecuting Aeneas in his own epic. She is also the patroness of Carthage, Rome's arch-rival in the race for empire after the death of Alexander the Great. And, of course, she tends to dislike heroes in general (see, for example, her vindictive torment of Heracles in Euripides' play of that name, lines 815–85). Her hatred, then, of Aeneas and his Trojans is multiply determined (see her wonderful opening tirade with its laundry list of grievances), and it is not merely a catalyst of epic action (like Apollo's in the *Iliad*; *Iliad* 1.10–15), nor is it temporary (like Poseidon's in the *Odyssey*; *Odyssey* 5.282–92, 380ff.; 9.522–30; 13.129–70): Juno's insatiable wrath is so pervasive that it comes to seem the poem's spine, its very plot.

Juno opens the poem, and she all but closes it. After her angry speech in Book 1, she immediately arranges for the storm at sea in

which Aeneas and his Trojans almost drown; in Book 2, she is
prominent among the gods who participate, in person and glee-
fully, in the destruction of Troy; Book 4 finds her colluding with
her enemy, Aeneas' mother, Venus, to keep Aeneas with Dido in
Carthage, thus preventing him from sailing off to Italy and found-
ing there a new Troy (Venus wants only to assure him temporary
safety in Carthage). In Book 5, as he nears his goal, Juno tries in
vain to engineer the burning of his ships. But it is in Book 7, when
Aeneas has completed his wanderings and has begun to establish
himself, that, acknowledging that all her efforts have proved futile,
her celestial rage turns hellish:

> But if my powers
> Are not great enough, why should I hesitate
> To seek help from any source whatever?
> If I cannot sway Heaven, I will awaken Hell!
> I concede Aeneas the rule of Latium,
> And Lavinia is his bride by iron fate,
> But to draw it out and delay the issue,
> That I may do, and destroy both nations.
>
> (7.378–85)

She understands well enough that she cannot truly alter fate, but
she knows she can still cause countless deaths among the Trojans
and Latins who are destined to be united, which means that she is
in effect fomenting a civil war (a pattern that will endure through
the centuries until, under Augustus, Rome and the Italians are, in
Virgil's lifetime, united once and for all). Her vindictiveness has
now grown so great that, thwarted from achieving any genuine
goal, she is committed to doing evil for the sake of evil. For this
purpose she summons Allecto, one of the Furies, from hell and
commands her to start a war between the Latins and the Trojans:
this Allecto proceeds to do with a joyful, demonic efficiency. It is
this perverted divinity and her handmaid from hell who are ulti-
mately responsible for what happens throughout the rest of the
poem, and it is she who, having dismissed Allecto and sent her
back to hell, becomes Discord incarnate as she flings open the
Gates of War. Having set her gratuitously evil project in motion,
Juno is relatively quiet in Books 8 through 11, but she makes a
spectacular reappearance in Book 12, where she once again man-
ages to disrupt a new treaty between the opposing sides and to
reactivate the (internecine) slaughter.

At last Jupiter persuades Juno to cease and desist her lethal med-dlings. He appeals to her vanity, he promises her that the Romans will come to accord her extraordinary worship. In short, he buys her off. She quickly concedes, letting her resentments go (12.996–1008). Or so it seems. Roman readers would have no trouble remembering that, despite her nominal capitulation, in the centu-ries to come she would side with Carthage against Rome in three wars. Her seeming conversion arises less from Jupiter's powers of persuasion than from narrative expediency: it is time for the story to end, for Aeneas to win, and for Turnus to die. But Juno's sub-mission and Jupiter's success in achieving it in no way answer the questions that Virgil had asked Jupiter a few hundred verses back:

> What god could now unfold for me
> So many bitter deaths, which poet could tell
> Of all the captains who met their many dooms
> Driven over the plain now by Turnus,
> Now by the Trojan hero? Did it please you,
> Jupiter, that nations destined to love
> In everlasting peace should clash so harshly?
>   (12.612–18)

This question about divine justice echoes another question, also unanswered, at the very beginning of the poem:

> Muse, tell me why the Queen of Heaven
> Was so aggrieved, her godhead so offended,
> That she forced a man of faultless devotion
> To endure so much hardship. Can there be
> Anger so great in the hearts of gods on high?
>   (1.12–16)

Both in the question to Jupiter and in the poem's final scenes, Virgil's presentation of theodicy remains clouded in a sinister uncertainty.

One thing Juno clearly represents in the *Aeneid* is fortune (a word often connected with her). As a poetic concept she stands for—and in the poem's narrative she produces—accidents, contin-gencies, bad luck. She utterly opposes the ordinances of providen-tial fate and contrives whenever possible to derail them—the more violently the better. In contrast, Jupiter represents, in an ambiguous, not wholly satisfying fashion, the power of providential fate, the justice and benevolence that supply the foundations for whatever is decent in the human condition. (Tribal god that Jupiter is, he also represents, of course, an incontestable validation of the Roman Empire.) The power of Juno's fortune cannot triumph over the power of Jupiter's fate, but (as Virgil's anguished question in Book 12 insinuates) Jupiter's fate cannot truly restrain the powers of darkness that Juno and her tamperings with fortune can unleash. One can argue, as the poem's denouement yearns to do, that all the accidents and contingencies, all the rotten, wretched luck that she invents, are, to recall the formulation of Alexander Pope, no more than "partial evils" that contribute to and are eventually gathered into a "universal good." But it is equally plausible that the bad contingencies are as real as they are prevalent and powerful, and that the providential wisdom that claims to transform them into itself is as likely as not to be a "noble lie," an illusion, a fiction useful when the tribe comes to (re)write its history, its victor's version of "how it happened." Seen in this latter way, Juno and Jupiter are evenly matched, and Virgil's divine machinery reveals a tragic dialectic at the heart of history, one that has room both for glory and for the voices of the vanquished and the oppressed.

Aeneas the Wanderer

In the first six books of the *Aeneid,* its hero replicates, in highly condensed form, the travels of the *Odyssey's* cunning, adventuresome, seriocomic hero. During the welcoming feast given him by Queen Dido of Carthage, Aeneas reluctantly yields to her request to hear about the fall of Troy and his search for the new homeland that numerous omens and prophecies have promised him. In Book 2 he recounts how the treacherous Greeks captured Troy, then indulged themselves in a savage spree of murder, looting, and burning. Troubled by these painful memories, he yet manages to tell of how he was barely able to rescue his son, his aged father, and his household gods and to lead them, together with the rest of the survivors, away from Troy into what turned out to be seven years of dangerous, baffling, and futile voyages. What most characterizes these self-narratives is their extraordinary self-effacement, a style of speech that is exactly counter to the fertile, energetic self-promotion that marks the stories effortlessly spun by Odysseus (that peerless confidence-man) whenever he finds it necessary or possible to recount or embellish or fabricate his adventures. The reader who remembers and expects here the swaggering brio of Aeneas' model in this section of the poem may be surprised and even disappointed by Aeneas as storyteller and hero of his own tale (in his *ABC of Reading*, Ezra Pound sketches a disgruntled reader who cries out in his exasperation: "Aach, a hero, him a hero? Bigod, I t'ought he waz a priest."). But however unheroic they may first strike us as being, Aeneas' laconic utterance and genuine humility are qualities of style and character that Aeneas manifests throughout his epic: here, precisely, the style is the man.

Our first impression of Aeneas in Book 1, when he is terrified that his ships are about to be sunk in the storm Juno has arranged for his destruction, is hardly auspicious. But he quickly recovers his self-possession and his courage once the storm has ended, and what sticks with us from the ensuing scenes are qualities that he will manifest hereafter throughout the poem: his humility (glory is not at all his highest priority), his remarkable instinct for self-sacrifice, and, most unexpected and most attractive of his virtues, his deep concern for the well-being of others. Some readers feel that he grows in discipline and in maturity as the poem progresses, but the degree of his composure and self-assurance seems more nearly a function of the situations he finds himself in. In Book 2, with his city in flames and falling to ruin all around him, he is at times all but hysterical with fear and rage—and too honest to try to conceal it. In Book 3, as he himself recounts it, the frustrations, the sinister people and places he meets with on his journeyings, and, finally, the sudden death of his father, Anchises, all combine to render him, for the most part, morose and querulous. In Book 4, Aeneas surprisingly and briefly imitates, in a somewhat pallid fashion, the robust and protracted philandering of Odysseus. Finally, in Book 6, he repeats his model's descent into the Underworld, but he manifests nothing of Odysseus' curiosity about the afterlife when he questions the newly dead or, after he recovers from his initial terror, his remarkable composure in dealing with the business of making his way through his gruesome ordeal and back out of it to the upper world. Aeneas, unlike Odysseus, behaves in the Underworld like a quiet spectator, or almost like a dutiful tourist, as he passes through the sights and sounds, familiar from Greek poetry, of the worst that hell has to offer. When he comes to the brighter spots in the afterlife and is briefly reunited with his father, Anchises, who has revealed to him, in a sort of splendid pageant, the outlines of his progeny's glory and of Rome's triumphant history, his responses to this amazing spectacle seem rather subdued: though we essentially see the glorious procession of Roman heroes through his eyes, our sense of what he thinks and feels about it is dim.

In Book 5, however, when, after successfully fleeing Dido and Carthage, he has reached Sicily, in imitation of Achilles in *Iliad* 23, he holds belated funeral games for his father, as the greatest of the Greek heroes had held them for his comrade Patroclus. This book shows Virgil's most faithful re-creation of Homer's matter and manner (it was Montaigne's favorite book of the *Aeneid*), and the sudden substitution here of Achilles as heroic model works flawlessly: with his father gone, and his mission resumed in earnest, he is in a position to behave in a more (conventionally) heroic manner than, for the most part, we have previously seen him behave. Here we find an Aeneas who is, for the first time, relaxed and gentle, but clearly in command. In this setting, on this occasion, he has become, finally and fully, the leader of his troops and the father of his people, not so much because he has achieved moral growth as because the condition in which he finds himself has altered.

It is his utter submission of himself to those duties that explains why the adjective *pius* most frequently qualifies his name, and why he automatically chooses it when introducing himself to his mother, Venus (who has wittily disguised herself as her arch-rival, the goddess Diana, a chaste huntress); "I am Aeneas, devoted to my city's gods" (1.461). The English word "pious" fails to address the range of the Latin word's connotations, which center on the purity of an individual's devotion to the performance of the obligations he has to members of his family, to his fellow citizens, and to the gods of his tribe. The word is peculiar because it combines, from a modern point of view, a state of mind that is almost legalistic in its concern with the ties that bind a person to his kin and his comrades and the supernatural powers that can help or harm the place he inhabits with kin and comrades; it also suggests, more subtly, the affection or sympathy (we get "pity" as well as "pious" from *pius*) that a person is likely to have for those, whether mortal or immortal, with whom his life is linked. This complex of feelings, at once familial, patriotic, and religious, may at first seem strange to us (though the closer we regard it the more familiar it may come to seem), yet it lies at the core of the Roman identity. The pious worshipper, in sacrificing his individual self to this widening collectivity of needs and duties and emotions becomes more than himself: he becomes the incarnation of his family, his tribe, and his nation; he becomes one with what was for a Roman the real absolute, the real eternity, the real good, namely, the Roman State in all its power and glory and hoped-for permanence.

In the tribulations he suffers in the first half of his epic, in his waverings and his vulnerability, Aeneas shows how hard is the process of accepting the irreversible commitment that Roman piety enjoins on Rome's citizens. Readers in the Middle Ages tended to read the first six books of the poem (it looks as though they were not much interested in the last six) as an allegory in which Aeneas as prototype of a Christian Everyman trudged wearily through temptation and spiritual peril until, at the moment when he plucked the golden bough before venturing down into hell, he was granted moral enlightenment and complete wisdom. But Aeneas does not pluck the golden bough and descend into hell in order to become wise. When the Sibyl of Cumae offers new prophecies of the ordeals that await him in Italy, he cuts her short (6.133–48). He has heard elsewhere about his destiny in Italy, and he is intent on obeying the order that Anchises had given him in a dream (5.820–39): he was to come down into the Underworld and learn what his father's shade had to tell him about his mission and its meaning. And when he meets with his father, his father greets him with these words: "You have come at last! I knew your devotion [*pietas*] / Would see you through the long, hard road" (6.813–14). Here begins the solemn scene in which the father of the family transfers his duties to the son who now becomes the new father of the family. The ghost of the father, in the scenes that follow, relinquishes his powers (and obligations) to his living son who, on his return to life on earth in the upper world, will be the present incarnation of the family's past and of its future. And Aeneas, ancestor of Julius and Augustus Caesar, this particular and fated man, now becomes the incarnation of Rome's future, the sire of its destiny and triumph, the paradigm of its pious sons for as long as Rome itself will endure. This is the place and moment when the wanderer ends his wanderings. In just a few pages, when he ascends to the upper world, he will be ready to assume his role as Rome's warrior, the supreme model of those who, in the coming centuries, will win its empire and whose spirits had paraded past him and Anchises in the final, haunting scene of Book 6.

Aeneas the Warrior

The second half of the *Aeneid* is often described as Iliadic, thus distinguishing it from the first half, where Odysseus was Aeneas' chief model. Books 7 through 12 are primarily concerned with the war between Aeneas, together with the new allies he finds in Italy, and the native Italians, led by Turnus, who regard Aeneas as an invader. One might therefore reasonably expect that Aeneas' heroic model will now become Achilles, but, paradoxically, this does not quite happen. As the invader of Italy, Aeneas seems to take on certain of Achilles' traits in specific situations, but as *pius* defender of hearth and family, he nevertheless often resembles Achilles' enemy, Hector. In contrast, it is Turnus, like Hector the champion of his invaded homeland, who frequently resembles Achilles. But whatever his similarities to Hector or to Achilles, Aeneas differs from conventional Homeric (or Roman) heroes in his seemingly fundamental aversion to warfare.

This quality of Aeneas must not be misunderstood: in no way is he to be thought of as some variety of pacifist (a concept bizarre in the extreme to the Roman mind) or as in any way lacking in bravery or martial excellence. Rather, efficient warrior that he is, he is essentially a man of peace. The day after his arrival in Latium, before he has begun to build a temporary settlement, he sends an embassy to the country's ruler, King Latinus, asking for peace. When this embassy has been warmly welcomed by Latinus, its spokesman asks only for a "safe strip of shore, / A little land for the gods of our country, / And water and air that are common to all" (7.276–78). Latinus happily grants this request, and the embassy returns to Aeneas bringing an offer of the peaceful outcome he had hoped for. We are not, and need not be, told how Aeneas receives this news. Instead, we immediately see and hear Juno's expected reaction to these events: she summons Allecto to incite hostilities, and once Allecto has completed her task, Juno opens the Gates of War and hurls Aeneas into a war he did not want.

Desperate for help, Aeneas goes to King Evander, an émigré from Greece who has founded a new city-state on the site where Rome itself will later stand. No sooner has Evander agreed to send his soldiers off under Aeneas' command than Venus signals him with thunder and lightning that she will soon be bringing the divine armor that she has prevailed on her husband, Vulcan, to create for him. Venus' signal shakes Aeneas from the gloomy ruminations that had taken hold of him as soon as Evander promised him the soldiers he had come for: he does not look forward to the carnage that is now close at hand and says to Evander:

> Ask not what the portents forebode,
> My dear host; in truth, do not ask. It is I

Who am summoned by heaven. . . .
Ah, the slaughter in store for the poor Laurentines!
What a price you will pay me, Turnus! How many
Shields and helmets and bodies of the brave
Will you, Father Tiber, roll beneath your waves?
Let them call for battle and break their treaty!
                              (8.605–7, 611–15)

These lines recall Aeneas' very first speech in the poem, his cry of
anguish when he thinks that he and his ships are about to be
destroyed in the storm and remembers the countless deaths that his
comrades had suffered years before when Troy fell to the Greeks.
In this passage, he seems to be making no distinction between the
imminent Trojan deaths and those of his enemies. It is not only the
brutality of the coming battles that sickens and grieves him here; he
is also saddened by and angered at the futility, the needlessness, of
a war that he had tried to avoid by the careful diplomacy of his
first overtures to Latinus. He does not yet, and never will, know
that Turnus is innocent of the outbreak of a war that Juno and her
henchwoman are guilty of having ignited; instead, even when he
blames Turnus, he manifests a touch of compassion for the man he
thinks guilty of causing the carnage he despises: "What a price you
will pay me, Turnus!" (8.612). This is an utterance shaped by an
angry pity; it is almost a cry of despair.

Aeneas figures only briefly in Book 9. When in Book 10 he
returns to Latium with his allies, before he and Turnus manage to
encounter one another, the action shifts to Evander's son, Pallas.
This young prince is enjoying enormous success in his debut as a
warrior when he meets up with Lausus, son of the ferocious Etrus-
can king, Mezentius. But before they can square off against each
other, Turnus rushes forward to save Lausus, challenges Pallas, and
quickly dispatches him. Having slain the young warrior, Turnus
strips the sword-belt from his corpse. Upon learning of Pallas'
death, Aeneas rushes off to avenge him:

He mowed down everything before him
With his sword, burning a broad path
Through the enemy, seeking you, Turnus,
Flush with slaughter. Pallas, Evander,
Everything swam in Aeneas' eyes—the table
He came to as a stranger, the right hands pledged.
                              (10.619–24)

This brief flash of picture-memory in Aeneas' mind's eye marks a crucial moment in the poem. Immediately after it, echoing Achilles in one of his most savage moments, Aeneas grabs eight young enemies whom he will later offer as human sacrifices at the funeral of Pallas. He then charges off after Turnus, slaughtering any Italian he meets in a killing frenzy worthy of Achilles at his most ferocious. But Juno has snatched Turnus out of the battle before Aeneas can get to him; cheated of the champion he wants to slay, Aeneas attempts to appease his vengeful wrath by killing any enemy he finds in his path.

It is Mezentius, Turnus' most formidable ally, whom he finally chances on. When Aeneas wounds Mezentius, Lausus rushes bravely to his father's defense, and Aeneas, just before he is forced to kill the young man, cries out to him:

> You're headed for death, Lausus! Why rush it
> By daring what's beyond your strength?
> Your filial devotion is blinding you.
>   (10.968–70)

As a son who loves his father and a father who loves his son, Aeneas, even as he threatens him, instantly recognizes his own best virtue in the young man who is about to die at his hands. And when, while driving his sword through Lausus' body,

> Anchises' son looked on his dying face,
> So strangely pale, he groaned in pity
> And stretched out his hand. There shone in that face
> The image of his own devotion to Anchises. . . .
>   "What now, poor boy,
> Can Aeneas give you for such glorious deeds?
> What is worthy of so great a heart?"
>   (10.982–88)

Moved by a curious sense of kinship with this enemy, shaken by compassion and admiration, Aeneas refuses to strip the corpse and lifts it tenderly from the ground. This peculiar mix of emotions, wherein *pietas* all but finds itself divided against itself, goes against both the epic and the Roman grain. It bespeaks both the poem's underground Epicurean current and a new kind of hero that it helps produce. It is this sensitivity, this paradoxical, emergent bias against violence, that makes Aeneas the strange kind of warrior he is and that defines the poem's harrowing final scene where, his emotions again in powerful conflict, he chooses, or is compelled, to disobey his better instincts.

The Shield of Aeneas: Virgil and History

By and large the characters in the *Aeneid* know little or nothing of the historical forces that are shaping the events in which they find themselves making the choices they make, performing the actions they perform. Aeneas himself never gets a real grasp of the extent of Juno's enmity toward him, and the teasing, ambiguous omens, dreams, and prophecies that he encounters before he reaches Italy serve mostly to baffle him. During his visit to the Underworld, however, his father's shade provides him with an elaborate sketch of the glorious history of the nation he will soon found in Italy when his war with its native population has ended:

> Now I will set forth the glory that awaits
> The Trojan race, the illustrious souls
> Of the Italian heirs to our name.
> I will teach you your destiny.
>   (6.896–99)

That said, a patriotic pageant, made up of souls destined to be reborn as great Romans in future ages, passes in review before Anchises, the Sibyl, and Aeneas. The procession begins with Aeneas' own as yet unborn son, Silvius, whose mother will be Aeneas' future wife, Lavinia; Silvius is followed by the early kings of Alba Longa who are followed in turn by Romulus, Rome's founder and first king: "Under his auspices, / . . . Rome will extend her renowned empire / To earth's horizons, her glory to the stars" (6.924–26). So far the procession is ordered according to a strict chronology, but at this point Anchises suddenly introduces the Julian clan, all of whom are descended from Aeneas' son, Ascanius (whose second name in Iülus), and from all the clan he singles out only two figures, Julius Caesar and

>   the man promised to you,
> Augustus Caesar, born of the gods,
> Who will establish again a Golden Age
> In the fields of Latium once ruled by Saturn
> And will expand his dominion

Beyond the Indus and the Garamantes,
Beyond our familiar stars, beyond the yearly
Path of the sun, to the land where Atlas
Turns the star-studded sphere on his shoulders.
                                        (6.939–47)

Anchises continues his prophecies of the role Augustus will play in
extending Rome's boundaries throughout the known world, boast-
ing that neither Hercules nor Bacchus in their wide and triumphant
journeyings will surpass the breadth of Augustus' dominions.
Anchises ends this segment of his revelations with a subtle rebuke
to what he apparently takes to be his son's hesitations about the
war in Latium he is about to undertake. Given the worldwide
empire that Aeneas' greatest heir will rule over, should Aeneas have
qualms about gaining a foothold in Italy? "And still we shrink
from extending our virtue, / And fear to take our stand in Auso-
nia?" (6.956–57).

Augustus is at once the centerpiece of Anchises' pageant and the
zenith of Rome's destiny. Although Rome and its emperors will
know greatness after Augustus is gone (like his adoptive father,
Julius, to his heavenly reward), it is Augustus who will rescue
Rome in its decadence from its enemies and from itself, it is he who
will both restore it to former glories and set it on its new and firmer
foundations. Having made this leap forward in time from Romulus
and Rome's beginnings to Virgil's (and Augustus') present,
Anchises then doubles back to his pageant and to the unborn souls
who will one day become the successors of Romulus, the kings
who will come after him. He then deftly skirts the expulsion of the
last (bad) king of Rome (6.970–73) to focus on the founding of the
Republic, the evolution of its "sweet liberty" (6.977), its slow,
patient conquest of Italy through a series of "defensive" wars, and
its steady string of victories over the Greeks and Carthaginians
who challenged its expansion throughout the Mediterranean.
These descriptions of the progress of the Republic's transformation
from small (agrarian) city-state into the center of its cosmopolitan
world empire are presented through a series of vivid, elliptical
images of great moments in Roman history.

It is hard to estimate how much Anchises expects his son to
understand and take away from the achronological, swirling suc-
cession of events, the blur of unknown names and faces that
Anchises offers to his gaze. But whatever he does or doesn't under-
stand, Aeneas doubtless gets the gist of the fabulous, confusing

spectacle his father presents him with because Anchises sums it up
with unforgettable clarity:

> Others will, no doubt, hammer out bronze
> That breathes more softly, and draw living faces
> Out of stone. They will plead cases better
> And chart the rising of every star in the sky.
> Your mission, Roman, is to rule the world.
> These will be your arts: to establish peace,
> To spare the humbled, and to conquer the proud.
>
> (6.1012–18)

Aeneas, since he is and will remain a Trojan, may be surprised to
find his father calling him a Roman. But he has perhaps heard the
name enough by now to guess what his father is driving at: Aeneas
himself is now Rome incarnate, and it is him and, through him, all
true Romans and most especially the man-god, Augustus, greatest
of them all, that Anchises is addressing as he explains to his son the
nature of Roman identity and of Rome's mission in the world.

If Aeneas' instruction had ended there, we might feel that he had
deciphered enough of the pageant's mysteries to grasp something of
the meaning of the Roman Empire and his place in it. But it doesn't
end there. Coming next to last in the pageant (again out of chrono-
logical order) is the great general Marcellus, The Sword of Rome.
And following him, the procession's final figure, is the young man
who will be the Sword's ancestor, another Marcellus, the son of
Augustus' own sister and his prospective heir. Aeneas is much
taken by this phantasm ("Beautiful in his gleaming armor / But
with downcast eyes and troubled brow," 6.1028–29) and asks his
father who he is. Anchises answers him tearfully. In verses that are
among the epic's most haunting, Anchises pronounces what is in
effect an elegy for the heir apparent, one of the *Aeneid*'s doomed
youths: "Fate will permit him on earth a brief while, / But not for
long" (6.1037–38). If Marcellus had not been fated to die just on
the brink of his early manhood, he was to have been, could have
been, should have been, a great warrior:

> If only you could shatter Fate, poor boy.
> You will be Marcellus! Let me strew
> Armfuls of lilies and scatter purple blossoms,
> Hollow rites to honor my descendant's shade.
>
> (6.1052–55)

As usual, we are not told what Aeneas feels about the extraordinary conclusion to this splendid vision of Rome's brightest and best. When the pageant vanishes with Marcellus, Anchises fills his son "with longing for the glory that was to come" (6.1060) by describing in detail the war he is about to embark on and by telling him "how to face or flee each waiting peril" (6.1063). Enflamed he may now be with a Homeric "longing for glory" (instead of his usual passion for duty), but by the time Aeneas finds himself embroiled in the war with Turnus and the Latins he seems to have forgotten most of what his father told him. In any case, when Anchises sends him and the Sybil through the Gate of Ivory back to the upper world we don't know what mood he is in or what he has understood about the world that he lives and fights and suffers in. There are numerous opinions about why he returns through the Gate of Ivory. Whatever Virgil's intention (it is well to remember that he has a special fondness for ambiguity), by placing the doomed Marcellus so near the Gate of Dreams (whether they are illusory or improperly interpreted) he shapes a mood that tints the close of Book 6 with an uncanny, ambivalent dissonance, one that clouds our sense of Aeneas' mission and perhaps his own sense of it as well.

In Aeneas' next and final vision of Roman history, uncertainty seems at first to have no place. Toward the end of Book 8, after Aeneas has concluded his alliance with Evander and is ready to battle the Latins, Venus brings Aeneas the new, divine armor that she has persuaded Vulcan to make for him. He receives these gifts from her hand with much of the gusto that Achilles shows when Thetis hands him his new armor ("he turned / The polished weapons the god had given him / Over and over in his hands, and felt / Pangs of joy at all its intricate beauty," *Iliad* 19.26–29). On taking up his weapons,

> Aeneas gloried
> In the gifts from heaven, in this high honor,
> And he could not satisfy his eyes as they moved
> From one part to another. He was lost in wonder
> As he turned each piece over in his hands
> And cradled it in his arms. . . .
>
> (8.704–9)

But here the similarities between Virgil's scene and its model end. On the shield of Achilles, the god Hephaestus has engraved the entire world: earth, ocean, the heavens, and their stars. Then, representing the human world, "he made two cities, peopled / And beautiful" (*Iliad* 18.528–29), one at peace and one at war. Up to this point, it looks as if Achilles' shield might be symbolizing the *Iliad* itself, which also shows peoples and their cities at peace and at war (but with a decided emphasis on war). But the rest of the shield, a little more than half of it, is devoted to the arts and pleasures of peace; fields being plowed and harvested, vineyards, farms and livestock, the business of living; it ends, rapturously, with young men and women in a joyful dance that portends matrimony and the renewal of the fertile world. There are various plausible ways of reading Achilles' shield, but a not unreasonable interpretation might be that the design on the shield of this best, most fearsome of Greek warriors explains what soldiers (him included, for all his glamorous individualism and obsession with glory) are supposed to be fighting to secure, namely, peace and its blessings for their compatriots and their children's children.

Vulcan's design is rather different. On the shield of Aeneas

> the Fire God had prophetically wrought
> The future of Italy, and Roman triumphs
> In the coming ages, every generation,
> In order, still to be born from the stock
> Of Ascanius, and all the wars they would fight.
> (8.716–20)

What the shield will offer Aeneas (and us), then, is a reprise of the parade of phantoms in Book 6. However, instead of being limited to memorializing military glory, it, like the shield of Achilles, will culminate in the blessings of peace. But this peace is not at all the peace that Homer imagined: the absence of war as the ideal condition that all humans yearn for. Instead, what Vulcan portrays at the center of Aeneas' shield is the imperial, universal peace (the *pax Augustana*) that Augustus established when he defeated Antony and Cleopatra and thereby put an end to Rome's hundred years of civic strife. Vulcan's pictures begin, much as Anchises' pageant had begun, with early Roman history, but he skips quickly from Ascanius to Romulus, devotes much of his space to Romulus' successors and to the great (dim) heroes of the early Republic, ending this segment with the fateful day when the Gauls actually sacked Rome (387 B.C.E.). Abruptly, he then includes a snippet of the Underworld:

Far below he set the hells of Tartarus,
The high gates of Dis, and the wages of sin.
You, Catiline, were hung from the frowning
Face of a cliff and trembled at the Furies
While Cato, set apart, gave laws to the good.
                                   (8.762–66)

Between them, Catiline, one of Rome's worst traitors, and Cato the
Younger, one of its greatest moral champions, summon up so
briefly that they function only to extinguish the ugly story of the
disintegration of the Republic in its last years, the turmoil and vio-
lence that both produced Augustus and was ended by him. It is this
sleight of hand that allows Vulcan (and Virgil), in another sudden
shift of mood and topic, to begin their depiction of the triumph of
Augustus, which will take up more than half of the rest of the
shield.

The sea-battle that made Augustus ruler of the world and
bringer of the peace it had longed for begins with a deceptive, lyri-
cal loveliness:

These scenes were lapped by the swelling sea,
Pure gold, yet the water was blue, and flecked
With whitecaps. Circling dolphins picked out in silver
Cut through the waves and their tails flicked the spume.
                                   (8.767–70)

At the fateful Battle of Actium, engraved on one side, stands Cae-
sar Augustus, leading a united Italy along with Rome and its peo-
ple, its senate and its gods, against Antony and his Egyptian wife,
who are figured on the opposite side, with all their maddened Ori-
ental hordes. Cleopatra has summoned the monstrous, bestial gods
of her kingdom to aid her, but, "chiseled in iron at the eye of the
battle" (8.802), ranged against them are Neptune, Minerva, Venus,
Mars, the Furies, Discord, and the war goddess Bellona. It is
Apollo, however, the god with whom Augustus most identified
himself, the god who would come to best symbolize the style of his
governance and his incontestable right to power, it is Apollo who
bends his bow, it is his arrow that puts an end to the Battle of
Actium. (Virgil's contemporary, the poet Propertius, provides us
with a delicious parody of this moment in his poem on Actium,
Elegies 4.6.) Terrified, the wicked Queen deserts Antony along
with her motley squadrons and is gathered up (like Dido before

her, whom she echoes in other ways) into a pretty, lyrical demise. "Pale as death," completing her flight to Egypt, she sails into the Nile where "The great rivergod had opened all the folds / Of his copious robe and welcomed the vanquished / Into the sheltering waters of his azure lap" (8.815–17).

Unlike the pageant of Book 6, the shield of Aeneas is carefully directed toward and ends vividly in pure narrative. This heavily stylized, condensed, elliptical representation of the Battle of Actium and its aftermath may be all that is left of the germ of an epic about Augustus that Virgil seems to have considered composing before he hit upon the (subtler, more artistic) idea of framing the story of Augustus, like a jewel in its setting, by the story of Aeneas. The picture of Augustus in triumph after his return to Egypt, benevolent and wise, graciously welcoming a grateful humankind as it throngs from all over the known world to do him homage (or rather to worship him) is possessed of a poetic beauty as splendid as it is delicate and concise. It is an astonishing, unforgettable portrait of the Augustan Peace.

But it is far from clear that Aeneas understands the meaning of Actium any better than he understands the rest of his shield (or any better than he had understood the Underworld pageant). He rejoices in the beauty of his armor when he first receives it, but we are told (8.715), even as he delights in it, that its design is "ineffable [*non enarrabile*]," beyond description or explanation. It is, of course, the perfection of the shield's craftsmanship, the beauty of the artifact, that is "ineffable," but what it represents is also beyond the power of art (both Vulcan's and poetry's) to imitate, to order, to clarify. And even it were not, even if the uncertainties and anomalies of history could be distilled through art to clarity, Aeneas still could not understand them:

Such was the design of the shield Vulcan made,
Venus' gift to her son. Aeneas was moved
To wonder and joy by the images of things
He could not fathom, and he lifted to his shoulder
The destiny of his children's children.

(8.840–44)

So different from the feelings he had back in Carthage when he gazed at the picture of the Trojan War, it is an ironic sort of joy he feels in the pictures of wars and triumphs that he does not understand and that he does not and cannot connect with the procession he saw in the Underworld. As he once lifted his father on his shoulders in their flight from Troy to a new homeland, so also he now hoists onto his shoulders these pictures (puzzling to him, clear to Augustus and to us) of a glorious future that he comprehends dimly if at all, one that his actions will ensure but that he will not live to partake of. At this moment, though he is near his goal, he is still what he was when we first glimpsed him, "exiled by Fate" (1.3), "a man battered / On land and sea" (1.4–5). Courageous, dutiful, compassionate, in proud possession of his beautiful and baffling shield, he is as much an existential Everyman as an epic hero when he departs from Evander's city to resume his struggles in a world whose workings and meanings he cannot grasp.

Virgil's first readers, of course, could read the shield expertly, and among them who more expertly than Augustus himself, the center of the shield, its real meaning, the man-god emperor who was to Aeneas little more than one of the more splendid of the ghostly creatures in the Underworld parade—that, and a mere name? As he read the shield, he, the real purpose of Aeneas' mission, Augustus would have seen nothing disconcerting in Aeneas' failure to understand the significance of the actions that he was, as an instrument of Fate, required to perform. Some of his contemporaries, however, probably did notice that fissure, and some of them may have sensed that it pointed to other places in the poem— among them, the poet's cry to Jupiter in Book 12, Anchises' elegy for Marcellus, Juturna's lament, Aeneas' encounter with Dido in the Underworld, his anguished speech over the corpse of Lausus— where the poem's patriotic grandeur conflicts with its more private, human face, moments in it when its sense of suffering outweighs its sense of imperial imperative, where Aeneas the human being and Aeneas the progenitor of all-conquering Rome split apart.

But there were probably more readers among Virgil's first readers (and there have been many more since) for whom, as for Augustus, such ambiguities were of no real importance. For these readers, any doubt about the centrality of Augustus on Aeneas' shield, and what they took to be his centrality in the poem, was unthinkable. Like any reader of Appian's *Civil Wars* (his terrifying history of Rome in the hundred years before the Battle of Actium), these readers knew in their blood and their bones why Augustus deserved to be, needed to be, at the center of a poem that celebrated Rome and its destiny. It was not hard to persuade them that his birth was a miracle, that his sudden intervention in Rome's self-destruction, just at the moment of what seemed its complete destruction, was providential. They understood why some Greeks hailed him as "savior" and were prepared to call him a god and to worship him as a god. For these readers, what might appear to be the poem's ambiguities, if they could not be explained (away), could be safely and easily ignored (after all, Virgil had not had a chance to put his finishing touches to his epic). So, for these readers, Augustus was at the center of Aeneas' shield because he became and remained and would remain the still center of Rome and its world, which was at the center of the universe and of history; he was the actuality toward which all the world's potentialities had always been moving.

Exactly what Virgil intended by the shield and by the poem that accords it such prominence we will never know. (One of its very best modern readers, the wonderful W. F. Jackson Knight, was so eager to learn what the poet really meant that he asked a friend to hold séances with a view to finding the answers to his questions "in the beyond.") We can assume that Virgil had some sympathy with those of his readers who would be pleased with the grandeur of his shield, who felt comfort in the world that Augustus had (as he claimed) rescued from ruin and remade, who felt unable to express their gratitude sufficiently and welcomed a poet and a poem that would say what they themselves were incapable of saying in praise of the return of law and order and the blessings of peace. But he may very well have shared some of the thoughts and feelings of those who paused to ponder those places in his poem where its tensions reveal themselves, where there glimmer, under the surfaces of the poem, worries about the fate of empires, about what happens when delight in prosperity turns into the dangerous notion that greed is good, and when joy in victory morphs into mere hubris. We cannot know whether he deliberately crafted those tensions, thus setting the truth of human misery against the truth of human achievement, or whether he was merely reflecting, merely recording (almost unconsciously), the tensions and uncertainties that continued to haunt Rome in the first decade of Augustus' reign, before it began to seem likely that he would *not* join his predecessors in being swept away in the chaos of Rome's recent history, before it began to seem possible, even probable, that the settlement he was planning would be successful and permanent.

Whether by his own design or as a reflection of anxieties in Rome's collective consciousness (whether he shared them or didn't), interwoven in the poem's epic texture, countervailing its celebration of the warrior in triumph, is the persistent memory of

the outcast, the exile, who speaks with the voice of the dispos-
sessed, of Trojan, not Roman, Aeneas. In recent years, some read-
ers, this reader among them, have been struck with what they take
to be Virgil's Epicurean strain and the deep, unfailing imprint on
his mind and art by Lucretius' *On the Nature of Things*. One line
from that poem could serve as a useful motto for this aspect of
Virgil's vision of the human condition: *"imbecillorum est aequum
miserarier omnes"* (5.1023), "it is just for all of us to feel compas-
sion for those who are weak." The *Aeneid* imagines how the
world, how any society, any time, anywhere, can be saved by
depicting (and celebrating) how Rome, Virgil's own (adopted) city,
was once saved. Though ambiguous about the nature of victory, it
is hardly contemptuous of prosperity and ordinary happiness. But
it is never forgetful of the prevalence of human suffering, it never
ignores the pain and the loss of the defeated or the huge cost of
victory, to the victor no less than to the vanquished. Aeneas is the
right hero for this strange, almost unepical epic, an odd and
improbable hero, perhaps, but more credible than many and more
admirable than most.

W. R. Johnson
University of Chicago

AENEID ONE

Arms I sing—and a man,
The first to come from the shores
Of Troy, exiled by Fate, to Italy
And the Lavinian coast; a man battered
On land and sea by the powers above   5
In the face of Juno's relentless wrath;
A man who also suffered greatly in war
Until he could found his city and bring his gods
Into Latium, from which arose
The Latin people, our Alban forefathers,   10
And the high walls of everlasting Rome.

Muse, tell me why the Queen of Heaven
Was so aggrieved, her godhead so offended,
That she forced a man of faultless devotion
To endure so much hardship. Can there be   15
Anger so great in the hearts of gods on high?

There was an ancient city, Carthage,
Colonized by Tyrians, facing Italy
And the Tiber's mouth far across the sea;
A city rich in resources, fierce in war,   20
And favored by Juno more than any other
Place on earth, even more than Samos. Here
Were her arms, her chariot; this was the city
The goddess cherished and strove to make
Capital of the world, if the Fates permitted.   25
But she had heard that a scion of Trojan blood
Would someday level Carthage's citadel;
That a Trojan people, an imperial power,
Would destroy Libya: so the Parcae
Were spinning out Fate. The Goddess   30
Brooded on this and on the Trojan War,
Which she herself, Saturnian Juno,
Had waged on behalf of her beloved Greeks,

Ever mindful of the Judgment of Paris—
The cause of the war—and her savage grief   35
Over her beauty scorned by that hateful race.
Nor could she forget the spiteful honor given
To ravaged Ganymede.
                  Incensed with these memories,
The Goddess kept the Trojan remnant
That had escaped the Greeks—and Achilles' rage—   40
Tossed all over the sea's expanse,
Far from Latium, doomed to wander
The circling waters year after year.

So massive was the labor of founding Rome.

Sicily had scarcely dropped out of sight,   45
And they were sailing joyfully on the open sea,
Bronze prows shearing the seaspume,
When Juno, nursing her heart's eternal wound,
Said to herself:

        "Am I to admit defeat,
Unable to keep these Trojans and their king   50
From Italy? Forbidden by the Fates, am I?
Pallas could burn the Argives' fleet
And drown all hands for one man's offense—
Oïlean Ajax's fit of passion.
She herself hurled Jupiter's fire from heaven,   55
Splintered the ships, churned up the sea,
And whirled up Ajax, exhaling flames
From his pierced lungs, and impaled him on a crag.
But I, who walk among the gods as their queen,
Sister of Jupiter and Jupiter's wife—I   60
Have to wage war for years on end
Against this one race. Who will worship Juno
After this, or bow down before her holy altars?"

Her heart inflamed, the Goddess went
To Aeolia, a country of clouds   65
And raging winds. Here in a vast cave
Aeolus rules the squalls and gales,
Keeping them chained in vaulted cells.
The indignant winds roar at their prison doors,

Rumbling deep in the mountain. But Aeolus   70
Sits on high and with his scepter calms
Their frenzied souls. If he did not,
They would swoop over land and sea
And through the deep sky, sweeping
Everything before them. Fearing just this,   75
The Father Almighty hid them away
In dark caves and piled above them
A mountain massif. And he gave them a king,
One who would know by chartered agreement
When to restrain and when to unleash them.   80
It was to Aeolus that Juno came as a suppliant:

"Aeolus, by order of the Father of Gods and Men
You calm the waves or provoke them with wind.
A race I despise sails the Tyrrhenian Sea,
Bringing Ilium's conquered gods to Italy.   85
Hit them hard with a storm and sink their ships,
Or scatter the fleet and litter the sea with corpses.
I have fourteen Nymphs with lovely bodies,
The most radiant of which, Deiopeia,
I will pronounce your wife, to have and to hold,   90
In return for this favor. She will live with you
All her years and bear you beautiful children."

And Aeolus:

            "It is yours to consider what you want,
My Queen, and mine to fulfill your commands.
To you I owe this modest realm and Jove's good will.   95
You grant me a seat at the table of the gods,
And you make me master of cloud and storm."

With that, he drove the butt of his spear
Against the cavernous mountainside, and the winds,
In battle formation, rushed out of all ports   100
And whirled over the earth. Swooping down,
They fell on the sea. Eurus and Notus
Churned up the depths, and with them Africus,
Whose dark squall line rolled huge waves shoreward.
The crews began to shout, the rigging creaked,   105
And then, in an instant, clouds stole the daylight

From the Trojans' eyes. Night lay black on the sea.
The sky's roof thundered and flashed with lightning,
And everywhere men saw the presence of death.

Aeneas' limbs suddenly went numb with cold.   110
He groaned and, lifting both palms to heaven, said:

"Three times, four times luckier were those
Who died before their parents' eyes
Under Troy's high walls! O Diomedes,
Bravest of the Greeks, if only I had been killed   115
By your right hand on Ilium's plain,
Where Hector went down under Achilles' spear,
Where huge Sarpedon lies, where the Simois rolls
So many shields and helmets caught in its current
And the bodies of so many brave heroes!"   120

As he was speaking a howling wind from the North
Struck against the sail. Waves shot to the stars.
The oars shattered. The prow swung around,
Exposing the side to the waves, and then
A mountain of water broke over the fleet.   125
The crews of some ships bobbed high on the crest,
While the wave's deep trough revealed to others
The deep seafloor churning with sand.
The South Wind twirled a trio of ships
Onto the Altars—the Italians' grim name   130
For the hulk of reef lurking under the sea.
The East Wind pushed another three ships
Into the shallows and ground them onto
The Syrtes' shoals, bedding them down
In pockets of sand. Another ship,   135
Which carried the Lycians and trusted Orontes,
Sank before Aeneas' own eyes. A wall of water
Crashed onto the deck, and the pilot flew headfirst
Into the sea. The ship spun around twice, three times,
Caught in a whirlpool that sucked it down quickly.   140
You could see men swimming here and there
In the vast gulf. Wicker shields, plaques,
And Trojan finery floated on the waves.
And now Ilioneus' strong ship, now Achates',
Now the ships that carried Abas and old Aletes   145

Were battered by the storm. Their joints sagged,
And they took on water through their splitting seams.

Meanwhile, the news filtered down to Neptune
Of the turmoil above. He heard the murmur
From the churning surface, and he felt   150
The still, bottom water rise in upheaval.
Lifting his serene face above the waves,
He peered out and saw Aeneas' fleet
Scattered, and the Trojans overwhelmed
By rough seas and the sky's downpour.   155
His sister's treachery was all too obvious.
Calling Eurus and Zephyrus, he said to them:

"Do you have so much confidence, Winds,
In your family connections? Do you dare
Overturn heaven and earth and raise tons of water   160
Up to the sky—without my divine sanction?
Why, I ought to . . . ! But settling the waves comes first.
You won't get off so lightly next time.
Now clear out of here! And tell your king this:
The sea and the trident were allotted to me,   165
Not to him. His domain is the outsized rock
That you and yours, Eurus, call home. Aeolus
Can puff himself up there, in his own hall,
And lord it over the prison of the winds."

Thus Neptune, and—no sooner said than done—   170
He calmed the sea, chased off the massed clouds,
And brought back the sun. Cymothöe and Triton,
Working together, pushed the ships off the jagged reef.
Neptune himself levered them up with his trident,
Cut channels through the shoals, and eased the swells,   175
His chariot's wheels skimming the whitecaps.

    Riots will often break out in a crowded assembly
    When the rabble are roused. Torches and stones
    Are soon flying—Fury always finds weapons—
    But then all eyes light upon a loyal citizen,   180
    A man of respect. The crowd stands still
    In hushed expectation. And with grave words
    He masters their tempers and calms their hearts.

So too the crashing sea fell silent, as its sire,
Surveying the watery expanse, drove his chariot   185
Under a clear sky, giving the horses free rein.

Aeneas' men, numb with fatigue,
Made for the nearest land, the coast of Libya.

They found a deep bay, across whose mouth
An island stands and makes a good port: 190
The waves that roll in from the open sea
Break on its sides and ripple on to shore.
The bay is flanked by high cliffs. Twin crags
Rise like threats toward the sky, but the water below
Is sheltered and silent. Above, shimmering woods,   195
And, rising higher, a dark grove with sinister shadows.
Opposite the looming crags is a cave,
With sweet-water springs and stone seats inside,
A haunt of the Nymphs. Sea-weary ships
Need not be tied in this harbor, nor moored   200
By hooked anchors that bite the seafloor.

Aeneas puts in here with the seven ships
That are left of his fleet. Lusting for dry land,
The Trojans disembark on the welcome beach,
Laying their brine-soaked bodies on the sand.   205
Achates strikes a flint and catches a spark
In leaves, then feeds the flames with dry tinder.
The men bring out whatever grain they can salvage
From the spoiled stores and, weary of it all,
Parch the kernels and grind grain on stones.   210

Aeneas now climbed up to an isolated point
With a view of the sea spread out below,
Hoping to see where the storm might have left
The Phrygian galleys of Antheus
Or of Capys, or to glimpse Caicus' armor   215
Mounted high on the stern. There was no ship in sight,
But he did see three stags browsing on the shore
And behind them an entire herd, feeding
In a long line down through the valley. Aeneas
Stood still, as did faithful Achates,   220
Who passed over feathered arrows and bow.
He brought down the leaders, each standing tall

With a thicket of antlers, and then he shot
At the herd itself, scattering them with his arrows
Into the woods. He did not stop shooting   225
Until he had triumphantly brought down
Seven good-sized animals, one for each ship.
Back at the port, Aeneas divided the meat
Among all of his men and distributed wine
That the hero Acestes had stored in jars   230
And given to them at their departure
From Sicily's shores. And then Aeneas
Spoke to his men to ease their hearts:

"Trojans! This is not our first taste of trouble.
You have suffered worse than this, my friends,   235
And God will grant an end to this also.
You faced Scylla's fury in her thundering crags
And braved the Cyclops' rocks. Recall your courage
And put aside your fear and grief. Someday, perhaps,
It will help to remember these troubles as well.   240
Through all sorts of perils, through countless dangers,
We are headed for Latium, where the Fates promise us
A peaceful home, and where Troy will rise again.
Endure, and save yourselves for happier times."

Aeneas said this, and though he was sick   245
With worry, he put on a good face
And pushed his anguish deep into his heart.
They set about preparing a feast from the kill.
Some did the skinning and butchering
And skewered the still quivering flesh on spits.   250
Others set cauldrons on the shore and tended fires.
The meal revived their strength. Spread out
Along the grass, they took their fill of old wine
And fat venison. When the feast was finished,
They talked long about their lost companions,   255
Hoping they were still alive, but fearing
They had met their end and would hear no more
When their names were called.
Loyal Aeneas grieved especially
For bold Orontes, and lamented in silence   260
The bitter loss of Amycus and Lycus,
Of brave Gyas and brave Cloanthus.

The day was at an end, and Jupiter
Was looking down from heaven's zenith
At the sail-winged sea and at the shores   265
Of all the peopled lands spread far and wide,
And as he looked he paused at the sky's pinnacle
And turned his luminous eyes toward Libya,
Pondering the world's woes. And Venus, sad,
Her eyes shining with tears, said to him: 270

"Lord of Lightning, eternal Ruler of Gods and Men,
What has my Aeneas done to offend you?
What have my Trojans done? They have suffered
One disaster after another, and still the whole world
Is barred to them to keep them out of Italy.   275
Surely someday, in the turning of time,
The Romans are to arise from this race.
They will continue Teucer's bloodline
And give birth to rulers who will hold
Earth and sea under their dominion.   280
You promised. What has changed your mind,
Father? That promise was what consoled me
At Troy's heartrending downfall. I balanced one fate
Against another. But the fortunes of these men,
After all their mishaps, have still not changed.   285
What end, O Lord, will you grant to their toils?
Antenor was able to escape the Greeks,
Cross safely over the Illyrian gulfs,
Pass the Liburnians' inmost realms,
And skirt the springs of the Timavus   290
Where it bursts through nine roaring mouths
And floods the fields under a sounding sea.
There he founded the town of Padua,
Settled his Teucrians, named his race,
And fixed the arms of Troy on a temple wall.   295
Now he is at rest and enjoys peaceful ease.
But we, your own flesh and blood,
To whom you have opened the heights of heaven,
Have lost our ships—O the infamy!—
And because of one deity's anger are betrayed   300
And disbarred from the shores of Italy.
Is this the reward for devotion? Is this
How you restore our ancestral power?"

Smiling at her with the look that calms storms
And clears the sky, the Father of Gods and Men   305
Kissed his daughter lightly and said:

"Spare your fears, Cytherean. Your people's destiny
Remains unmoved. You will see Lavinium
And its promised walls, and you will raise
Great-souled Aeneas to the stars on high.   310
I have not changed my mind. Your son—
I will speak at length, since you are so worried,
Unrolling Fate's scroll and revealing its secrets—
Your son will wage a great war in Italy,
Crush barbarous nations, and set up laws   315
And city walls for his own people, reigning
In Latium until three summers have passed
And three winters since the Rutulians' defeat.
But the boy Ascanius, surnamed Iülus—
His name was Ilus while Ilium still stood—   320
Will be in power for thirty great cycles
Of the rolling months, will move his throne
From Lavinium, and build the mighty walls
Of Alba Longa. This kingdom will endure
For three hundred years under Hector's race,   325
Until Ilia, Vesta's royal priestess,
Pregnant by Mars, shall give birth to twins.
Then Romulus, proud in the tawny hide
Of the wolf who nursed him, will continue
The lineage, build the walls of Mars,   330
And call the people, after his own name,
Romans. For these I set no limits
In time or space, and have given to them
Eternal empire, world without end.
Even Juno, who in her spite and fear   335
Now vexes earth, sea, and sky, shall adopt
A better view, and with me cherish the Romans,
Lords of the world, the people of the toga.
That is my pleasure. And there will come a time
As the years glide on, when the descendants   340
Of Trojan Assaracus shall subdue
Glorious Mycenae, Phthia, and Argos.
From this resplendent line shall be born
Trojan Caesar, who will extend his Empire

To the Ocean and his glory to the stars,   345
A Julian in the lineage of great Ilus.
And you, Venus, free at last from care,
Will someday welcome him into heaven,
Laden with Oriental spoils of war,
And his name too will be invoked in vows.   350
Then war shall be no more, and the ages
Will grow mild. Grey-haired Faith, and Vesta,
And Quirinus with his brother Remus
Will make laws. The Gates of War,
Iron upon bolted iron, shall be closed,   355
And inside, impious Fury will squat enthroned
On the savage weapons of war, hands bound tight
Behind his back with a hundred brazed knots,
Howling horrible curses from his blood-filled mouth."

Thus Jupiter, and from heaven he dispatched   360
Mercury, Maia's winged son, so that Carthage,
With its newly built towers, would lie open
To welcome the Trojans, and that Dido,
In her ignorance of Fate, would not ban them
From her land. The god wings his way   365
Through the vast sky, quickly touches down
On Libya's shore, and just as quickly
Accomplishes his mission. At the god's will
The Phoenicians put aside their fighting spirit,
And, above all, the Queen conceived   370
A great benevolence toward the Trojans.

Aeneas, meanwhile, aware of his duty,
Was up thinking the whole night through.
When Dawn kissed his face with light, he resolved
To set forth and explore the strange coastline   375
To see which way the wind had blown him
And to see who lived there, man or beast,
In the untilled land that lay before him.
Then, he would report back to his men.
He hid the fleet under a rocky overhang   380
Steeped in a forest's shimmering shade.
Then he strode forth, with Achates
His only companion, gripping in his hand
A pair of javelins tipped with flared iron.

And there, in the middle of the forest,   385
Was his mother, coming toward him.
She looked and dressed like a young woman
And bore a huntress's weapons. She could have been
A Spartan girl, or Harpalyce of Thrace,
Who outruns horses and the Hebrus' rapids.   390
A supple bow was slung over her shoulders
In the style of a huntress, and she let her hair
Fly loose in the wind. Her flowing robe was cinched up
In a knot, offering a glimpse of her knees.
She spoke first:

        "Have either of you seen   395
Any of my sisters? They're sporting quivers
And lynx hides. They may have wandered here,
Or are hot on the trail of a frothing boar."

Thus Venus, and the son of Venus responded:

"I've neither heard nor seen any of your sisters.   400
But how should I address you, Maiden? Your face
Is hardly mortal, and your voice does not sound human.
Surely you are a goddess. Apollo's sister?
One of the Nymphs? Whoever you are, Goddess,
Be gracious to us, lighten our burden,   405
And tell us, under what sky are we now?
Into what part of the world have we been tossed?
We are strangers in a strange land, lost,
Driven here by the wind and immense seas.
Many victims will fall by my hand at your altars."   410

And Venus:

        "I am hardly worthy of such honor.
It is customary among Tyrian girls
To carry quivers and lace on high scarlet boots.
What you see around you is Tyrian country
And a Punic city from Agenor's bloodline,   415
But it borders on Libya, a warlike nation.
Dido rules here, having left her city, Tyre,
To escape from her brother. It's a long story,
Full of intrigue, but I will sum it up for you.

Dido's husband, Sychaeus, was the richest man   *420*
In Phoenicia, and loved dearly
By ill-starred Dido. Her father, with good omens,
Had given her to him untouched and virgin.
But her brother, Pygmalion, who ruled the land,
Was a most wicked man. A feud rose up   *425*
Between the two men, and impious Pygmalion,
Blind with gold-lust and contemptuous
Of his sister's love, secretly cut down Sychaeus
Before the altars, alone and off guard.
The villain hid his crime for a long time   *430*
And with many pretenses cruelly kept alive
Poor Dido's vain hopes. But the actual ghost
Of her unburied husband visited her dreams,
Lifting his pale face in wondrous ways.
He showed her the bloodstained altars,   *435*
Bared his pierced chest, and revealed the crime
At the dark heart of the noble house.
Then he urged her to flee the country,
And, to aid her journey, he showed her where
An ancient, secret treasure was buried,   *440*
Untold tons of silver and gold. Roused by all this,
Dido prepared for flight, joined by others
Who either feared or hated the cruel tyrant.
They commandeered ships, loaded them with gold,
And all the wealth of avaricious Pygmalion   *445*
Was shipped out to sea. A woman did this.
They arrived at the place where now you see
The soaring walls of a new city—Carthage.
They bought as much land as they could surround
With the hide of an ox, and so its name Byrsa.   *450*
But who are you? From what shores did you sail,
And where are you going?"

      Faced with such questions,
Aeneas sighed and drew his voice from deep within:

"Goddess, if I were to start from the beginning
And tell you the whole tale of our suffering,   *455*
Dusk would gather over the dying day.
We are from Troy. Perhaps the name
Of that ancient city means something to you.

We have wandered the seas, and a storm
Has driven us to the coast of Libya.   460
I am Aeneas, devoted to my city's gods,
Refugees I rescued from enemy hands,
And my ship's most precious cargo. My fame
Has reached the heavens above. My quest
Is for Italy to be our fatherland, and to found   465
A race descended from Jove most high.
I embarked on the Phrygian sea with twenty ships,
My mother charting my course
As I pursued my destiny. Scarcely seven
Have survived the winds and the waves.   470
Lost, destitute, I wander the Libyan desert,
A man expelled from both Europe and Asia."

Venus would not endure any further self-pity
And interrupted him in mid-complaint:

"Whoever you are, I can hardly believe   475
You draw your breath cursed by the gods.
After all, here you are at our Tyrian town.
Just get yourself to the Queen's doorstep.
I foretell that your ships and comrades are safe,
Driven to shore by winds from the North—   480
Unless I've learned nothing about reading birds.
Observe the serenity of those twelve gliding swans.
An eagle, Jove's bird, swooped down from above
And disturbed their flight in the open sky,
But now they are flying in a long line again.   485
Some have landed, and you can see the others
Looking down for a good place to alight.
Just as those birds, in formation again,
Sport with wings whirring, rimming the sky
And issuing their song, so too your ships,   490
With their hearty crews, are either in port
Or entering the harbor under full sail.
Well, go on. Just let your feet follow the road."

She spoke, and as she turned, her neck
Shone with roselight. An immortal fragrance   495
From her ambrosial locks perfumed the air,
Her robes flowed down to cover her feet,
And every step revealed her divinity.

Aeneas knew his own mother, and his voice
Fell away from her as she disappeared: *500*

"You! Do you have to cheat your son
With empty appearances? Why can't we
At least embrace and talk to each other
In our own true voices?"

                              With this rebuke,
Aeneas turned toward the city.   *505*
Venus, for her part, enclosed both her son
And his companion in a dark cloud,
Cloaking them in mist so that none would see them
As they walked along and so detain them
With questions about their reasons for coming.   *510*
And then she was gone, aloft to Paphus,
Happy to see her temple again, where Arabian
Incense curls up from one hundred altars
And fresh wreaths of flowers sweeten the air.

The two heroes, meanwhile, followed the path   *515*
And ascended a hill high above the city.
Looking down, Aeneas was amazed
At the sheer size of the place—once a few hovels—
The city gates, the bustle on the paved streets.
The Tyrians were hard at work, building walls,   *520*
Fortifying the citadel, rolling boulders by hand,
Marking out sites for houses with trenches.
As Aeneas watched, they made laws, chose officials,
Installed a senate. Some were dredging
The harbor, others laying the foundation   *525*
For a theater, carving huge columns out of a cliff
To grace the stage that was yet to be built—

    Like bees under an early summer sun
    Leading a new swarm out to the wildflowers,
    Or stuffing honey into the comb,   *530*
    Swelling the cells with nectar, or unloading
    The pollen other bees bring to the stall,
    Or warding off the worthless brood of drones:
    The busy hive seethes with all their activity
    And the fragrant honey is redolent of thyme.   *535*

"Happy are they whose walls are rising."

Thus Aeneas, as he surveyed the city's heights.
And then, hidden in the miraculous cloud
He mingled with the citizens, invisible to all.

At the city's center there was a shady grove.   540
It was here the Phoenicians when they made land,
Refugees from the surge and storms of the sea,
Had dug up the token foretold by Juno,
The head of a spirited horse, an augury
Of success in war and a prosperous people.   545
Here Sidonian Dido had dedicated
A huge temple to Juno, rich with offerings
And the goddess's presence. A bronze threshold
Surmounted the steps; the joints and beams glowed
With bronze, and bronze doors slowly groaned open   550
On heavy hinges. It was in this grove that Aeneas
Could finally relax; here he first dared
To hope for safe harbor and have confidence,
After all his trials, in a turn for the better.
For while he was waiting for the Queen,   555
Touring the temple, marveling at the city's
Great good fortune and at the work
Of various artisans blended together,
He saw pictured on the walls the whole Trojan War,
Whose fame had already spread through the world.   560
There were the sons of Atreus, there Priam,
And there Achilles, raging at each of them.
Aeneas stopped and said with tears in his eyes:

"Is there any place on earth, Achates,
Not filled with our sorrows? Look,   565
There is Priam! Here, too, honor matters;
Here are the tears of the ages, and minds touched
By human suffering. Breathe easy, my friend.
Troy's renown will yet be your salvation."

                              Thus Aeneas,
And he fed his soul on empty pictures,   570
Sighing, weeping, his face a flood of tears
As he scanned the murals of the Trojan War.

On one panel the Greeks are in full retreat,
With the Trojan youth hard on their heels.
In the other direction crested Achilles   575
   Bears down on the Trojans with his chariot.

A little farther on he sees through his tears
The snowy canvas of Rhesus' tents,
His camp betrayed in their first night at Troy
And savaged by the blood-soaked son of Tydeus,   580
Who then drove the fiery steeds of Rhesus
To the Greek camp, before they ever tasted
   Trojan fodder or drank from the Xanthus.

On another panel Troilus, just a boy
And no match for Achilles in combat,   585
Has lost his armor and is being dragged
By his stampeding horses. Fallen backward
From his empty chariot, he still holds the reins
While his neck and hair trail in the dust
   And the plain is scored by the tip of his spear.   590

Meanwhile, Trojan women, their hair streaming,
Are going to the temple of implacable Pallas,
Bearing a robe and beating their breasts
In supplication. The goddess's head is turned away,
   And she keeps her eyes fixed on the ground.   595

And now Achilles has dragged Hector
Three times around the walls of Troy
And is selling the lifeless body for gold.
Aeneas is choked with grief when he sees the spoils,
The chariot, the corpse of his friend,   600
   And Priam stretching out weaponless hands.

And now Aeneas recognizes himself
In close combat with the foremost Achaeans
And sees the eastern ranks, dark Memnon's armor,
And Penthesilea among her thousands of Amazons   605
With their crescent shields. Burning with fury,
She binds a golden belt below one naked breast,
   A warrior queen daring to do battle with men.

While Aeneas' gaze was fixed on these marvels,

The Queen was making her way to the temple,   610
The most beautiful Dido, and as she walked
A throng of youths crowded around her.

On the Eurotas' banks or the ridges of Cynthus
Diana leads the dances, and a thousand Oreads
Circle around her this way and that. A quiver   615
Hangs from her shoulder, and as she treads
She towers above the other goddesses,
And Latona's heart beats with secret joy.

So too Dido, moving through their midst,
Urged on the work of building a kingdom.   620
Then, under the temple's vaulted entrance
And flanked by guards, she ascended her throne.
She was making laws for her people,
Distributing duties or assigning them by lot,
When suddenly Aeneas saw, coming toward him   625
In a crowd, Antheus, Sergestus, and brave Cloanthus
Along with other Trojans whom the black storm
Had scattered and driven to distant shores.
Aeneas was stunned, Achates too, with joy and fear.
They burned with desire to clasp hands with them   630
But were confused and uncertain of the situation.
They kept themselves hidden inside the cloud
And watched. What has happened to their comrades?
On what shore did they leave their ships?
Why have they come here? These are chosen men   635
From all the ships, making for the temple
With loud cries and prayers for indulgence.

When they had entered and were allowed to speak,
The eldest, Ilioneus, calmly began:

"Queen, whom Jupiter has permitted   640
To found a new city and to curb with justice
The arrogance of the surrounding tribes,
We are Trojans, blown by winds over the sea.
In our misery we pray you to prohibit
The burning of our ships. Spare a pious race,   645
And look with grace upon our fortunes.
We have not come to pillage your homes

And carry the booty down to the shore.
There is no such violence in our hearts
And no such arrogance in a conquered race.   650
There is a place the Greeks call Hesperia,
An ancient land, strong in war and rich in soil.
Oenotrians once lived there. Now, it is said,
A younger race has named it Italy
After their leader. We were on course   655
For that land, when a sudden squall
Rose up—Orion behind it—and drove us
Onto blind shoals, scattering our ships
Amid trackless rocks and overwhelming waves.
We few drifted along and came to your shores.   660
But what race of men is this? What land
Is so barbarous that it allows this conduct?
We are denied access to the very shore!
These warmongers forbid us to set foot
On the border of their land. You may scorn   665
Our common humanity and mortal arms,
But the gods will remember good and evil.
We had a king, Aeneas, no one more just
Or devoted, no one greater in battle.
If Fate still preserves him, if he still breathes   670
The sky's pure air and does not yet lie with the shades,
We have no fear, nor would you regret
Being first to contend with him in courtesy.
          There are cities in Sicily too, and arms,
And a hero of Trojan blood, Acestes.   675
Allow us to beach our storm-battered fleet,
To mill planks and trim oars from your woods,
So that if we find our comrades and leader,
And we are destined to go to Italy, to Italy
And to Latium we may gladly set forth.   680
But if all is lost, and you, noble father
Of the Trojan people, have gone down
In the Libyan sea, and Iülus
Is our hope no more, then at least we can seek
The straits of Sicily—whence we came here—   685
And our homes there, with Acestes as our king."

Thus Ilioneus, and all the Trojans
Murmured in approval.

Dido, eyes lowered, responded briefly:

"Fear no more, Teucrians, ease your hearts.   690
Stern necessity and my kingdom's newness
Force me to such measures to protect our frontier.
Who does not know of Aeneas and Troy,
Of that city's warriors and its exploits,
Of the conflagrations of that great war?   695
Punic hearts are not so dull and unfeeling,
Nor is Tyre so far from the course of the sun.
Whether you choose great Hesperia, land of Saturn,
Or Sicily, the realm of Acestes,
I will speed you safely on your journey.   700
Or would you like to settle here, share my kingdom?
The city I am founding is yours. Draw up your ships.
Trojan and Tyrian I will treat the same.
I only wish that Aeneas himself were here,
Driven in by the same South Wind. Be sure   705
I will dispatch our best men to scour the coast
And search every corner of Libya.
He may have been cast ashore and
May be wandering now in some wood or town."

Aeneas and Achates, alert to every word,   710
Had long been burning to burst from the cloud,
And now Achates turned to Aeneas and said:

"What do you think, Goddess-born? You see
That all is safe, our ships and men restored.
Only one is missing, and he went down in the gulf   715
Before our own eyes. Everything else agrees
With your mother's words."

                              He had scarcely finished
When the enveloping cloud parted
And dissolved into thin air. There stood Aeneas,
Gleaming in the clear light, his face and shoulders   720
Like a god's. His mother breathed upon him
The radiance of youth, breathed glory on his hair,
And she gave his eyes an exultant luster
Like the sheen of hand-rubbed ivory,

Or Parian marble, or silver set in gold.   725
Unforeseen, unexpected, he addressed the Queen:

"The man you seek is before you. I am
Aeneas, of Troy, saved from Libyan seas.
Dido, you alone have pitied Ilium's
Unutterable woes, and now you offer us—   730
The remnant left by the Greeks, outworn
By every misfortune on land and sea,
A destitute band—you offer us
A share of your city and your home.
We do not have the means to render worthy thanks,   735
Nor do any Trojan survivors anywhere
In the wide world. May the gods—
If any powers above look down on the pious,
If there is any justice anywhere—may the gods
And your good conscience reward you   740
As you deserve. What happy age bore you?
What noble parents gave birth to such a child?
While rivers run to the sea, while shadows
Move over mountainsides, while the sky
Pastures the stars, ever shall your honor,   745
Your name, and your praises endure,
Whatever the lands that summon me."

Aeneas spoke, and he reached out
For dear Ilioneus with his right hand,
Serestus with his left, and then the others,   750
His brave Gyas and brave Cloanthus.

Dido, stunned by his sudden appearance
And his great ill fortune, responded:

"Goddess-born, what misfortune has plagued you,
What force has driven you onto savage coasts?   755
You, then, are Aeneas, whom Venus bore to Anchises
Near the waters of the Simois river in Troy?
I remember well when Teucer came to Sidon,
Exiled by his father and seeking new realms
With the aid of Belus, my own father,   760
Who was waging war in Cyprus then,
Establishing his power in that rich land.

Since that time I have known about Troy,
Known you by name, and the Pelasgian leaders.
The Trojans' enemy sang Troy's praises   765
And wanted it known that he was of Trojan stock.
And so, young men, come under my roof.
My fortune too has long been adverse
But at last has allowed me to rest in this land.
My own acquaintance with suffering   770
Has taught me to aid others in need."

Thus Dido, and as she led Aeneas into her palace
She proclaimed sacrifices in his honor
In all the temples. Meanwhile, she sent
To his comrades on the shore twenty bulls,   775
A hundred boars with great, bristling backs,
And as many fat lambs with their dams,
The day's joyful gifts.
                      The palace gleamed
With luxurious furnishings as the great hall
Was being prepared for a banquet: 780
Coverlets embroidered with royal purple,
Heavy silver on the tables, gold cups engraved
With the heroic deeds of a long lineage
Stretching back to the origin of the race.

But Aeneas' love for his son, Ascanius,   785
Would not allow his mind to rest. He sent
Achates, on the run, to the ships
To report the news and to bring the boy
Back to the city. Ascanius was all Aeneas' care.
He also told Achates to bring presents   790
Snatched from ruined Ilium: a mantle
Stiff with gold-stitched figures, and a veil
Fringed with saffron acanthus, both worn
By Helen, who brought them from Mycenae—
Wondrous gifts from her mother, Leda—   795
When she sailed for Troy and her illicit wedding;
The scepter, too, of Priam's eldest daughter,
Ilione; and a pearl necklace; and a coronet
With a double band of jewels and gold.
And so Achates hurried off to the ships.   800

Venus, meanwhile, was busily concocting
Another scheme. She would send Cupid—
Transformed to look just like Ascanius—
To come in the place of that sweet boy
And with his gifts enflame the Queen's heart   805
And infiltrate her bones with fire.
The Cytherean feared this dubious union,
Tyrians speaking two tongues. She chafed
Under Juno's arrogance, and at nightfall
Her anxiety mounted. She turned, therefore,   810
To the winged God of Love and spoke to him:

"My son, my strength and my power, you alone
Scorn your father's Typhoean lightning blasts,
And so to your godhead I come on bended knee.
You know how your brother, Aeneas,   815
Is beaten about the sea by Juno's wrath,
And you have often grieved at my grief for him.
Phoenician Dido now has him, and detains him
With soft words. I dread the outcome
Of Juno's hospitality. She will not be idle   820
During this great turn of events. And so,
I plan to catch the Queen off guard and by guile
Encircle her with passion, so that no power
Can change her, and she will be bound to me,
By her great love for my Aeneas.   825
Now here is how I think you can do this.
The young prince, my pride and joy and all my care,
Is preparing to go, at his father's summons,
To the Sidonian city, bearing such gifts
As have survived the sea and the flames of Troy.   830
I will wrap him in slumber and tuck him away
In my sacred shrine, either high on Cythera
Or on Idalium, so that he will never know
Of my trickery or get in the way.
For a single night, no more, feign his looks.   835
Boy that you are, wear the boy's familiar face.
And when amid the royal feast and flowing wine
Dido, her joy knowing no bounds, takes you
Onto her lap, embraces you and plants
Sweet kisses on your mouth, breathe into her   840
Your secret fire and poison her unobserved."

Love obeyed his dear mother, donned his wings,
And walked off joyously with Iülus' gait.
Iülus himself Venus bathed in the waters
Of calm repose and, holding him to her breast,   845
Lifted him up to Idalia's high groves,
Where soft marjoram breathed upon him,
Nestled in blossoms sweet in the shade.

And so Cupid, obedient to his mother's word,
And delighting in the company of Achates,   850
Carried the royal gifts to the palace.
When he arrived, the Queen had already
Taken her place amid gorgeous tapestries,
Reclining on a golden couch in the great hall.
Father Aeneas and the Trojan youth gathered   855
And were made to recline on purple coverlets.
Servants poured water on their hands, served bread
From baskets, and brought them soft napkins.
There were fifty maids working in the kitchen
To prepare all the banquet's dishes in order   860
And to keep the hearth-fire for the Penates.
Another hundred, and as many male servants,
All the same age, laid the food on the table
And set out the cups.
     The Tyrians too
Crowded the festive hall and were told to recline   865
On embroidered couches. They marveled
At Aeneas' gifts, and they marveled at Iülus,
At the god's glowing complexion, at the words
He feigned, and at the robe and the veil
Elaborately stitched with saffron acanthus.   870
Dido especially, doomed to a wretched end,
Could not satisfy her soul. The ill-fated Phoenician
Burned with desire when she gazed at the boy
And was equally moved at the sight of the gifts.
The boy, when he had hung on Aeneas' neck   875
And satisfied the deluded father's love,
Went to the Queen. And she clung to him
With all her heart, her eyes were riveted on him,
And she cuddled him on her lap. Poor Dido.
She had no idea how great a god had settled there.   880
Mindful of his Acidalian mother,

Little by little he began to blot out Sychaeus
And tried to captivate with a living passion
Her slumbering soul and her heart long unused.

At the first lull in the feast the tables were cleared.   885
Great bowls were set out and crowned with wine.
The palace grew loud, and the guests' voices
Echoed through the halls. Glowing lamps
Hung down from the fretted gold ceiling,
And flaming torches vanquished the night.   890
Dido called for a heavy gold drinking bowl
Crusted with jewels and filled it with wine—
A bowl used by Belus and Belus' descendants.
Then silence reigned in the great hall again.

"Jupiter, Lord of Hospitality,   895
Grant that this day be a happy one
For Tyrians and Trojan travelers alike,
And may our children remember it!
May Bacchus, giver of joy, be near,
May Juno bless us, and may all Tyrians   900
Favor our gathering with grace and good cheer."

Dido prayed and then poured a drop
Onto the table. After this libation,
Her lips were the first to touch the bowl's rim.
Then she passed it to Bitias with a challenge,   905
And he promptly drained the foaming bowl,
Soaking himself in the brimming gold.
Then the other lords drank.
                         Long-haired Iopas,
A bard taught by mighty Atlas,
Now sounded his golden lyre.
                         He sang   910
Of the wandering moon and the sun's toils,
Of the origin of human and animal kind,
Of how rain falls and why lightning flashes,
Of Arcturus, the Bears, and the misty Hyades,
Of why the winter sun rushes down to Ocean,   915
And why long winter nights are so slow to end.

The Tyrians applauded again and again,
And the Trojans joined in. And Dido,

Unhappy woman, prolonged the night
With varied conversation   920
And drank deeply the long draught of love.
She asked about Priam over and over,
Asked much about Hector, wanted to know
What armor Memnon wore when he arrived,
What the horses of Diomedes were like,   925
And how great was Achilles.

                    "Still better,"
She cries, "Tell us, my dear guest,
The whole story from the beginning—
The treachery of the Greeks, the downfall
Of your people, and your own wanderings.   930
Seven summers have now seen you roving
Through every land and over all the seas."

AENEID TWO

The room fell silent, all eyes on Aeneas,
Who from his high couch now began to speak:

"My Queen, you are asking me to relive
Unspeakable sorrow, to recall how the Greeks
Pulled down Troy, that tragic realm   5
With all its riches. I saw those horrors myself
And played no small part in them. What Myrmidon
Or Dolopian, what brutal soldier of Ulysses
Could tell such a tale and refrain from tears?
And now dewy night is rushing from the sky,   10
And the setting stars make sleep seem sweet.
But if you are so passionate to learn
Of our misfortunes, to hear a brief account
Of Troy's last struggle—although my mind
Shudders to remember and recoils in pain,   15
I will begin.

Broken by war and rebuffed by the Fates
For so many years, the Greek warlords
Built a horse, aided by the divine art
Of Pallas, a horse the size of a mountain,   20
Weaving its ribs out of beams of fir.
They pretended it was a votive offering
For their safe return home. So the story went.
But deep within the Horse's cavernous dark
They concealed an elite band, all their best,   25
Stuffing its huge womb with men at arms.

Within sight of Troy lies a famous island,
Tenedos, prosperous while Priam's kingdom stood,
Now just a bay with poor anchorage for ships.
The Greeks sailed there and hid on the desolate shore;   30
They were gone, we thought, sailed off to Mycenae.

26

And so all of Troy shook off its long sorrow.
The gates were opened. It was a joy to visit
The Doric camp, the abandoned beachhead,
The deserted sites. Here the Dolopians   35
Pitched their tents, here fierce Achilles,
Here lay the ships, here were the battle-lines.
Some of us gaped at the virgin Minerva's
Fatal gift, amazed at the massive Horse.
Thymoetes wanted it dragged inside the walls   40
And installed in the citadel. Treason perhaps,
Or Troy's doom was already in motion.
But Capys, and other wiser heads, urged us
To either pitch this insidious Greek gift
Into the sea, or burn it on the spot, or else   45
Pierce and probe the belly's hidden hollows.
The crowd took sides, uncertain what to do.

And now Laocoön comes running down
From the citadel at the head of a great throng
And in his burning haste he cries from afar: 50

'Are you out of your minds, you poor fools?
Are you so easily convinced that the enemy
Has sailed away? Do you honestly think
That any Greek gift comes without treachery?
What is Ulysses known for? Either this lumber   55
Is hiding Achaeans inside, or it has been built
As an engine of war to attack our walls,
To spy on our homes and come down on the city
From above. Or some other evil lurks inside.
Do not trust the Horse, Trojans! Whatever it is,   60
I fear the Greeks, even when they bring gifts.'

With that, he hurled his spear with enormous force
Into the vaulting belly of the beast. The shaft
Stood quivering, and the hollow insides
Reverberated with a cavernous moan.   65
If we had not been on the gods' wrong side,
If we had been thinking right, Laocoön
Would have driven us to hack our way into
The Greek lair, and Troy would still stand,
And you, high rock of Priam, would remain.   70

But at that moment a band of Dardan shepherds
Came up with loud shouts, dragging to the king
A prisoner with his hands bound behind his back.
This man had deliberately gotten himself captured
With one purpose in mind, to open Troy to the Greeks,   75
Ready to either work his deceits or face certain death.
The Trojan youths streamed in from all sides
To see the captive and jeer at him.
                               Hear now
The treachery of the Greeks, and from one offense
Learn all their evil.
                      The man stood in full sight   80
Of the crowd, dismayed, unarmed, and glancing
Around at the ranks of men he cried out:

'Ah, what land, what sea, can receive me now,
What will be my final wretched fate?
I have no place among the Greeks,   85
And the Trojans are clamoring for my blood.'

At this our mood changed, and we prodded him
To tell us what he meant. Who were his people,
And what was he counting on to save him
Now that he was our prisoner? Finally,   90
He stopped trembling and began to speak:

'Come what may, King, I will tell you all
And not deny, first, that I am a Danaan.
Fortune may have damned Sinon to misery,
But she will not make him a liar as well.   95
You may have heard the name Palamedes,
Belus' glorious son, whom the Greeks
Condemned to death, under false charges,
Because he opposed the war. He was innocent.
Now they mourn him, now that he is dead.   100
He was my kinsman, and my father,
A poor man, sent me here in his company
When I was just a boy. While Palamedes
Was still in good standing, still thrived in council,
I too had somewhat of a name, some honor.   105
But when through the malice of cunning Ulysses
(Everyone knows this) he passed from this world,

I was a ruined man and dragged on my life
In darkness and grief, eating my heart out
Over the fate of my innocent friend.   110
Nor was I silent, but I raved
That if I ever had the chance, ever returned
As victor to Argos, I would have my vengeance.
My words aroused resentment, and my life
Was now infected. Ulysses made it his mission   115
To terrorize me with countless new charges,
Sowing rumors in everyone's ears, searching
In his guilt for weapons against me. In the end
He found Fortune's tool, Calchas the soothsayer—
But you don't want to hear all this. And why   120
Should I stall? If you paint all Greeks
With the same stripe, if "he's Achaean"
Is all you need to hear, take your vengeance
At once. This is what the Ithacan would want,
And what Atreus' sons would pay dearly for.'   125

Now indeed we burned to know more,
Strangers as we were to infamy so great
And to Greek guile. Trembling, he went on:

'Weary with the long war, the Greeks
Often wanted to quit Troy and sail home.   130
If only they had! But stormy weather
And rough seas would scare them from leaving.
And when they'd hammered together
The maple horse, the sky rumbled even more.
Anxious, we sent Eurypylus to consult   135
The oracle of Phoebus Apollo,
And he brought back these dismal words:
You placated the winds with a virgin's blood
To come, O Danaans, to the shores of Troy.
Your return must be won with an Argive life.   140
When the god's words reached the army's ears
Everyone was dazed, and an icy fear
Seeped into their bones. Which man was doomed,
Whom would Apollo claim? The Ithacan
Dragged Calchas out into the roaring crowd   145
And demanded to know what heaven portended.
Many divined that this despicable ploy

Was aimed at me and saw what was coming.
Five days and five more the seer sat in his hut,
Silent, refusing to sentence anyone to death.   150
Finally, forced by the Ithacan's cries,
Calchas broke his silence and, as agreed,
Doomed me to the altar. Everyone approved,
And the ruin each had feared for himself
They bore well when it devolved upon one.   155

'And now the dark day dawned. The salted grain,
The sacral headbands were being prepared
For my ritual slaughter, when, I confess,
I broke my bonds and snatched myself from death.
I skulked all night in a muddy swamp,   160
Hidden in the sedge, holding my breath
Until they sailed. Now I have no hope
Of seeing my homeland, my sweet children,
The father I long for. And the Greeks
May make them pay for my escape, poor things,   165
And by their death expiate my sin.
And so I pray, by whatever powers above
Still witness Truth, and by any Faith we men
Still have uncorrupted, show mercy
To a suffering soul, guiltless and wronged.'   170

We spared him for his tears and pitied him
Of our own accord. Priam himself ordered
His shackles removed and spoke to him kindly:

'Whoever you are, take no further thought
Of the Greeks. You are one of us now.   175
But tell me, and speak the whole truth:
Why did they erect this monstrous horse?
Who devised it, and to what purpose?
Is it a religious offering or an engine of war?'

Thus Priam. And Sinon, the consummate liar,   180
Lifting his unchained hands to the stars:

'Eternal fires of heaven, I summon you
And your inviolable Power to witness,
And you altars and nefarious blades

Which I escaped, and you consecrated fillets   185
Which as victim I wore: it is just for me
To break the sacred oaths of the Greeks,
Just to abhor those men, and to lay bare to the sky
Every secret they would conceal. I am bound
By no law of my country. But you, Troy,   190
Stand by your word and keep your faith,
If what I say proves to be your salvation.

'From the war's beginning, Pallas Athena
Was the Greeks' entire hope. But when
Wicked Diomedes and Ulysses,   195
With his criminal mind, entered
Her high temple, murdered the guards,
And stole the fateful Palladium,
Daring to handle her virgin fillets
With bloodstained fingers—then   200
The Danaans' fortunes began to falter,
Their strength was broken, and the goddess
Turned her back on them. Tritonia
Gave us clear portents of her displeasure.
As soon as her statue was set up in camp,   205
Flames glittered from her upturned eyes,
Sweat poured down her limbs, and three times
She flashed up from the ground, miraculous,
Holding her shield and quivering spear.
Calchas at once began to prophesy: 210

"The Greeks must attempt a retreat by sea.
Troy cannot be taken by Argive weapons
Until they seek new omens in Argos
And return the godhead carried away
In curved keels over open water."   215

'They are sailing over to Mycenae now,
And when they have recruited soldiers and gods
They will recross the water all unforeseen.
So Calchas sifted the omens and counseled the Greeks
To erect this Horse, in expiation   220
Of the Palladium's theft and the godhead wronged.
And he ordered them to build its oaken bulk
Up to the sky, so it could not be brought

Through the city's gates or walls and there protect
The Trojan people under the old religion.   225
For if you lay violent hands
Upon this offering to Minerva,
Destruction will fall—may the gods turn this omen
Against the Greeks—upon Priam's realm.
But if your hands bring it into the city,   230
Asia will wage war upon Pelops' walls,
And this fate awaits our children's children.'

And so through Sinon's treacherous art
His story was believed, and we were taken
With cunning, captured with forced tears,   235
We whom neither great Diomedes
Nor Achilles of Larissa could subdue,
Nor ten years of war, nor a thousand ships.

What happened next was more horrible still
And threw us into deepening chaos.   240
Laocoön, serving by lot as Neptune's priest,
Was sacrificing a great bull at the god's altar,
When we saw, coming from Tenedos
Over the calm water, a pair of serpents—
I shudder to recall them—making for shore.   245
Trailing huge coils they sheared through the sea,
And their bloody crests arched over the waves
As they writhed and twisted in the seething surf.
They were almost ashore. Their eyes
Were shot with blood and fire, and their tongues   250
Hissed and flickered in their open mouths.
We scattered, pale with fear, as the sea-snakes
Glided through the sand straight for Laocoön.
First, they entwined the priest's two sons
In great looping spirals, and then they sank their fangs   255
Into the boys' wretched bodies and began to feed.
Then they seized Laocoön as he ran to their aid,
Weapon in hand, and lashed their scaly bodies
Twice around his waist and twice around his neck,
Their heads reared high. As the priest struggled   260
To wrench himself free from the knotted coils,
His headbands were soaked with venom and gore,
And his horrible cries reached up to the stars.

Wounded by an ill-aimed blow, a bull will bellow
As it flees the altar and shakes the axe from his neck.   265

So too Laocoön. But the twin serpents
Slithered off to the high temple of Pallas
And took refuge at the grim goddess's feet,
Vanished behind the disk of her shield.

An inhuman terror coiled through our hearts.   270
Shuddering with horror, everyone said Laocoön
Had received the punishment he deserved
For wounding the sacred wood of the Horse
With his accursed spear. All proclaimed
The Horse should be drawn to Minerva's temple   275
And her godhead appeased. We breached the walls,
Everyone girding themselves for the work,
And set wheels beneath the feet of the Horse.
A noose was made taut around its neck
And the fateful contraption inched up the battlements,   280
Pregnant with arms. Boys and unwed girls
Circled around it, singing hymns
And touching the rope with glee. On it moved,
Gliding like a threat into the city.
O my country! O Ilium, home of the gods!   285
O walls of Troy famed in war! Four times
At the very threshold of the city gate
The Horse halted, and four times
Weapons clattered in its belly. Yet we pressed on
Mindlessly, blind with passion, and installed   290
The ill-starred monster on our high holy rock.
Even then Cassandra opened her lips
Against the coming doom, lips cursed by a god
Never to be believed by the Teucrians,
And we pitiful Trojans, on our last day,   295
Wreathed the shrines of the gods with flowers.

The sky turned, and night swept up from Ocean,
Enfolding in its great shadow earth and heaven—
And the Myrmidons' treachery. The Trojans
Spread out along the wall were dead silent now,   300
Slumber entwining their weary limbs,
And the Argive fleet started to sail from Tenedos

Through the silent, complicit moonlight,
Making for the shore they knew all too well.
The flagship raised a beacon, and at this signal   305
Sinon, cloaked by the gods' unjust decrees,
Stealthily unlocked the pine trapdoor,
And the Horse released from its open womb
The enclosed Danaans, glad to push themselves out
Of the hollow oak into the cool night air,   310
Thessandrus and Sthenelus and grim Ulysses—
Sliding down the rope—Acamas and Thoas,
Achilles' son, Neoptolemus, great Machaon,
Menelaus, and Epeos himself,
The fabricator of the insidious horse.   315
They fanned out through a city drowned in sleep,
Slit the guards' throats, opened all the gates,
And joined as planned the invading Greeks.

At that late hour, when sleep begins to drift
Upon fretful humanity as grace from the gods,   320
Hector appeared to me in my dreams,
Pitiful spirit, weeping, black with blood
And dust from the ruts of Achilles' chariot,
Thongs piercing his swollen ankles. Ah,
How he looked, how different from that Hector   325
Who returned to Troy wearing Achilles' armor,
The Hector who threw fire on the Danaan ships!
His beard was matted, his hair clotted with gore,
And he bore all the wounds he had received
Fighting before his country's walls. In my dream   330
I blurted out to him these tearful words:

'Light of Dardania, Troy's finest hope,
What has delayed you? From what shores have you come
To answer our prayers? We have suffered
Many losses since you left us, Hector.   335
Yet, we have labored on, and now we see you
At the end of our strength. Why has your face
Been defiled, and what are these wounds I see?'

My empty questions meant nothing to him.
With a heavy sigh from deep within, he said: 340

'Run, child of the goddess, save yourself
From these flames! The enemy holds the walls.
Great Troy is falling. Enough has been given
To Priam and his country. If Pergamum's height
Could be defended by a hero's hand,   345
Its defense would have been this hand of mine.
Troy commends to you the gods of the city.
Accept them as companions of your destiny
And seek for them the great walls you will found
After you have wandered across the sea.'   350

He spoke, and brought out from the sanctuary
Great Vesta, her chaplets, and her eternal fire.

By now the lamentation in the city
Had grown to such proportions that it reached
My father Anchises' house, secluded though it was   355
Among the pines. The sickening sound of battle
Startled me from sleep, and I climbed to the roof
And stood at the very top, upright and listening.

   It was as if the South Wind were fanning fire
   Through the fields, or a mountain torrent had leveled   360
   The farmlands and swept away the oxen's tillage,
   Flattening the hedgerows, and I was a shepherd
   Listening in the dark from some towering rock.

Then the truth was revealed. The Danaans' treachery
Lay open before me. Deïphobus' great house   365
Was collapsing in flames, as was Ucalegon's
Next door. The Sigean straits burned
With the inferno's reflected light.
Men's shouts rose with the shrill sound of horns.
Out of my mind, I took up arms—no battle plan,   370
But my soul burned to gather a war party
And storm the citadel. Rage and fury
Sent my mind reeling, and my only thought
Was how glorious it is to die in combat.

At that moment Panthus, priest of Apollo,   375
Ran up to my door, dragging his grandson
Away from Greek swords, the sacred images
Of our vanquished gods clutched in his arms.

'Where is the fighting thickest, Panthus?
What position should we try to hold?'

                        My words   380
Were scarcely out when he answered, groaning:

'Troy's last day and final hour have come.
We are Trojans no more. Ilium is no more.
The great glory of the Teucrians is gone.
Jupiter in his rage has given all to Argos,   385
And Greeks are lords of our burning city.
High stands the Horse, pouring forth armed men,
And Sinon, insolent in victory,
Sets fires everywhere. Thousands of troops,
As many as ever came from Mycenae,   390
Are at the wide-open gates. Others patrol the streets.
A line of unsheathed, glistening steel
Stands ready for slaughter. Our night guard
Is barely resisting and fighting blind.'

Panthus' words and will of the gods   395
Drove me through the inferno of battle
Wherever the grim Fury called, wherever
The roars and shouts rose to the sky.
Falling in with me in the moonlight
Were Rhipeus and Epytus, one of Troy's best,   400
Hypanis and Dymas, a little throng now,
And young Coroebus, son of Mygdon.
He had come to Troy in those last days,
Madly in love with Cassandra, and brought
Aid to Priam, a sturdy son-in-law. Poor boy,   405
If only he had listened to the warnings
Of his raving bride.
When I saw them close ranks, eager for battle,
I began:

        'Brave hearts—brave in vain
If you are committed to follow me to the end—   410
You see how we stand. All the gods
Who sustained this realm are gone, leaving
Altar and shrine. You are fighting to save
A city in flames. All that is left for us

Is to rush onto swords and die. The only chance   415
For the conquered is to hope for none.'

This added fury to the young men's courage.
Like wolves in a black mist, blind with hunger,
Their whelps waiting with dry throats, we passed
Through the enemy's swords to certain death   420
And held our course to the city's center.
Ebony night swirled around us. Who could tell
That night's carnage, or match it with tears?
The ancient city fell, that had for many years
Been queen. Corpses lay piled everywhere,   425
In the streets, the houses, the hallowed thresholds
Of the temples. And it was not only Trojans
Who paid in blood. At times the vanquished
Felt their valor pulse through their hearts,
And the conquering Greeks fell. Raw fear   430
Was everywhere, grief was everywhere,
Everywhere the many masks of death.

Androgeos offered himself to us first.
Heading up a large company of Greeks,
He mistook us for an allied band and called: 435

'On the double, men! What took you so long?
We're burning and looting Pergamum here,
And you're just arriving from the ships?'

He realized at once from our tentative reply
That we were the enemy. He froze, choked   440
On his own words, and then tried to backpedal,

> Like a man who has stepped on a snake
> Hidden in briars and in sudden terror cringes
> When it rears and puffs out its purple hood.

Androgeos was shaking and backing away   445
When we charged and hedged them in.
Unfamiliar with the terrain, they panicked.
And we cut them down, Fortune smiling
On our first effort. Flushed with success,
Coroebus cried:

'Let's follow Fortune's lead   450
And exchange our armor for Danaan gear.
Who cares if this is deceit or valor?
The enemy will supply us with weapons.'

With that he put on Androgeos' plumed helmet,
Hefted his emblazoned shield, and hung   455
An Argive sword by his side. So too Rhipeus,
Dymas, and my other boys, their spirits high
As they armed themselves in new-won spoils.
We moved out, mingling with the Greeks
And with gods not ours. In the blind night   460
We engaged in many skirmishes, and sent
Many a Greek into the jaws of Orcus.
Some scattered to the safety of the shore
And the ships. Others, like terrified children,
Climbed back up into the belly of the Horse.   465

Never rely on the gods for anything
Against their will. The next thing we saw
Was Cassandra, Priam's daughter,
Being dragged, hair streaming, from the shrine
Of Minerva's temple, lifting to heaven   470
Her burning eyes—her eyes only,
For her tender hands were bound. Coroebus
Could not endure this. He threw himself
Into the midst of the band, determined to die.
We closed ranks and charged, but were overwhelmed.   475
First, our countrymen targeted our uniforms,
The misleading crests on our Greek helmets,
Picking us off from the roof, a piteous slaughter.
Then the Greeks themselves, grunting with anger
At the attempted rescue of Cassandra,   480
Came at us from all sides, Ajax most viciously,
Then the two sons of Atreus and Ulysses' men.

It was like a hurricane when winds clash
From every direction, Winds West and South
And the East proud with his colts of Dawn.   485
The forests groan, and Nereus foams with rage
As he stirs with his trident the lowest depths.

The men we had routed with our stratagem
In the dim of night rematerialized, the first
To recognize our mendacious shields   490
And discordant accents. We were outnumbered.
Coroebus fell first, killed by Peneleos
At the war goddess's altar. Then Rhipeus,
Of all Teucrians the most righteous (but the gods
Saw otherwise) went down. Hypanis   495
And Dymas were run through by friends;
And you, Panthus, neither your piety
Nor Apollo's fillet protected you
When you fell. O ashes of Ilium!
O last flames of my people! Be witness   500
That in your fall I shunned neither fight nor chance,
And had my fate been to die by Greek hands
I had earned that fate. We were torn from there,
Iphitus, Pelias, and myself, we three,
Iphitus heavy with years, Pelias slowed   505
By a wound from Ulysses. Without pause
We were called by the clamor to Priam's house.

Here was an enormous battle, so intense
It was as if there was no fighting anywhere else,
And men were not dying throughout the city.   510
Here we saw the War God unchained. Greeks
Scrambled to the roof, and the threshold
Was besieged by a bulge of shields. Ladders
Hugged the walls, and men inched their way
Upward on the rungs, left hands holding up shields   515
Against projectiles, right hands clutching
Posts and battlements. Above, the Trojans
Tore down the towers and all the rooftop
To use as missiles—they saw the end was near—
Defending themselves to the death, rolling down   520
Gilded rafters, their fathers' splendors of old.
Other troops, swords drawn, massed around the doors,
Blocking the entrances. Our pulses quickened
With new energy to protect the palace
And come to the aid of our vanquished men.   525

There was a secret entry in the rear,
A passageway through Priam's palace

By which Andromache, poor soul,
Would come unattended to her husband's parents
While Troy still stood and lead her boy,   530
Astyanax, to see his grandfather.
I scaled the roof, where the Teucrians
Were lobbing their useless missiles to little effect.
Rising to the sky from the roof's sheer edge
Stood a tower from which all Troy   535
Could once be seen, and in the distance
A thousand Greek ships and their beachhead camp.
We pried at its upper stories with our swords
Until the joints gave way, wrenched it loose,
And sent it crashing down like rolling thunder   540
Onto the ranks of the Greeks. But more Greeks
Kept coming, and more stones kept falling.

Framed by the portal to the entrance court
Pyrrhus stood in his glory, haloed in bronze,

> *As a snake raised on poison basks in the light*   545
> *After a cold winter has kept him underground,*
> *Venomous and swollen. Now, having sloughed*
> *His old skin, glistening with youth, he puffs out*
> *His breast and slides his lubricious coils*
> *Toward the sun, flicking his three-forked tongue.*   550

At his side loomed Periphas, and Automedon,
Once Achilles' charioteer, now the armor-bearer
Of Achilles' son. Massed around them
Were all the tough troops from Scyros,
Hurling torches onto the roof as they closed in   555
On Priam's palace. Pyrrhus led the charge,
Cleaving through the solid threshold
With a battle-axe, tearing the brass-bound doors
From their hinges, and hatcheting a hole
The size of a window in a huge oaken panel,   560
Revealing all the house in a grim tableau.
Open to view were the long halls; laid bare
Was the inner sanctum of Priam
And the kings of old, who now saw
Armed men standing on their very threshold.   565

A tumultuous roar tore through the house;
Its vaulted halls echoed with women's wails,
And the din reverberated to the golden stars.
Trembling matrons roamed lost through the rooms,
Clinging to the doors, lips pressed against them.   570
Pyrrhus moved on with all his father's might,
And nothing could stop him. The gate gave way
Before the battering ram, and the doors,
Wrenched from their sockets, fell to the floor.
The Greeks forced their way in, butchered   575
The Trojans who stood up against them,
And filled the whole space with their soldiery,

> Worse than a river bursting through its banks,
> The water churning in overwhelming fury,
> Flooding the fields and sweeping herds and folds   580
> Over the plain.

                    I saw with my own eyes
Neoptolemus, lusting for slaughter,
And Atreus' two sons, there on the threshold.
I saw Hecuba, with her hundred daughters,
And Priam, polluting with his blood   585
The very altars he had consecrated himself.
Those fifty bedchambers, that promise of offspring,
The doorposts proud with barbarian gold—
All lost. The Greeks held what the fire spared.

And what, you may ask, was Priam's fate?   590
When he saw that his city had fallen,
The doors of his palace shattered,
And the enemy at his very hearth,
The old man slung his long-unused armor
Over his trembling shoulders, strapped on   595
His useless sword, and, bound to die,
Charged the enemy.
                    In the middle of the palace,
Under heaven's naked wheel, an enormous altar
Lay beneath the branches of an ancient laurel
Whose shade embraced the household gods.   600
In this sacred place Hecuba and her daughters
Huddled like doves driven by a black storm,

Clutching the gods' images. But when she saw
Priam himself clad in the armor of his youth,
She cried out:

    'My poor husband,   *605*
What insanity has driven you
To take up these weapons? Where
Are you rushing to? The hour is past
For defense like this, even if my Hector
Were still here. Come to this altar, please.   *610*
It will protect us all, or you will die with us.'

Hecuba said these things, took the aged man
In her arms, and placed him on the holy seat.

And now Polites, one of Priam's sons,
Pursued by Pyrrhus, came running   *615*
Through the colonnades, wounded.
When he reached the vast atrium
Pyrrhus was breathing down his neck,
And yet he slipped away to face his parents' eyes.

There he fell, Pyrrhus' spear in his back,   *620*
And poured out his life in a pool of blood.
Then Priam, in death's grip as he was,
Did not hold back his anger or spare his voice.

'For this heinous crime,' he cried, 'this outrage,
May the gods in heaven—if there is in heaven *625*
Any spirit that cares for what is just and good—
May the gods treat you as you deserve
For making me watch my own son's murder
And defiling with death a father's face.
Not so was Achilles, whom you falsely claim *630*
To be your father, in the face of Priam his foe,
But honored a suppliant's rights and trust,
And allowed the bloodless corpse of Hector
Burial, and sent me back to my own realm.'

And the old man threw his feeble spear. Its tip *635*
Clanged against the bronze of Pyrrhus' shield
And dangled uselessly from its boss. And Pyrrhus:

'Then you can take this news to my father,
The son of Peleus. Be sure to tell him
About my sad behavior and how degenerate   640
His son has become. Now die.'

                         So saying,
He dragged Priam, trembling and slipping
In his son's blood, up to the altar. Winding
His left hand in the old man's hair, with his right
He lifted his flashing sword and buried it   645
Up to its hilt in his side. So ended Priam,
Such was his fated doom, as Troy burned
Before his eyes and Pergamum fell.
Once the lord of so many peoples,
The sovereign of Asia, he lies now   650
A huge trunk upon the shore, head severed
From his neck, a corpse without a name.

Then an awful sense of dread enveloped me.
I stood in a daze, and there rose before me
The image of my dear father, the same age   655
As the wounded king whom I was watching
Gasp out his life. Before me rose Creüsa,
Abandoned, the pillaged house, and the plight
Of little Iülus. I looked around
For my troops. They had all deserted me.   660
Too fatigued to fight, they had either jumped
To a welcome death or dropped limply into the flames.

Now I alone was left, when I saw,
Hiding in the shadows of Vesta's shrine,
Helen, daughter of Tyndareus. The bright fires   665
Gave me light as I wandered here and there
Casting my eyes over everything.
Fearing the Trojans' anger for Troy's fall,
The vengeance of the Greeks, and the wrath
Of her deserted husband, Helen, destroyer   670
Alike of her own country and ours,
This detestable woman, crouched by the altars.
My soul flared with a burning desire
To avenge Troy and make her pay for her sins.

'So she will look upon Sparta unscathed   675
And enter Mycenae as a triumphant queen?
She will get to see her husband and home,
Her parents and children, attended
By Trojan women and Phrygian slaves?
Was it for this that Priam was slaughtered,   680
Ilium burned, and our shore soaked with blood?
Never! Although there is no heroic name
In killing a woman, no victory,
I will be praised for snuffing out evil
And meting out justice. And it will be sweet   685
To quench my soul with vengeful fire
And satisfy my people's ashes.'

I was carried away by this frenzy, when,
Shining through the dark in a halo of light,
My mother appeared before my eyes, more clearly   690
Than ever before, revealing herself
As a radiant goddess, just as the great ones
In heaven see her, so beautiful, so tall.
She caught me by the hand and, in grace,
Spoke these words from her pale-rose lips: 695

'What anguish is behind this uncontrollable rage?
Why so angry, my son? And where has your love
For our family gone? Will you not first see
Where you left your father, Anchises,
Feeble with age, or whether Creüsa   700
And your child, Ascanius, are still alive?
They are surrounded by Greek soldiers
And but for my loving care would have died
In the flames by now, or the swords of the enemy
Would have tasted their blood. It is not   705
The detestable beauty of Tyndarean Helen
Or sinful Paris that is to blame. No, it is the gods,
The remorseless gods, who have ruined Troy
And burnt the topless towers of Ilium.
See for yourself. I will dispel the mist   710
That enshrouds you and dulls your mortal vision.
You might not trust your mother otherwise,
And disregard her kind instructions.

Here,
Where you see piles of rubble, stones
Wrenched from stones, and plumes of smoke and dust,   715
Is Neptune, shaking the walls he has pried up
With his great trident and uprooting the city
From its foundations. Over here, Juno,
Ferocious in her iron vest, first to hold
The Western Gates, summons with her usual   720
Fury reinforcements from the ships.
And now look up. Tritonian Pallas
Is already seated on the highest towers,
Glowing from a thunderhead, grim
With her Gorgon. The Father himself   725
Gives the Greeks courage and strength
And incites the gods to oppose the Trojans.
Hurry away, my son, and end your struggle.
I will bring you safely to your father's door.'

And she plunged into night's shadows.
                              Dire faces,   730
Numinous presences hostile to Troy, now loomed
In the darkness visible.

To my eyes it seemed that all Ilium
Was sinking in flames, and Neptune's Troy
Was being overturned from its base.   735

    It was just like an ancient mountain ash
    That woodsmen are straining to fell. Iron axes
    Ring thick and fast on its trunk, hacking it through,
    And it threatens to fall, nodding from its crest,
    Its foliage trembling, until, bit by bit,   740
    Overcome with wounds, it gives one last groan
    And torn from the hillside comes crashing down.

I descended and, guided by a god,
Somehow got through fire and foe.
Weapons gave way; the flames receded.   745

When I reached the doors of my father's house,
My old home, I sought him first and wanted
More than anything to lift him up

Into the mountains—but he refused
To draw out his life and suffer exile   750
With Troy in ashes.

                    'You are young,'
He cried, 'and still strong; you must take flight.
If the gods wanted to prolong my life
They would have preserved this home of mine.
It is enough and more that I have seen   755
Such destruction once before and have survived
One capture of my city. Say farewell
To my body lying just as it is
And depart. I shall die by my own hand.
The Greeks will pick over my spoils and pity me.   760
Loss of burial is light. Despised by heaven
And useless, I have lived too many years
Since the Lord of Gods and Men breathed winds
Of lightning upon me and touched me with fire.'

He kept repeating words such as these   765
And would not move. We were all in tears,
My wife, Creüsa, Ascanius, all our household,
Pleading with my father not to compound
Our desperate plight and destroy us with him.
He refused, and remained just as he was.   770
I reached for my gear, wanting only to die.
What hope was there for deliverance now?

'Did you think I could leave without you, Father?
How could such a thing come out of your mouth?
If it pleases the gods that nothing be left   775
Of this great city, and if you are determined,
If it is your pleasure, to throw yourself
And all of us into Troy's holocaust—
The door to that fate is wide open. Pyrrhus,
Grimed with Priam's gore, will be here soon;   780
Pyrrhus, who mutilates the son
Before the father's eyes, butchers the father
Like a beast at the altar. O my merciful mother,
Was it for this you saved me from the enemy,
So I could see the enemy in my own home   785
And Ascanius, and my father, and Creüsa

Slaughtered in each other's blood?
                              To arms, men!
The last light calls the vanquished. Take me back
To the Greeks. Let me start the battle again.
Never this day shall we all die unavenged!'   790

Once more I strapped on my sword, gripped my shield
In my left hand, and was hurrying out of the door,
When Creüsa embraced my feet at the threshold
And held up little Iülus to his father, saying:

'If you go to die, take us with you,   795
To whatever fate. But if experience has taught you
To rely on your weapons, guard first this house.
To whom do you leave us, little Iülus,
Your father, and me, once called your wife?'

Her voice filled the house with moaning,   800
And then, without warning, a strange portent
Flickered between the faces and hands
Of Iülus' anxious parents: a light tongue of flame
Gleaming above his head. Harmless to the touch,
It licked his soft locks and grazed his temples.   805
Trembling with fear, we shook the fire from his hair
Quickly and doused the holy flames with water.
But my father, Anchises, enraptured,
Raised his eyes to the stars above
And lifted his hands and his voice to heaven: 810

'Almighty Jupiter, if you are moved
By any prayers, only look upon us,
And if by our piety we have earned it,
Give us your aid and confirm this omen.'

His aged words had just finished, when suddenly   815
Thunder crashed on our left, and a star
Shot down from the sky, sliding through the dark
And trailing a luminous flood of sparks.
We watched it glide over the palace roof
And bury its splendor in Ida's forest,   820
Leaving a shining furrow in its wake.
The air reeked with sulfur all around.

Overwhelmed, my father lifted himself up
In adoration of the star and spoke to heaven:

'No more delay. I follow, and where you lead,   825
There I am. Gods of our fathers, save this house,
Save my grandson. Yours is this omen,
In your power is Troy. And now, my son,
I am ready to go as your companion.'

He spoke, and now the sound of the fire   830
Could be heard more clearly, and the inferno
Rolled its seething heat ever closer.

'Come, dear Father, onto my shoulders now.
You will not weigh me down, and come what may
We will face it together, peril or salvation.   835
Little Iülus will walk beside me, and my wife
Will walk in my footsteps some distance behind.
Now listen to me, all of my household:
Just outside the city there is a mound,
And a temple of Ceres, long deserted.   840
Beside these stands an ancient cypress
Worshiped by my ancestors for many years.
There, by our separate ways, we will meet.
Take into your hands, Father, the sacred gods
Of our country. It would be a sacrilege   845
If I touched them before I washed away
The bloody filth of battle in a living river.'

This said, I spread upon my shoulders
A golden lionskin and bent to my burden.
Little Iülus held my hand and kept up,   850
Although his stride could not match his father's,
And my wife followed behind.
                              We kept
To the shadows and I undisturbed before
By any number of weapons thrust my way
And whole platoons of Greeks, now was frightened   855
By every breeze and startled by every sound,
Afraid for my companion and my burden.

We were nearing the gates, and it looked like

We had made it through, when suddenly
The sound of marching feet drifted on the wind.   860
Squinting through the gloom, my father cried:

'Run for it, Son! They're getting close.
I can see the bronze glitter of their shields.'

I panicked. Some malignant spirit
Robbed me of my wits, for while I ran   865
Down back alleys, leaving the familiar streets,
My wife, Creüsa, was taken from me
By some evil fortune. Had she stopped,
Or got lost and sat down exhausted?
I never saw her again, didn't even look back   870
Or think of her behind me until we arrived
At the mound by Ceres' ancient temple.
When finally we were all gathered there,
She alone was missing. No one had seen her,
Not her husband, not her son, no one.   875
What man or god did I not accuse
In my delirium? What crueler thing
Had I seen in our overturned city?
I entrusted Ascanius, Anchises,
And the gods of Troy to my companions   880
And hid them in a bend of the valley.
Myself, I strapped on my glittering armor
And went back to the city, hell-bent
On running every risk again,
Combing through all of Troy,   885
And putting my life on the line once more.

I started at the walls and the dark gate
Where I had escaped and retraced my steps
Through the night, looking everywhere by torchlight.
Everywhere there was fear. The very silence   890
Was terrifying. Then I turned homeward,
In case, just in case, she had gone there.
The Greeks were there in force, and the house
Consumed with fire. Fanned by the wind,
It spiraled up past the eaves and gnawed at the roof,   895
Blasting the sky with its heat. I moved on
And saw once more the palace of Priam

On the citadel. There, in the empty court
Of Juno's sanctuary, stood Phoenix
And dire Ulysses, chosen to guard the spoils,   900
Treasures from every part of Troy, ripped
Out of burning temples—tables of the gods,
Solid gold bowls, and plundered robes—
All in a heap. Boys and trembling matrons
Stood around in long rows.   905

I even risked casting my voice into the night
And filled the streets with shouts, calling
'Creüsa' over and over again
In my misery, all in vain.
                              But as I rushed
Through the empty shells of buildings, frantic   910
To find her, there rose before my eyes
The sad ghost of Creüsa herself, an image
Larger than life. I was transfixed,
My hair stood on end, and my voice choked.
Then she spoke to me and calmed my fears: 915

'What good does it do, my sweet husband,
To indulge in such mad grief? These things
Do not happen without the will of the gods.
You may not take your Creüsa with you;
The Lord of Olympus does not allow it.   920
Long exile is yours, plowing a vast stretch
Of sea. Then you will come to Hesperia,
Where the Lydian Tiber runs gently
Through fertile fields. There, happy times,
Kingship, and a royal wife shall be yours.   925
Dry your tears for your beloved Creüsa.
I shall not look upon the proud domains
Of the Myrmidons or Dolopians,
Nor go to be a slave for Greek matrons,
I, a Trojan woman, and wife of the son   930
Of the goddess Venus. No,
The Great Mother keeps me on these shores.
Farewell, and keep well your love for our child.'

Creüsa spoke, and then left me there,
Weeping, with many things yet to say.   935

She vanished into thin air. Three times
I tried to put my arms around her; three times
Her wraith slipped through my hands,
Soft as a breeze, like a vanishing dream.

The long night was spent, and at last   940
I went back to rejoin my people.

I was surprised by the great number
Of new arrivals I found, women and men,
Youth gathered for exile, a wretched band
Of refugees who had poured in from all over,   945
Prepared to journey across the sea
To whatever lands I might lead them.
The brilliant morning star was rising
Over Ida's ridges, ushering in the day.
The Greeks held all the city gates.   950
There was no hope of help. I yielded
And, lifting up my father, sought the mountains."

*Book 3 is omitted. Aeneas continues his story. Having built a fleet, Aeneas
sails from Troy with his band of refugees. They stop in Thrace, but are
warned off by the ghost of Polydorus, Priam's youngest son, who was killed
by the king of Thrace. Sailing on they arrive at Delos, where Aeneas consults
the oracle of Apollo, who tells him to seek his ancient homeland. Anchises
thinks the oracle means Crete, but after attempting to settle there the Tro-
jans realize that Italy is their true homeland and they sail on. They are
attacked by the Harpies in the Strophades and finally arrive in Buthrotum, in
northwest Greece, where they are welcomed by Priam's son Helenus and
his wife, Andromache, the widow of the Trojan hero Hector. Following
Helenus' advice the Trojans sail to Italy and then to Sicily, where they
encounter the Cyclops Polyphemus. Acestes gives them hospitality in
Drepanum, and there Anchises dies. When the fleet sails from Sicily they are
caught in the storm that takes them to Carthage. Aeneas finishes his story.*

AENEID FOUR

But the Queen, long sick with love,
Nurses her heart's deep wound
With her pounding blood, and dark flames
Lick at her soul. Thoughts of Aeneas—
The man's heroic lineage, his noble character—   5
Flood her mind, his face and words transfix
Her heart, and her desire gives her no rest.

When Dawn had spread the sunlight over earth
And dispelled night's damp shadow from the sky,
Dido, deeply troubled, spoke to her sister: 10

"Anna, my nightmares would not let me sleep!
This guest who has come to our house—
His looks, the way he carries himself, his brave heart!
He has to be descended from the gods. Fear
Always gives away men of inferior birth.   15
What the Fates have put him through at sea,
The wars he painted, fought to the bitter end!
If I were not unshakable in my vow
Never to pledge myself in marriage again
After death stole my first love away—   20
If the mere thought of marriage did not leave me cold,
I might perhaps have succumbed this once.
Anna, I must confess, since my husband,
Poor Sychaeus, fell at my brother's hands
And stained our household gods with blood,   25
Only this man has turned my eye,
Only he has caused my heart to falter.
I recognize the old, familiar flames.
But may the earth gape open and swallow me,
May the Father Almighty blast me   30
Down to the shades of Erebus below
And Night profound, before I violate you,
O Modesty, and break your vows.

The man who first joined himself to me
Has taken my love with him to the grave."   35

Thus Dido, and her tears wet her bosom.

And Anna:

       "O sister dearer than light itself,
Will you waste your youth in spinsterhood
Alone and grieving, never to taste love's joys,
The sweetness of children? Do you think   40
Any of this matters to ghosts in the grave?
True, in your mourning no potential husbands
Have caught your eye, neither back in Tyre
Nor here in Libya. You've looked down your nose
At Iarbas and Africa's other heralded chieftains.   45
But does it make sense to resist someone you like?
Has it crossed your mind just where you've settled?
The Gaetulians, invincible in war,
And Numidian horsemen are on one frontier.
Just off the coast are the Syrtes' quicksand shoals,   50
Desert to the south, and wild Barcaean nomads
Ranging all over. Need I mention the war clouds
Gathering over Tyre, and your brother's threats?
I think the providential gods, with Juno behind them,
Have blown these Trojan ships our way.   55
With a husband like this, what a city, Sister,
What a kingdom you would see rise! With Trojan allies
What heights of glory our Punic realm would climb!
Just beg the gods' indulgence, and when you have
Good omens from the sacrifices, pamper   60
Your guests, and invent reasons for them to linger:
'Stormy Orion vexes the dim sea, your ships
Are battered, the weather just won't cooperate.'"

With these words Anna fanned the flames of love
That flickered in Dido's heart and gave resolve   65
To her wavering mind, dissolving her sense of shame.

First they make the rounds at shrines, soliciting
Divine approval. To Ceres the lawgiver, Apollo,
And father Bacchus the sisters slaughter

Choice sheep in perfect rituals. But they honor   70
Above all Juno, goddess of marriage. Dido herself,
With her great beauty, holds the wine-bowl
And pours it out between a glossy heifer's horns.
She glides past statues of gods to rich altars,
Ushers in each day with offerings, consults in awe   75
The steaming entrails of disemboweled bulls.
But what do prophets know? How much can vows,
Or shrines, help a raging heart? Meanwhile, the flame
Eats her soft marrow, and the wound lives,
Silent beneath her breast.

                 Dido is burning.   80
She wanders all through the city in her misery,
Raving mad,

        like a doe pierced by an arrow
     Deep in the woods of Crete. She is unwary,
     And the arrow, shot by a shepherd who has no idea
     Where it has landed, finds the animal,   85
     And as she runs all through the Dictaean forest
     The lethal shaft clings to her flank.

                     So too Dido.

Now she leads Aeneas on a tour of the walls,
Shows him what the wealth of Sidon can build.
She begins to speak, but her voice cracks.   90
As dusk comes on her royal desire is a banquet.
Mad to hear once more the labors of Ilium,
She demands the story again, and again she hangs
On every word. When her guests have left,
And the waning moon has set, and the westering stars   95
Make slumber sweet, she pines away
In the empty hall, lying alone on Aeneas' couch,
Seeing and hearing him although he is gone.
Or she holds little Ascanius in her lap
To fill in the features of Aeneas' face   100
And in this way cheats her unspeakable love.

The half-built towers rise no higher, the men no longer
Drill at arms or maintain the city's defensive works.

All work stops, construction halts on the huge,
Menacing walls. The idle derricks loom against the sky.   *105*

When Jove's dear wife saw Dido so lovesick
That her good name no longer mattered to her
As much as her passion, she approached Venus and said:

"An outstanding victory! What a memorable display
Of divine power by you and your little boy,   *110*
Two devious deities laying low a single woman!
Your fear of Carthage and your suspicion
Of its noble houses hardly escapes me, my dear.
But to what purpose? Why are we at odds?
Why not instead work out a lasting peace—   *115*
Sealed with a royal marriage? You have what you want:
Dido burning with love, her very bones enflamed.
I propose, therefore, that we rule this people jointly,
With equal authority. Dido can submit
To a Trojan husband, with Carthage as her dowry."   *120*

The Goddess of Love detected a ploy
To divert power away from Italy
And to Libyan shores. She responded this way:

"Only a fool would refuse such an offer
And prefer to oppose you—provided, of course,   *125*
That your plan meets with success. But I remain
A little unclear about the intentions of Fate.
Does Jupiter want the Tyrians and Trojans
To form one city? Does he approve
This mingling of races? You are his wife,   *130*
And so you should persuade him. Lead on,
And I'll follow."

                 And the Queen of Heaven:

"Leave that to me. Now listen, and I'll outline
Exactly how we will deal with the business at hand.
Aeneas and the most unfortunate Dido   *135*
Are preparing a woodland hunt for tomorrow,
As soon as Titan lifts his luminous head

And dissolves with his rays the curtains of the world.
Just as the beaters start flushing out game
I'll pour down a black rain laced with hailstones   140
And make all the heavens rumble with thunder.
The hunters will scatter in the enveloping gloom,
And Dido and Aeneas will find themselves
In the same cave. I will be there too,
And with your consent I will unite them   145
In holy matrimony. This will be their wedding."

The Cytherean approved and nodded her assent,
Smiling all the while at Juno's treachery.

Dawn rose from the river Ocean,
And at first light the hunting party   150
Spills out from the gates with nets and spears.
Massylian horsemen and keen hounds surge ahead,
But the Carthaginian nobles await their Queen.
She pauses at the threshold of her chamber
While her stallion, resplendent in purple and gold,   155
Champs the foaming bit. Finally, she steps forward
With her retinue, wearing a Phoenician cloak
Finished with embroidery. Her quiver is gold,
Her hair is bound in gold, and the purple cloak
Is pinned with a clasp of gold.
                            Then out ride   160
The Trojans with Iülus, excited to be among them.
Aeneas himself, handsome as a god,
Takes the lead and joins his troops to Dido's.

> *In winter Apollo leaves Lycia and the streams*
> *Of Xanthus and goes to his birth-isle, Delos.*   165
> *There he renews the circling dances,*
> *And Cretans, Dryopes, and painted Scythians*
> *Whirl around his sacred altars while the god*
> *Paces the ridges of Mount Cynthus, braiding*
> *His flowing hair with soft leaves and gold,*   170
> *And the arrows rattle in the quiver on his back.*

                            No less majestic
Was Aeneas, and his face shone with equal glory.

When they came into the high, trackless hills,
Mountain goats, dislodged from the rocks above,
Ran down the ridges. Elsewhere, herds of deer   *175*
Streamed across open country, kicking up
Billows of dust in their flight from the hills.
Young Ascanius rode his spirited mount
Up and down the valleys, in high spirits himself,
Chasing deer and goats but hoping all the while   *180*
That something less tame, a wild boar or tawny lion,
Would come down from the mountains.

Meanwhile, the sky begins to rumble,
And a rainstorm, turning to hail, sweeps in.
The Tyrians and Trojans, with Iülus among them,   *185*
Venus' own dear grandchild, scatter through the fields
In search of shelter. Streams gush down the mountain,
And Dido and the Trojan leader make their way
To the same cave. Earth herself and bridal Juno
Give the signal. Fires flash in the Sky,   *190*
Witness to their nuptials, and the Nymphs
Wail high on the mountaintop. That day
Was the first cause of calamity and of death
To come. For no longer is Dido swayed
By appearances or her good name. No more   *195*
Does she contemplate a secret love. She calls it
Marriage, and with that word she cloaks her sin.

Rumor at once sweeps through Libya's great cities,
Rumor, the swiftest of evils. She thrives on speed
And gains power as she goes. Small and timid at first,   *200*
She grows quickly, and though her feet touch the ground
Her head is hidden in the clouds. The story goes
That Mother Earth, vexed with the gods, bore this
One last child, a sister to Coeus and Enceladus.
Fast on her feet, her beating wings a blur,   *205*
She is a dread, looming monster. Under every feather
On her body she has—strange to say—a watchful eye,
A tongue, a shouting mouth, and pricked-up ears.
By night she wheels through the dark skies, screeching,
And never closes her shining eyes in sleep.   *210*
By day she perches on rooftops or towers,
Watching, and she throws whole cities into panic,

As much a hardened liar as a herald of truth.
Exultant now, she fills the people's ears
With all kinds of talk, intoning fact and fiction: 215
Aeneas has come, born of Trojan blood;
Dido, impressed, has given him her hand,
And now they indulge themselves the winter long,
Neglecting their realms, slaves to shameful lust.
The loathsome goddess spreads this gossip   220
Far and wide. Then she winds her way to King Iarbas,
And with her words his rage flares to the sky.

Iarbas, a son of Jupiter Ammon
By a Garmantian nymph the god had ravished,
Had built in his vast realm a hundred temples   225
For his Father, and on a hundred altars
Had consecrated sacred fire, an eternal flame
In honor of the gods. Blood from sacrificial victims
Clotted the soil, the portals bloomed with garlands,
As Iarbas, they say, insane with jealousy at Rumor's   230
Bitter news, knelt at these altars surrounded by gods,
Upturned his palms and prayed, prayed to his Father:

"Almighty Jupiter, to whom the Moors now offer
Libations of wine as they feast on brocaded couches—
Do you see these things? Why should we shudder   235
At you, Father, when you hurl your thunderbolts,
Or when lightning flashes blindly in the clouds
And stammering thunder rolls through the sky?
This woman, a vagrant in my land, who established
Her little town on a strip of coast we sold to her,   240
With acreage on lease—this woman has spurned
My offers of marriage and embraced Aeneas as her lord.
And now this Paris, with his crew of eunuchs,
The bonnet on his pomaded hair tied with ribbons
Beneath his chin, makes off with the prize   245
While we, who bring offerings to temples—
Your temples—are worshiping an empty name."

So Iarbas prayed, clutching the altar.
And the Almighty heard him, and turned his eyes
To the royal city and the lovers oblivious   250
Of their better name.

Then Jupiter said to Mercury:

"Go now, my son, summon the Zephyrs,
Glide down on your wings and speak to the Trojan
Idling in Carthage. He seems to have quite forgotten,
In his infatuation, the cities given him by Fate.   *255*
Carry my words down through the rushing winds.
This is not the man his lovely mother promised us.
Not for this did she rescue him twice from the Greeks,
But that he should be the one to rule Italy, a land
Pregnant with empire and clamorous for war,   *260*
And produce a race from Teucer's high blood,
And bring all the world beneath the rule of law.
If his own glory means nothing to him, if he will not
Take on this labor for his own fame's sake,
Does he begrudge Ascanius the towers of Rome?   *265*
What is he hoping for? Why does he linger
Among a hostile people and have no regard
For Ausonia's race and Lavinian fields?
In sum, he must sail. That is my message."

Jupiter had spoken, and his son prepared   *270*
To fulfill his commands. He bound on his feet
The golden sandals whose wings carry him over
Landscape and seascape in a blur of wind.
Then he took the wand he uses to summon
Pale ghosts from Orcus or send them down   *275*
To Tartarus' gloom—the same wand he uses
To charm mortals to sleep and make sleepers awake
And unseal the dead's eyelids. Holding this wand
He now rides the wind, sailing through thunderheads.
As he flies along, he makes out the summit   *280*
And steep slopes of Atlas, who shoulders the sky.
His pine-clad head is forever dark with clouds
And beaten by storms. Snow mantles his shoulders,
And icy streams drip from his frozen grey beard.
Mercury glided to a halt here, poised in the air,   *285*
And then gathered himself for a dive to the sea,
Where he skimmed the waves

like a cormorant
That patrols a broken shoreline hunting for fish.

And so the god flew from the mountain giant, Atlas,
(Whose daughter, Maia, was Mercury's mother)   *290*
And came at last to the beaches of Libya.

The wing-footed messenger stepped ashore,
And when he reached the huts he saw Aeneas
At work, towers and houses rising around him.
His sword was enstarred with yellow jasper,   *295*
And from his shoulders hung a mantle blazing
With Tyrian purple, a splendid gift from Dido,
Who had stitched the fabric with threads of gold.

Mercury weighed in at once:

                              "Are you, of all people,
Laying the foundations of lofty Carthage   *300*
And building a beautiful city—for a woman?
What about your own realm, your own affairs?
The ruler of the gods—and of all the universe—
Has sent me down to you from bright Olympus,
Bearing his message through the rushing winds.   *305*
What are you thinking of, wasting your time in Libya?
If your own glory means nothing to you,
Think of the inheritance you owe to Ascanius—
A kingdom in Italy and the soil of Rome."

With these words on his lips, Mercury vanished   *310*
Into thin air, visible no more to human eyes.

Aeneas stood there amazed, choking with fear.
He bristled all over, speechless, astounded,
And he burned with desire to leave that sweet land,
In awe of the commandment from the gods above.   *315*
But what should he do? What can he say
To the Queen in her passion? How will he choose
His opening words? His mind ranges all over,
Darting this way and that, and as he weighs
His options, this seems the best choice: *320*
He calls his captains, Mnestheus, Sergestus,
And brave Serestus, and he orders them
To prepare the fleet for silent running, get the men
To the shore and the gear in order, but conceal

The reason for this change of plans. Meanwhile,   325
He explains that—since good Dido knows nothing
And would never dream that a love so strong
Could ever be destroyed—he himself will find
A way to approach her, the proper occasion
To break the news to her gently.
                              The captains   330
Were more than happy to fulfill his commands.

But the Queen (are lovers ever really fooled?)
Had a presentiment of treachery. Fearing all
Even when all seemed safe, she was the first
To detect a shift in the wind. It was evil Rumor   335
Who whispered that the fleet was preparing
To set out to sea.
                    She went out of her mind,
Raging through the city

                    as wild and furious
       As a maenad when the holy mysteries have begun,
       Her blood shaking when she hears the cry "Bacchus!"   340
       In the nocturnal frenzy on Mount Cithaeron,
       And the mountain echoes the sacred call.

Finally she corners Aeneas and says:

"Traitor! Did you actually hope to conceal
This crime and sneak away without telling me?   345
Does our love mean nothing to you? Does it matter
That we pledged ourselves to each other?
Do you care that Dido will die a cruel death?
Preparing to set sail in the dead of winter,
Launching your ships into the teeth of this wind!   350
How can you be so cruel? If Troy still stood,
And you weren't searching for lands unknown,
You wouldn't even sail for Troy in this weather!
Is it me? Is it me you are fleeing?
By these tears, I beg you, by your right hand,   355
Which is all I have left, by our wedding vows,
Still so fresh—if I have ever done anything
To deserve your thanks, if there is anything in me
That you found sweet, pity a house destined to fall,

And if there is still room for prayers, I beg you,   *360*
Please change your mind. It is because of you
The Libyan warlords hate me and my own Tyrians
Abhor me. Because of you that my honor
Has been snuffed out, the good name I once had,
My only hope to ascend to the stars.   *365*
To what death do you leave me, dear guest
(The only name I can call the man
I once called husband)? For what should I wait?
For my brother Pygmalion to destroy my city,
For Gaetulian Iarbas to lead me off to captivity?   *370*
If you had at least left me with child
Before deserting me, if only a baby Aeneas
Were playing in my hall to help me remember you,
I wouldn't feel so completely used and abandoned."

Dido finished. Aeneas, Jupiter's message   *375*
Still ringing in his ears, held his eyes steady
And struggled to suppress the love in his heart.
He finally made this brief reply:

                    "My Queen,
I will never deny that you have earned my gratitude,
In more ways than can be said; nor will I ever regret   *380*
Having known Elissa, as long as memory endures
And the spirit still rules these limbs of mine.
I do have a few things to say on my own behalf.
I never hoped to steal away from your land
In secret, and you should never imagine I did.   *385*
Nor have I ever proposed marriage to you
Or entered into any nuptial agreement.
If the Fates would allow me to lead my own life
And to order my priorities as I see fit,
The welfare of Troy would be my first concern,   *390*
And the remnants of my own beloved people.
Priam's palace would still be standing
And Pergamum rising from the ashes of defeat.
But now the oracles of Gryneian Apollo,
Of Lycian Apollo, have commanded with one voice   *395*
That the great land of Italy is my journey's end.
There is my love, my country. If the walls
Of Carthage, vistas of a Libyan city,

Have a hold on you, a Phoenician woman,
Why do you begrudge the Trojans   400
A settlement in Ausonia? We too have the right
To seek a kingdom abroad.
                          The troubled ghost
Of my father, Anchises, admonishes me
Every night in my dreams, when darkness
Covers the earth, and the fiery stars rise.   405
And my dear son, Ascanius—am I to wrong him
By cheating him of his inheritance,
A kingdom in Hesperia, his destined land?
And now the gods' herald, sent by Jove himself,
(I swear by your head and mine) has come down   410
Through the rushing winds, ordering me to leave.
I saw the god myself, in broad daylight,
Entering the walls, and heard his very words.
So stop wounding both of us with your pleas.
It is not my own will—this quest for Italy."   415

While he is speaking she looks him up and down
With icy, sidelong glances, stares at him blankly,
And then erupts into volcanic fury:

"Your mother was no goddess, you faithless bastard,
And you aren't descended from Dardanus, either.   420
No, you were born out of flint in the Caucasus,
And suckled by tigers in the wilds of Scythia.
Ah, why should I hold back? Did he sigh as I wept?
Did he even look at me? Did he give in to tears
Or show any pity for the woman who loved him?   425
What shall I say first? What next? It has come to this—
Neither great Juno nor the Saturnian Father
Looks on these things with impartial eyes.
Good faith is found nowhere. I took him in,
Shipwrecked and destitute on my shore,   430
And insanely shared my throne with him.
I recovered his fleet and rescued his men.
Oh, I am whirled by the Furies on burning winds!
And now prophetic Apollo, now the Lycian oracles,
Now the gods' herald, sent by Jupiter himself,   435
Has come down through the rushing winds
With dread commands! As if the gods lose sleep

Over business like this! Go on, leave! I'm not
Arguing with you any more. Sail to Italy,
Find your kingdom overseas. But I hope,   440
If there is any power in heaven, you will suck down
Your punishment on rocks in mid-ocean,
Calling Dido's name over and over. Gone
I may be, but I'll pursue you with black fire,
And when cold death has cloven body from soul,   445
My ghost will be everywhere. You will pay,
You despicable liar, and I will hear the news;
Word will reach me in the deeps of hell."

With these words she breaks off their talk
And in her anguish flees from the daylight   450
And out of his sight, leaving him there
Hesitant with fear, and with so much more to say.
Her maids support her as she collapses, take her
To her marble room, and lay her on her bed.

Aeneas, loyal and true, yearns to comfort her,   455
Soothe her grief, and say the words that will
Turn aside her sorrow. He sighs heavily,
And although great love has shaken his soul,
He obeys the gods' will and returns to the fleet.

Then the Trojans redouble their efforts   460
And haul their ships down all along the shore.
Keels are caulked and floated, leafy tree limbs
Are brought in for oars, and beams left rough
In the men's impatience to leave. You could see them
Streaming down from every part of the city.   465

> *Ants, preparing for winter, will busily plunder*
> *A huge pile of seeds and store it in their nest.*
> *The black line threads through the fields as the insects*
> *Transport their spoils on a narrow road through the grass.*
> *Some push the huge grains along with their shoulders,*   470
> *Others patrol the line and keep it moving,*
> *And the whole trail is seething with their work.*

What was it like, Dido, to see all this? What sighs
Escaped your lips, when from your high tower

You saw the shoreline crawling with Trojans,   475
And the sea roiled with the shouts of sailors?

Cruel Love, what do you not force human hearts to bear?
Again Dido collapses into tears, again feels compelled
To beg Aeneas and to bow down to Love,
Lest she leave something untried and so die in vain: 480

"Look at them, Anna, scuttling across the shore,
Streaming down from every direction. The canvas
Can hardly wait for the breeze, and the sailors
Are laughing as they hang the sterns with garlands.
I had the strength to foresee this sorrow,   485
And I will have the strength to endure it, Sister.
There is one more thing I will ask of you.
You are the only one that traitor befriended,
Confiding in you even his deepest feelings.
Only you will know the best way to approach him.   490
Go, my dear, bend your knee before our archenemy.
Tell him I never joined the Greek alliance at Aulis
To burn down Troy, never sent my warships
To Pergamum, nor defiled his father's ashes
Or disturbed his ghost. Why, then, does he refuse   495
To admit my words into his obstinate ears?
What is his hurry? Is he too rushed to grant
The final request of his wretched lover:
To wait for favorable winds for his flight?
I am no longer asking for our marriage back—   500
The marriage he betrayed—nor that he do without
His precious Latium or relinquish his realm.
All I want is time, some breathing room for my passion,
Until Fate has taught me how the vanquished should grieve.
Beg from him this last favor, Sister. If he grants it,   505
I will pay it back with interest—by my death."

Thus Dido's prayer, and her sister sadly
Bore it to Aeneas, then bore it again. Unmoved
By her tears, he made no response to her words.
Fate stood in the way, and a god sealed the man's ears.   510

*Alpine winds swoop down from the North
And struggle to uproot an ancient oak.*

They blow upon it from every side until its leaves
Strew the ground and the strong trunk-wood creaks.
But the tree clings to the crag, and as high as its crown   515
Reaches to heaven, so deep do its roots sink into the earth.

So too the hero, battered with appeals
On this side and that. His great heart feels
Unendurable pain, but his mind does not move,
And the tears that fall to the ground change nothing.   520

And now Dido, in awe of her doom,
Prays for death. She is weary of looking upon
The dome of heaven, and, furthering her resolve
To leave the light, she saw as she placed offerings
On the incense-fumed altar a fearful omen: 525
The holy water turned black, and the wine,
When she poured it, congealed into gore.
She told no one of this, not even her sister.
There was more. Dido had in the palace
A marble shrine to her deceased husband,   530
A shrine she honored by keeping it wreathed
With snow-white wool and festal fronds.
Now she heard, or seemed to hear, her husband's voice,
When dusk had melted the edges of the world,
Calling her. And the owl, alone on the rooftop,   535
Would draw out its song into an eerie wail.
And the sayings of seers from days gone by
Would fill her with terror. And then in her sleep
A fierce Aeneas would pursue her as she raved.
And then she would be alone, abandoned forever,   540
Forever traveling a long, lonesome road
Through a desert landscape, searching for her Tyrians—

Like mad Pentheus when he sees the maenads,
And sees a double sun and a duplicate Thebes;
Or like Orestes stalked by Furies on an empty stage,   545
Pursued by his mother with torches and snakes
While the avenging Fiends lurk in the doorway.

And so Dido, worn down by grief, went mad.
Determined to die, she worked out by herself
The time and the means, and only then   550

Did she address her sister, hiding her plan
Behind a face radiant with serenity and hope:

"O Sister, I have found a way—be glad for me—
Either to get him back or free myself from love.
On the shore of Ocean, near the setting sun,   555
Lies farthest Ethiopia, where gigantic Atlas
Turns on his shoulders the star-studded heavens.
A priestess from there, of the Massylian tribe,
Has been presented to me. She guarded the sanctuary
Of the Hesperides, protected the golden apples   560
On their tree, and feasted the dragon
On honey and the poppy's drowsy opium.
She claims her incantations can set hearts free
Or plunge them into the depths of despair,
All as she chooses. She can stop rivers cold,   565
Make the stars turn backward, and conjure up
The spirits of night. You will hear the ground bellow
Under your feet, see elms stroll down mountains.
I swear by the gods, Anna, and by your dear head,
I am reluctant to resort to black magic. Still,   570
Build a pyre secretly in the central courtyard
Under the open sky and pile upon it
The weapons our impious hero left
On our bedroom walls, and all his forgotten clothes,
And the marriage bed that was my undoing.   575
It will do me good to destroy every reminder
Of that evil man—as the priestess told me."

She fell silent, and the color drained from her face.

In spite of everything, her sister Anna
Did not believe that Dido was inventing   580
These strange rites to disguise her own funeral.
She could not conceive of passion so great
And feared no worse for Dido now
Than at the death of Sychaeus.
                    And so,
Anna prepared the pyre.   585

But the Queen, out in the open courtyard—
Where the pyre now reared heavenward,

Vast with billets of pine and sawn oak—
Hangs the place with garlands and funeral fronds.
Upon the bed she arranges his clothes, the sword   590
That he left, and his picture, knowing well
What was to come.
            There were altars
Around the courtyard, and the priestess
Shook her hair out free and chanted thunderous prayers
To three hundred gods, to Erebus and Chaos,   595
To three-bodied Hecate and Diana's three faces,
Virgin huntress, Moon, and pale Proserpina.
She sprinkled water as being from Avernus
And with a bronze knife harvested by moonlight
Herbs selected for their milky, black poison.   600
She calls for the love charm of a newborn foal
Torn from his forehead before his mother can eat it.
Dido herself, sacred cakes of barley in her pious hand,
Stands close to the altars, one foot unsandaled,
Her dress unbound. Then she calls to witness,   605
As one about to die, first Gods and then Stars
Who share Destiny's secrets. And then she prays
To whatever Power makes a final reckoning
For lovers who love on unequal terms.

It was night, and all over earth weary bodies   610
Lay peacefully asleep. Woods and wild seas
Had fallen still, and the stars were midway
In their gliding orbits. Ox and meadow were quiet,
And all the brilliant birds who haunt
The lapping lakes and tangled hedgerows   615
Were nestled in sleep under the dark, silent sky.

But not Dido, unhappy heart. She never drifted off
Into sleep, nor let night settle on her eyes or breast.
Her anxiety mounts, and her love surges back
And seethes, wave after wave on a furious sea.   620
At last she breaks into speech, debating in her heart:

"What am I doing? Should I entertain once more
My former suitors—and hear them laugh at me?
Go begging for a marriage among the Nomads,
After scorning their proposals time and again?   625

Shall I follow the Trojans' fleet and be subject
To their every command? After all, aren't they
So grateful for the help I gave them
That they could never forget my past kindnesses?
Even if I wanted to, who would let me on board,   630
Welcome someone so hated onto their ships?
Poor Dido, do you not yet appreciate
The treachery bred into Laomedon's race?
What then? Shall I crew with the Trojans
Cruising cheerfully away, all on my own?   635
Or should I, at the head of my own Tyrian fleet,
Give them pursuit, order my people to hoist sail
Into the wind again, a people I could scarcely persuade
To abandon their city back in Phoenicia?
No, Dido, die as you deserve, end your sorrow   640
With a sword.
        You, my dear sister, caving in to my tears,
First loaded my frenzied soul with these sorrows
And put me in the enemy's path. It was not my lot
To live a blameless life as a widow, as free
As a wild thing, untouched by these cares.   645
I have not kept my vow to Sychaeus' ashes."

As these cries erupted from Dido's heart,
Aeneas, bent on leaving, with everything in order,
Was catching some sleep on his ship's high stern,
And in his sleep he had a vision of Mercury,   650
Returning to him in the same form as before,
The same voice and face, the same golden hair
And graceful body—and, as before, with a warning:

"Goddess-born, how can you sleep in a crisis like this?
Are you blind to the perils surrounding you,   655
Madman? Don't you hear a sailing breeze blowing?
Dido's heart revolves around evil. Determined
To die, she seethes with tides of raw passion.
Will you not flee now, while flight is still possible?
You will soon see this sea awash with timbers   660
And the shore in flames—if Dawn finds you
Lingering here. Push off, then, without delay.
A woman is a fickle and worrisome thing."

And with these words he melted into the dark.

Aeneas was deeply shaken by this apparition.   665
He tore himself from sleep and woke his crew:

"On the double, men, unfurl those sails
And get to the benches! A god has come down
From heaven again, urging us to cut the cables
And get out of here as fast as we can.   670
We will follow you, Holy One, whoever you are,
And gladly obey your commands again.
Be with us once more, grant us your grace,
And set propitious stars in the sky before us."

He spoke, drew his sword   675
Flashing from its sheath, and severed
The stern cable. Aeneas' fervor
Spread through the fleet. They ran to their posts
And shoved off from the shore, blanketing the sea
With their hulls. Leaning into the oars,   680
They swept the blue water and churned it to foam.

Dawn left Tithonus' saffron bed
And sprinkled the world with early light.
The Queen, in her tower, watched the day whiten
And saw the fleet moving on under level sails.   685
She knew the shores and harbors were empty,
The oarage gone. She beat her lovely breast
Three times, four times, and tore her golden hair.

"O God!" she said. "Will he get away,
Will this interloper make a mockery of us?   690
To arms, the whole city, after him!
Launch the fleet! Bring fire, man the oars!
What am I saying? Where am I?
What has come over me? Oh, Dido, only now
Do you feel your guilt? Better to have felt it   695
When you gave away your crown. Behold
The pledge, the loyalty, of the man they say
Bears his ancestral gods, bore on his shoulders
His age-worn father! Could I have not torn him
Limb from limb and fed him to the fishes?   700

Murdered his friends? Minced Ascanius himself
And served him up as a meal to his father?
The battle could have gone either way: What of it?
Doomed to die, whom did I have to fear?
I should have torched his camp with my own hands,   705
Annihilated father and son and the whole race,
And thrown myself on top of the conflagration.
     O Sun, fiery witness to all earthly deeds,
And Juno, complicit in my unhappy love,
Hecate, worshiped with howls at midnight crossroads,   710
Avenging Furies, and gods of dying Elissa—
Attend to this, turn the force of your wrath
Upon sins that deserve it—O hear my prayer!
If this criminal is destined to make harbor again,
If this is what the Fates and Jupiter demand,   715
May he still have to fight a warlike nation,
Be driven from his land and torn from Iülus.
May he plead for aid and see his people slaughtered.
And when he has accepted an unjust peace,
May he not enjoy his reign or the light of day   720
But die before his time and lie unburied
On a desolate shore. This is what I pray for.
These last words I pour out with my blood.
And you, my Tyrians, must persecute his line
Throughout the generations—this your tribute   725
To Dido's ashes. May treaties never unite
These nations, may no love ever be lost between them.
And from my bones may some avenger rise up
To harry the Trojans with fire and sword,
Now and whenever we have the power.   730
May coast oppose coast, waves batter waves,
Arms clash with arms, may they be ever at war,
They themselves and their children forever."

Dido said these things and then set her mind
On a quick escape from the hated light. She exchanged   735
A few words with Barce, Sychaeus' nurse; her own
Was black ashes back in the old country.

"Dear Nurse, bring my sister Anna here.
Have her sprinkle her body with river water
And bring along the victims for expiation. You   740

Come with her, and wreathe your brows with wool.
I intend to complete the rites to Stygian Jove
That I have begun, and so end my troubles,
And to send the Trojan's pyre up in flames."

She spoke. The old woman quickened her step.   745
Dido trembled, panicked at the enormity
Of what she had begun. Eyes bloodshot,
Blotched cheeks quivering, pale with looming death,
She burst into the innermost part of the house,
Climbed the pyre like a madwoman, and unsheathed   750
The Trojan sword—a gift not sought for such a use.
The sight of the familiar bed and the clothes he wore
Made her stop in tears. Struggling to collect herself,
She lay upon the couch and spoke her final words:

"Love's spoils, sweet while heaven permitted,   755
Receive this soul, and free me from these cares.
I have lived, and I have completed the course
Assigned by Fortune. Now my mighty ghost
Goes beneath the earth. I built an illustrious city.
I saw my walls. I avenged my husband   760
And made my evil brother pay. Happy,
All too happy, if Dardanian ships
Had never touched our shores!"

                    Dido spoke,
And pressing her face into the couch:

"We will die unavenged, but we will die.   765
This is how I want to pass into the dark below.
The cruel Trojan will watch the fire from the sea
And carry with him the omens of my death."

With these words on her lips her companions saw her
Collapse onto the sword, saw the blade   770
Foaming with blood and her hands spattered.
A cry rises to the roof, and Rumor
Dances wildly through the shaken town.
The houses ring with lamentation
And the wails of women. Great dirges   775
Hang in the air. It was as if Carthage itself

Or ancient Tyre had fallen to the enemy,
And flames rolled through the houses of men
And over the temples of the gods.

Anna, in great distress, heard the cries.   780
She rushed through the crowd, clawing her face
With her nails, and beating her breasts
With her fists, and then spoke to her dying sister:

"So this is what it was all about, Sister.
You cheated me, didn't you? This is what   785
Your pyre was for, your altars, your fire—
To deceive me. What should I lament first,
Deserted like this? Did you scorn my company
In death? You should have called on me
To share your fate, to die by the sword   790
With the same agony, at the same moment!
Did I build this pyre with my own hands
Calling upon the gods of our fathers,
So that when you were lying upon it like this
I would not be here? Cruel! You have destroyed   795
Yourself, me, the Sidonian elders, and your city.
     Ah, let me bathe her wounds, and if any last breath
Still lingers on her lips, let me catch it on mine."

She had reached the top of the pyre by now
And was holding her sister close to her bosom,   800
Sobbing as she used her dress to stanch
The blood's dark flow. Dido, trying to lift
Her heavy eyes, grew faint again. The wound hissed
Deep in her chest. Three times she struggled
To prop herself upon her elbow,   805
Three times she rolled back on the bed.
With wandering eyes she sought the light
In heaven's dome and moaned when she found it.

Then Almighty Juno, pitying Dido's long agony
And hard death, sent Iris down from Olympus   810
To free her struggling soul from its mortal coils.
Her death was neither fated nor deserved
But before her day and in the heat of passion.
Proserpina had not yet plucked from her head

A golden lock, nor allotted her a place   815
In the Stygian gloom. And so Iris flew down
Through the sky on sparkling, saffron wings,
Trailing in the sunlight a thousand changing hues,
And then stood above Dido's head.

                                      "This offering
I consecrate to Dis and release you from your body."   820

As soon as she had cut the lock, all the body's warmth
Ebbed away, and Dido's life withdrew into the winds.

Book 5 is omitted. Aeneas and the Trojans leave Carthage, and a storm drives them back to Drepanum in Sicily where Acestes again receives them. Aeneas holds funeral games to mark the first anniversary of his father's death. Meanwhile, Juno inspires the Trojan women, weary from seven years of wandering, to burn the ships, but Jupiter douses the fire with rain. The ghost of Anchises appears to Aeneas and acting on his advice, Aeneas allows any of the Trojans who so wish to remain in Sicily. Aeneas sails with the fleet for Italy. Venus asks Neptune to ensure a safe voyage for her son. Neptune agrees but demands a human life in return. Aeneas' helmsman Palinurus becomes drowsy, falls overboard, and is killed by savages when he swims ashore.

AENEID SIX

Aeneas wept as he spoke, and let the fleet
Glide along until it reached Cumae. Keels
Backed into the long arc of Euboean beach,
Prows seaward, as the anchors bit
Into the sea's shelving floor. Crews flashed ashore 5
Onto the banks of Italy. Some kindled fire
From veins of flint, some foraged timber
From the wilderness, others located streams.
But Aeneas, on a mission of his own,
Sought the high, holy places of Apollo 10
And the Sibyl's deeps, the immense caverns
Where the prophetic god from Delos breathes
Into her mind and soul and opens the future.
Aeneas and his men were soon within
The groves of Trivia and under golden eaves. 15

Daedalus once, fleeing Minoan Crete
On beating wings, trusted himself
To the open sky, an unused path,
North toward the Bears and a light landing
On this Chalcidian height, 20
And dedicated here his airy oarage
To you, Phoebus, and founded this temple.

On the doors, the murder of Androgeus
And the annual penalty for the Athenians,
Seven of their sons offered for sacrifice. 25
The urn stands ready, the lots are drawn. Opposite,
Rising from the sea, the island of Crete,
Raw passion for a bull, and Pasiphaë
In her furtive position, raising her knees.
And there too the mixed breed, the Minotaur, 30
Hybrid monument to unspeakable desire.
Here the Labyrinth winds its inextricable course,
And here is Daedalus himself, pitying

Princess Ariadne's great love, unraveling
The twisted skein of the maze, guiding Theseus'   35
Blind footsteps with a thread. And you also,
Icarus, would have played a great part
In this masterpiece, if grief had allowed:
Twice the artist attempted your fate in gold,
Twice the father's hands fell.

                        Aeneas' eyes   40
Would have scanned every last detail.
But Achates, sent ahead, was back,
And with him was Deïphobe, Glaucus' daughter,
Priestess of Phoebus and Trivia. A figure
Of divine awe, she had this to say to Aeneas: 45

"This is no time for looking at pictures.
You should be sacrificing seven bulls
From a sacred herd, and seven chosen sheep."

She spoke, and when Aeneas' men
Had seen to the sacrifice the priestess   50
Called the Trojans under the looming temple.

The flank of that Euboean cliff was carved
Into a hundred cavernous mouths, gaping orifices
That roar the Sibyl's oracular responses.
The virgin priestess greeted them at the threshold: 55

"It is time to demand your destiny. The god! Behold,
The god!"

           And as she spoke there before the gates
Her color changed, her hair spread out
Into fiery points, she panted for air,
And her breast heaved with feral madness.   60
She was larger than life now, and her voice
Was no longer human, as the god's power
Took possession of her:

                  "You hesitate
To pray, hesitate, Aeneas of Troy?
The great mouths of this thunderstruck hall   65
Will not open until you pray."

                    And she was silent.
Fear seeped like icy water through the Trojans' bones,
And their lord poured forth his heart in prayer:

"Phoebus, who has always pitied Troy
In its darkest times, who guided the arrow   70
From Paris' hand into the body of Achilles,
And who guided me through so many seas
Pounding so many distant shores,
The remote Massylian tribes, the lands
Fringed by the shoals of the Syrtes—   75
Now at last we have in our grasp
The ever-receding shore of Italy.
May Troy's fortune follow us no farther.
You also, gods and goddesses
Whom Ilium's great glory offended,   80
May now justly spare the Dardan race.
And you, most holy prophetess, who hold
The future in your mind, grant the realm
That has been pledged to me by Fate,
Grant that the Teucrians settle in Italy   85
With the wandering, harried gods of Troy.
Then to Phoebus and Trivia I will dedicate
A temple of solid marble and holy days
In Phoebus' name. And a great shrine
Awaits you in our realm, gracious priestess,   90
An inner sanctum where I will deposit
Your prophecies and the mystic sayings
Told to my people and ordain your priests.
Only do not entrust your verses to leaves,
Playthings swirling when the wind gusts,   95
But chant them out loud."

                    Aeneas finished.
But the priestess had not yet taken Apollo's
Bit in her mouth, and she convulsed like a maenad
Monstrous in the cave, desperate to shake
The great god from her breast. All the more,   100
Though, he tired her rabid mouth, tamed
Her wild heart, and molded her to his will.
And now the cave's hundred mouths

Opened of their own accord and transmitted
The oracle's response through the empty air: 105

"You have escaped the perils of the sea,
But perils more grave await you on land.
The Dardanians will enter Lavinium—
Be sure of that—but will wish they had never come.
War, I see horrible war, and the Tiber   110
Foaming with blood. You will have another
Simois and Xanthus, another Doric camp.
A second Achilles has been born in Latium
To a goddess mother, and Juno will
Continue to afflict the Teucrians,   115
While you, a suppliant, shall beg for help
Throughout Italy. And the cause
Of all this suffering for the Trojans
Shall be once more a foreign bride,
An alien marriage.   120
Do not yield, but oppose your troubles
All the more boldly, as far as your fate
And fortune allow. Salvation will come first
From where you least expect it—
A Greek city will open wide its gates."   125

In words such as these the Sibyl of Cumae
Chanted eerie riddles from her shrine
In the echoing cave, shrouding truth
In darkness, as Apollo shook the reins
And twisted the goad in her raving heart.   130
As soon as her frenzy ceased, and her lips
Were hushed, the Trojan hero began:

"Virgin priestess, trouble of any kind,
However strange, no longer surprises me.
I expect it, and I have thought this through.   135
I ask for one thing. It is said that here
Are the dark lord's gate and the murky swamp
Of Acheron's backwater. Let me pass.
Open the sacred doors and show me the way,
So that I might see my father face to face.   140
I saved him, I carried him on my shoulders
Through fire and a thousand enemy spears.

He was at my side through the long journey,
Sharing the perils of sea and sky, crippled
As he was, beyond what his age allowed.   145
It was his pleas that convinced me to come
As suppliant to you. Pity father and son,
Gracious one, for you have the power.
Not in vain did Hecate appoint you
Mistress of the groves of Avernus.   150
If Orpheus could call forth his wife's ghost,
Enchanting the shades with his Thracian lyre,
If Pollux could ransom his brother, taking turns
With death, traveling the way so many times—
Not to mention Theseus and Hercules.   155
I too am descended from Jove most high."

So Aeneas prayed, clutching the altars.
And the Sibyl answered:

                    "Goddess-born son
Of Trojan Anchises, the road down
To Avernus is easy. Day and night   160
The door to black Dis stands open.
But to retrace your steps and come out
To the upper air, this is the task,
The labor. A few, whom Jupiter
Has favored, or whom bright virtue   165
Has lifted to heaven, sons of the gods,
Have succeeded. All the central regions
Are swathed in forest, and Cocytus
Enfolds it with its winding, dark water.
But if you have such longing, such dread desire   170
To cross the Styx twice, twice to see
Black Tartarus, and if it pleases you
To indulge this madness as a sacred mission,
Listen to what you must do first.
Hidden in a darkling tree there lies   175
A golden bough, blossoming gold
In leaf and pliant branch, held sacred
To the goddess below. A grove conceals
This bough on every side, and umber shadows
Veil it from view in a valley dim.   180
No one may pass beneath the earth

Until he has plucked from the tree
This golden-leaved fruit. Fair Proserpina
Decrees it be brought to her as a gift.
When one bough is torn away another   185
Grows in its place and leafs out in gold.
Search it out with your deepest gaze
And, when you find it, pluck it with your hand.
It will come off easily, of itself,
If the Fates call you. Otherwise you will not   190
Wrench it off by force or cut it with steel.
Farther, there lies unburied (ah, you do not know)
The lifeless body of your friend,
Defiling the entire fleet with his death
While you seek counsel at my doorstep.   195
Bear him to his resting place and bury him
In the tomb. Then lead black cattle here
As first victims to expiate your sins.
Only then will you see the Stygian groves
And realms closed to the living."

                              She spoke,   200
Closed her lips, and said no more.

                         Aeneas
Left the cave and walked on with downcast eyes,
Pondering these mysteries. Loyal Achates
Walked with him, just as worried, and the two
Talked with each other, trying to sort out   205
Which comrade might be dead, whose unburied body
The seer spoke of. Then they came to the shore
And saw on the beach the body of Misenus,
Dead before his time—Misenus, son of Aeolus,
Second to none at rousing men to war   210
With his bugle's call. He had been the companion
Of great Hector and fought at his side,
As good with a spear as he was with his horn.
But when Achilles deprived Hector of life,
Misenus joined the ranks of Aeneas,   215
Unwilling to follow a lesser hero.
But today he had been sounding a conch shell,
Making it blare and sing like the sea, insanely
Challenging the gods to a contest. Triton

Was jealous and, if the tale is true, caught   220
The man and drowned him in the rocks and surf.
And so they gathered around and mourned,
And Aeneas led the echoing dirge,
Since this also was his duty. Then,
In tears, they hurried to carry out   225
The Sibyl's orders, piling up trees
For his tomb's altar and rearing it skyward.
Then into the primeval forest, the deep lairs
Of wild things—and down fell the pines,
The ilex rang with the axe, ash logs and oak   230
Were split with wedges, and enormous trunks
Rolled down the mountainside.

                         Aeneas
Led the way in this work also, wielding
The same tools and cheering on his men.
But his heart was heavy, and as he gazed   235
At the deep woods a prayer came to his lips:

"Let the golden bough show itself now
On a tree in this forest, since the prophetess
Was all too right about you, Misenus!"

He had scarcely spoken when twin doves   240
Came fluttering down from heaven
Before his very eyes and settled
On the green grass. Aeneas' mind soared
When he saw his mother's birds, and he prayed:

"Show me the way, float on the air to the heart   245
Of the forest, where the earth lies soft
In the shadow of the radiant bough
And you, Goddess and Mother, do not fail me
In these doubtful times."

                    And he stood quietly,
Watching, tracking their direction in the trees.   250
The doves, as they fed, flew only as far
As someone following could keep them in sight.
But when they came to the jaws of Avernus,
With its foul smell, they ascended swiftly,

And then, gliding down through the limpid air,   255
They sat side by side on their chosen perch,
A tree through whose branches there shone
A discordant halo, a haze of gold.

> *During winter's cold, deep in the woods,*
> *Mistletoe blooms with strange leafage*   260
> *On a tree not its own and entwines*
> *The burled branches with its yellow fruit.*

Such was the gold seen on the dark ilex,
And so rustled its foil in the gentle breeze.
Aeneas seized it at once, and though the bough   265
Hesitated, he broke it off eagerly and brought it
Safely back beneath the Sibyl's roof.

The Trojans were still lamenting Misenus
There on the shore, performing final rites
For thankless ash. First, they built a huge pyre   270
Out of resinous pine and split oak,
Then trimmed its sides with gloomy foliage
And set up before it funereal cypresses.
They adorned the top with glittering arms.
Others heated water in bronze cauldrons   275
And bathed and anointed the cold body.
A cry went up. And then they placed the corpse,
Wet with their tears, onto the couch
And draped it with his familiar purple robes.
A small group lifted the heavy bier,   280
A poignant service, and with eyes averted
In ancestral manner, lit the fire. Flames crackled
Around the gifts heaped on the pyre—frankincense,
Platters of food, bowls filled with olive oil.
After the embers collapsed and the flames   285
Died away, they doused the remnant
Of glowing ash with wine. Corynaeus
Gathered the bones and placed them in an urn.
Then he circled the company three times,
Sprinkling them with water fresh as dew   290
From an olive branch, and so purified the men.
Then he spoke some last words. Aeneas,
In an act of piety, heaped above Misenus

A huge burial mound—with the hero's arms,
Horn, and oar—beneath a soaring hill   *295*
That is still called Misenus
And will bear that name throughout the ages.

The funeral was finished. Aeneas turned all his attention
To the Sibyl's commands.

                    There was a deep cave
With a jagged, yawning mouth, sheltered   *300*
By a dusky lake and a wood's dark shade.
Over this no winged thing could fly, so putrid
And so foul were the fumes that issued
From the cave's black jaws and rose to the sky
(And so the Greeks called the place Avernus).   *305*
Here the priestess set in line four black bulls,
Poured wine upon their brows, and plucked
The topmost bristles from between their horns.
They set them on the sacred fire as first offerings,
Calling on Hecate, mistress of the moon   *310*
And of Erebus below. Others slit the bulls' throats
And caught their warm blood in bowls
While Aeneas himself sacrificed a lamb,
Black-fleeced, to Night, the Eumenides' mother,
And to Earth, her great sister. To you,   *315*
Proserpina, he offered a barren heifer.
Then began a sacrifice to the Lord of Styx,
As at night's darkest hour the hero lay
Carcasses of bulls on the altars, pouring rich oil
On their burning entrails. But, look, under   *320*
The threshold of the rising sun the ground rumbled.
The wooded ridges trembled, and dogs howled
As through the gloom the goddess drew near.

                          "Begone,
Begone, you uninitiated!" shrieked the seer.
"Stand off from the grove! And you, Aeneas,   *325*
Onto the road and unsheathe your sword. Now
Is the time for courage and a heart of iron."

She spoke, then plunged wildly into the cave,
And Aeneas matched her stride for stride.

Gods of the world below, silent shades,   330
Chaos and Phlegethon, soundless tracts of Night—
Grant me the grace to tell what I have heard,
And lay bare the mysteries in earth's abyss.

On they went, shrouded in desolate night,
Through shadow, through the empty halls   335
Of Dis and his ghostly domain, as dim

> *As a path in the woods under a faint moon*
> *When Jupiter has buried the sky in gloom*
> *And night has stolen color from the world.*

Just before the entrance, in the very jaws   340
Of Orcus, Grief and avenging Cares
Have set their beds. Pale Diseases
Dwell there, sad Old Age, Fear, Hunger—
The tempter—and foul Poverty,
All fearful shapes, and Death and Toil,   345
And Death's brother Sleep, Guilty Joys,
And on the threshold opposite, lethal War,
The Furies in iron cells, and mad Strife,
Her snaky hair entwined with bloody bands.

In the middle a huge elm stands, spreading   350
Its aged branches, the abode of false Dreams
That cling to the bottom of every leaf.
At the doors are stabled the monstrous shapes
Of Centaurs, and biform Scyllas, and Briareus
With a hundred heads, the Lernaean Hydra,   355
Hissing horribly, the Chimaera armed with flame,
Gorgons, Harpies, and the hybrid shade of Geryon.
Suddenly panicked, Aeneas drew his sword
And turned its edge against their advance,
And if his guide had not observed   360
That they were hollow, bodiless forms,
Flitting images, he would have charged
And slashed vainly through empty shadows.

From here a road led to the Tartarean waters
Of Acheron, where a huge whirlpool,   365
Churning with mire, belched all its sand

Into Cocytus. The keeper of these waters
Was Charon, the grim ferryman, frightening
In his squalor. Unkempt hoary whiskers
Bristled on his chin, his eyes like flares   370
Were sunk in flame, and a filthy cloak hung
By a knot from his shoulder. He poled the boat
Himself, and trimmed the sails, hauling the dead
In his rusty barge. He was already old,
But a god's old age is green and raw.   375

And now a whole crowd rushed streaming
To the banks, mothers and husbands, bodies
Of high-souled heroes finished with life,
Boys and unwed girls, and young men
Placed upon the pyre before their parents' eyes.   380

> *As many as leaves that fall in the woods*
> *At autumn's first frost, as many as birds*
> *That teem to shore when the cold year*
> *Drives them over the sea to sunny lands.*

There they stood, begging to be the first   385
Ferried across, hands stretched out in love
For the farther shore. But the grim boatman
Culled through the crowd, accepting some,
But keeping the others back from the sand.

Aeneas, shocked by this mob of souls, said: 390

"What does this mean, priestess, the spirits
Crowding to the river? How is it decided
That some must leave the banks while others
Sweep the bruised water with oars?"

And the priestess, ancient of years: 395

"Son of Anchises and true son of the gods,
You are looking at the lagoons of Cocytus
And the river Styx, by whose name
Even the gods fear to swear falsely.
The crowd you see are the unburied dead;   400
The ferryman is Charon; his passengers

Are the dead entombed. He may not carry
Any across the raucous, dread water
Until their bones are at rest. Else,
A hundred years they must roam the shoreline   405
And only then may return to cross these shoals."

The son of Anchises stopped in his tracks,
Pondering all this, and pitied in his heart
Their unjust lot. He saw among them,
Sad and bereft of death's due, Leucaspis,   410
And Orontes, captain of the Lycian fleet,
Overwhelmed by the storm that engulfed their ships
As they sailed the windy seas out of Troy.

And now there came Palinurus, who
While reckoning their course from Libya   415
By the stars had fallen from the stern
Into the waves. Aeneas hardly knew him,
Forlorn in the deep gloom, but finally
Recognized him and called out:

                    "Palinurus,
What god tore you from us and plunged you   420
Into the open sea? Apollo, never before
Found false, deluded me when he foretold
You would escape the sea and reach Ausonia."

And Palinurus:

                    "Delphi did not mislead you,
My captain, nor did any god drown me.   425
The rudder I was holding to steer our course
Ripped apart, and as I fell headlong I
Dragged it down with me. I swear by the wild sea
I was not so afraid for myself as for your ship,
Afraid that stripped of its gear and its pilot overboard   430
It might founder and sink in the heavy weather.
Three stormy nights the South Wind drove me
Over boundless seas. As the fourth dawn broke
I rode the crest of a wave and sighted
Italy. I fought my way toward land and thought   435
I had safety in my grasp. I hooked my fingers

On a crag of shore, but weighed down
By my dripping clothes I was easy prey
For a band of marauders. Wind and surf
Now roll my body along the tide line.   440
By the sweet light and the air of heaven,
By your father, by the promise Iülus holds,
Save me from these woes, Aeneas unconquered!
Either cast earth upon me—it is in your power
If you sail back to Velia—or if your divine mother   445
Shows you how (surely it is not your plan
To sail the great Styx without divine power),
Give me your hand and take me with you
Across these waves, so that I may at least
Find in death my final resting place."   450

Thus Palinurus, and the Sibyl answered him:

"Where did you get this outrageous desire?
Are you, unburied, to look upon the Styx,
The Furies' stream, and approach these shores
Unbidden? Stop hoping that the gods' decrees   455
Can be bent with prayer. But hear this
And bear it in your heart as consolation.
The neighboring peoples, in cities far and wide,
Will be driven by portents to appease your bones,
Will build a tomb, and to the tomb will tender   460
Solemn offerings, and forever the place
Will be called Palinurus."

By these words
His anguish was relieved, his grief dispelled.
And the land rejoices in the name Palinurus.

Continuing their journey, they drew near the river.   465
Out on the water the boatman saw them
Heading to the bank through the silent wood,
And before they could speak he rebuked them:

"Hold it right there, whoever you are
Coming to our river in arms! Why are you here?   470
This is the Land of Shadows, of Sleep

And drowsy Night. Living bodies
May not be transported in this Stygian keel.
I was not happy to take Hercules
Across the lake, or Theseus and Pirithoüs,   475
Invincible sons of the gods though they were.
One of them wanted to drag off in chains
The Tartarean watchdog from Pluto's throne—
And dragged him off trembling. The others tried
To carry off the queen from the bedroom of Dis."   480

Apollo's prophetess responded briefly:

"There is no such treachery here. Calm down.
Our weapons offer no threat of violence.
The giant watchdog may howl from his cave
Eternally and frighten the bloodless shades.   485
Proserpina may keep her chastity intact
Within her uncle's doors. Aeneas of Troy,
Famed as a warrior and man of devotion,
Goes down to his father in lowest Erebus.
If this picture of piety in no way moves you,   490
Yet this bough" (she showed it under her robe)
"You must acknowledge."

                        Charon's engorged rage
Subsided. No more was said. Marveling
At the venerable gift, the fateful bough
So long unseen, he turned the dark-blue prow   495
Toward shore. There he cleared the deck,
Pushed the shades from the benches, and laid out
The gangplank. He took aboard his hollow boat
Huge Aeneas. Groaning under his weight,
The ragtag craft took on water. At last,   500
The swamp crossed, the ferryman disembarked
Hero and seer unharmed in the muddy sedge.

Crouching in a cavern on the farther shore
Cerberus made these regions resound,
Barking like thunder from all three of his throats.   505
The seer, close enough now to see the snakes
Bristling on his necks, flung a honeyed cake
Laced with drugs into his ravenous jaws.

Cerberus snatched it from the air and then
Went slack, easing his huge, limp bulk   510
To the ground, stretching out over all his den,
Dead to the world. Aeneas entered the cave
And left behind the water of no return.

Now came the sound of wailing, the weeping
Of the souls of infants, torn from the breast   515
On a black day and swept off to bitter death
On the very threshold of their sweet life.
Nearby are those falsely condemned to die.
These places are not assigned without judge
And jury. Minos presides and shakes the urn,   520
Calls the silent conclave, conducts the trial.

In the next region are those wretched souls
Who contrived their own deaths. Innocent
But loathing the light, they threw away their lives
And now would gladly bear any hardship   525
To be in the air above. But it may not be.
The unlovely water binds them to Hell,
Styx confines them in its nine circling folds.

Not far from here the Fields of Lamentation,
As they are called, stretch into the vastness.   530
Here those whom Love has cruelly consumed
Languish concealed in sequestered myrtle glades,
Sorrow clinging to them even as they wander
These lost paths in death. In this region of Hell
Aeneas makes out Phaedra, Procris,   535
And mournful Eriphyle, displaying the wounds
She received from her son. He sees Evadne
And Pasiphaë and, walking with them,
Laodamia, and Caeneus, a young man once,
Now a woman, returned to her original form.   540
And among them, her wound still fresh,
Phoenician Dido wandered that great wood.
The Trojan hero stood close to her there
And in the gloom recognized her dim form

   As faint as the new moon a man sees,   545
   Or thinks he sees, through the evening's haze.

He broke into tears and spoke to her
With tender love:

               "Oh, Dido, so the message was true
That you were dead, that you took your own life
With steel. Was I really the cause of your death?   *550*
I swear by the stars, by the powers above,
And by whatever faith lies in the depths below,
It was not my choice to leave your land, my Queen.
The gods commanded me to go, as they force me now
With their high decrees to go through this shadowland,   *555*
This moldy stillness, the abyss of Night.
I could not believe that I would cause you
Such grief by leaving. Stop! Don't turn away!
Who are you running from? Fate will never
Let us speak with each other again."   *560*

With such words Aeneas tried to soothe
Her burning soul. Tears came to his eyes,
But Dido kept her own eyes fixed on the ground,
As unmoved by his words as if her averted face
Were made of flint or Marpesian marble.   *565*
Finally she left, a stranger to him now, and fled
Into a darkling grove, where her old husband,
Sychaeus, comforted her and returned her love.
But Aeneas, struck by the injustice
Of her fate, wept as he watched her   *570*
Disappear, and pitied her as she went.

Aeneas and the Sibyl now made their way
To the farthest fields, a place set apart
For the great war heroes. Here Diomedes
And renowned Parthenopaeus met Aeneas,   *575*
And the pale shade of Adrastus. And here,
Lamented on earth and fallen in war,
Were many Dardanians. Aeneas moaned
When he saw their long ranks:
Glaucus, Medon, and Thersilochus,   *580*
Antenor's three sons; Polyboetes,
Priest of Ceres, and Idaeus,
Still with his chariot, still bearing arms.
They crowded around him, right and left,

And it was not enough for these shades   585
To have seen him: they want to linger,
To walk beside him and learn why he came.
But as soon as the foremost Danaans
And the battalions of Agamemnon
Saw Aeneas' arms flashing in the gloom,   590
They trembled with fear. Some turned to run,
As if fleeing again to their beachhead camp.
Others tried to shout, but their voices,
Thin and faint, mocked their gaping mouths.

And here Aeneas saw Deïphobus,   595
Son of Priam, his whole body mangled
And his face cruelly mutilated, shredded,
And both hands gone. His ears had been torn
From the sides of his head, and his nostrils lopped
With a shameful wound. Aeneas scarcely   600
Recognized him as he trembled, struggling
To hide his brutal disfigurement. He paused
But then addressed him in familiar tones:

"Deïphobus, mighty warrior
Of Teucer's high blood, who took delight   605
In such torture? Who dared treat you like this?
Word reached me that on that last night, weary
With endless slaughter of Greeks, you fell
On a heap of tangled corpses. I set up for you
An empty tomb on the Rhoetian shore   610
And called three times upon your ghost.
Your name and your arms guard the place.
You, my friend, I could not see, nor bury you
In your native soil before I had to leave."

And Priam's son responded:

                              "My friend,   615
You have left nothing undone but have paid
All that is due to Deïphobus' shade.
My own fate, and that lethal Spartan woman,
Plunged me into this misery. She left
These memorials! You know how we spent   620
That last night in delusive joy. You know,

You remember all too well. When the Horse
Leapt to the city's high, holy place, its womb
Heavy with infantry, Helen feigned
A ritual dance and led the Trojan women   625
Crying in ecstasy around Pergamum's heights
While she herself held the huge, blazing torch
That signaled the Greeks from the citadel.
I was asleep in our ill-starred bedroom,
Worn out with care, wrapped in slumber   630
As peaceful as death, while Helen,
My incomparable wife, was busy removing
Every weapon from the house and even slipped
My trusty sword from under my head.
Then she called Menelaus inside,   635
Hoping this would please her lover
And wipe out the memory of her old sins.
Why draw it out? They burst into my room,
Ulysses with them, the evil counselor.

                              O Gods,
If my face is pious enough to pray for vengeance   640
Make the Greeks pay in kind!
                         But you,
Tell me now, what has brought you here,
Alive? Were you driven here while roaming the sea,
Or by Heaven's command? Why do you visit
The drear confusion of this sunless realm?"   645

While they were talking, Dawn had climbed
High up the sky in her roselight chariot,
And they might have spent all their allotted time
On these matters had not the Sibyl warned:

"Night is coming on, Aeneas, yet we   650
Weep away the hours. Here is the place
Where the road splits into two. To the right,
Winding under the walls of great Dis,
Is the way to Elysium. But the left road
Takes the wicked to their punishment   655
In Tartarus."

      Deïphobus responded:

"Do not be angry, great priestess. I will go
And return to my place in the shadows. But you,
Glory of our race, go. Go to a happier fate."

And on this word he turned away.   660

Aeneas suddenly looked back and saw,
Under a cliff to the left, a great fortification
Surrounded by a triple wall and encircled
By a river of fire—Phlegethon—
That rolled thunderous rocks in its current.   665
The Gate was flanked by adamantine columns
That could not be destroyed by any force,
Human or divine. High on a tower of iron,
Tisiphone sat, draped in a bloody pall,
Sleeplessly watching the portal night and day.   670
Groans, the crack of the lash, iron clanking,
And dragging chains grated on the ear.
Stunned by the noise, Aeneas froze in his tracks.

"What evil is here, priestess, what forms of torture,
What lamentation rising on the air?"   675

And the Sibyl began:

              "Teucrian hero,
No virtuous soul may ever set foot
On this accursed threshold, but when Hecate
Made me mistress of the groves of Avernus
She showed me all of the punishments   680
The gods inflict.
              Cretan Rhadamanthus
Rules this iron realm. He queries each soul,
Hears his lies, and forces him to confess
The sins whose atonement he has postponed,
In his deluded vanity, until too late. At once,   685
Tisiphone pounces upon the guilty soul
With her avenging scourge, brandishing
Glaring serpents in her left fist as she calls
Her sister Furies. Then, metal grinding
Upon metal, slowly open the Gates of Hell.   690
Do you see the face of the Fury who guards

The vestibule? The Hydra lurking within
Is much worse—fifty gaping black throats.
      Then there is the pit of Tartarus itself,
Plunging down into darkness twice as deep   695
As Olympus is high. Here Earth's ancient brood,
The Titans, struck down by the thunderbolt,
Writhe in the abyss. And here too I saw
The twin sons of Aloeus, the Giants who tried
To tear open the sky and pull Jupiter down.   700
And I saw Salmoneus suffering torment
For aping the Olympian's thunder and lightning.
Torches shaking, he drove his chariot
Through all the cities of Greece in triumph,
And he brought his show of smoke and mirrors   705
Home to Elis, demanding a divinity's honors
For mimicking with bronze and horses' hooves
The inimitable rumble of thunderheads.
But the Father Almighty hurled his bolt—
No smoky torch—through the thick clouds   710
And blasted the sinner into perdition.
And Tityos is there, another son of Earth,
His body stretched over nine full acres,
And a monstrous vulture with a hooked beak
Gnaws away at his immortal liver   715
And tortured entrails, pecking deep for its feasts.
The bird lives in his bowels while his flesh,
Like his pain, is renewed endlessly.
And then there are the Lapiths, Ixion
And Pirithoüs, above whom a black rock   720
Totters, ever about to fall. Before their eyes
A banquet fit for a king is spread,
And high festive couches gleam with gold.
Reclining there, the eldest Fury
Keeps their hands from touching the table,   725
Rearing up with a torch and roaring 'No!'
      Here are those who hated their brothers,
Struck a parent, or betrayed a client;
Those who hoarded the wealth they had won,
Saving none for their kin (the largest group this);   730
Those slain for adultery; those who did not fear
To desert their masters in treasonous war—
All these await their punishment within.

Do not ask its form, or what fortune undid them.
Some roll huge stones, or hang outstretched   735
On the spokes of a wheel. Theseus sits
And will sit forever. Phlegyas in his agony
Lifts his voice through the gloom, admonishing all:
'Learn justice, beware, do not slight the gods.'
This one sold his country for gold and installed   740
A tyrant; another made and unmade laws
For a price. This one went to his daughter's bed.
All dared a great crime, and did what they dared.
Not if I had a hundred mouths, a hundred tongues,
And a voice of iron, could I recount   745
All the crimes or tell all their punishments."

Thus the aged priestess of Apollo.

"But come, pick up your pace, and complete
What you came for," the Sibyl continued. "Hurry!
I see the walls forged by the Cyclopes   750
And the gates in the archway opposite, where
We have been told to place our offering."

They went side by side down dusky paths
And drew near the doors. Aeneas
Stood on the threshold, sprinkled his body   755
With fresh water, and fixed the bough in place.

The offering to the goddess complete,
Aeneas and the Sibyl now came
To regions of joy, the green and pleasant fields
Of the Blissful Groves. Air and sky   760
Are more spacious here, and the light shines
With an amethyst glow. The land here knows
Its own sun and stars.
                        Some are at exercise
On the grassy wrestling ground, some contend
On the yellow sand, others tread a dance   765
And chant a choral song. And Orpheus,
In the long robes of a Thracian priest,
Accompanies them on his seven-toned lyre,
Plucking notes with his fingers and ivory quill.
Here too is the ancient race of Teucer,   770

A people most fair, high-souled heroes
Born in better times—Ilus, Assaracus,
And Dardanus, founder of Troy.

                          Aeneas
Wonders at their weapons and chariots,
Mere phantoms, and yet their spears   775
Stand fixed in the ground, and their horses
Graze unyoked over all the plain.
The pleasure they took in arms and chariots
When they were alive, in keeping sleek horses,
Is still theirs now beneath the earth.   780
And he sees others, to the right and left,
Scattered on the grass, feasting, or singing
Songs of joy in a fragrant grove of laurel
Where the Eridanus rolls its mighty waters
Through forests to the world above.
                         Here too are those   785
Wounded fighting in their country's defense,
Those who in life were priests and poets,
Bards whose words were worthy of Apollo;
Also, those who enriched life with inventions
Or earned remembrance for service rendered—   790
Their brows bound with bands as white as snow.
When they had gathered around, the Sibyl
Addressed them, Musaeus especially,
Who stood head and shoulders above the others:

"Tell me, blessed souls, and you, best of poets,   795
Which part of this realm harbors Anchises?
For him we have crossed the rivers of Erebus."

The great soul Musaeus answered her briefly:

"We have no fixed homes but dwell in shadowed
Groves, recline on riverbanks, and live in meadows   800
Freshened by streams. But if you so wish,
Over this ridge I can show you an easy path."

He led them up and pointed out to them
Shining fields below. The pair went down.

Anchises, deep in a green valley, was reviewing   *805*
As a proud father the souls of his descendants
Yet to be born into the light, contemplating
Their destinies, their great deeds to come.
When he saw his son striding toward him
Through the grass, he stretched out   *810*
His trembling hands, tears wet his cheeks,
And these words fell from his lips:

"You have come at last! I knew your devotion
Would see you through the long, hard road.
I can look upon your face, and we can hear   *815*
Each other's familiar voices again.
I have been counting the hours carefully
Until this day, and my love has not deceived me.
All the lands and seas, all the dangers
You have been through, my son! How I feared   *820*
You would come to harm in Libya."

And Aeneas:

"You, Father, your sad image,
Kept appearing to me, leading me here.
Our ships stand offshore in the Italian sea.
Let me hold your hands in mine, Father,   *825*
Do not pull away from my embrace!"

As Aeneas said this he began to weep.
Three times he tried to put his arms
Around his father's neck. Three times
His father's wraith slipped through his hands,   *830*
As light as wind, as fleeting as a dream.

While they talked in this sequestered valley
A secluded grove caught Aeneas' eye.
A stream drifted past its rustling thickets—
The river Lethe—and around it hovered   *835*
Nations of souls, innumerable

> *As bees on a cloudless summer day*
> *That settle upon wildflowers in a field*
> *And swarm so thickly around the white lilies*
> *That the whole meadow hums and murmurs.*   *840*

Aeneas was shaken at the sight
And asked, in his ignorance, the reason
For this congregation. What was the river,
And who were the men crowding its banks?
Father Anchises answered: 845

"These are souls owed another body by Fate.
In the ripples of Lethe they sip the waters
Of forgetfulness and timeless oblivion.
I have been longing to show them to you,
The census of my generations, so that you   850
May rejoice as I do at finding Italy."

"Father, can it be that souls go from here
To the world above and return again
To their gross bodies? What is this yearning
For these poor souls to taste the light?"   855

Aeneas asked this.

                    "I will tell you, my son,
And not keep you in doubt."

                    Anchises answered,
And he revealed the mysteries one by one.

"First, heaven and earth, the sea's expanse,
The moon's bright globe, the sun and stars   860
Are all sustained by a spirit within.
Every part is infused with Mind,
Which moves the Whole, the source of life
For man and beast and all winged things
And the monsters of the marmoreal deep.   865
A divine fire pulses within those seeds of life,
A celestial energy, but it is slowed and dulled
By mortal frames, earthly bodies doomed to die.
And so men fear and desire, sorrow and exult,
And, shut in the shade of their prison-houses,   870
Cannot see the sky. Nor, when the last gleam
Of life flickers out, are all the ills
That flesh is heir to completely uprooted,
But many corporeal taints remain,

Ingrained in the soul in myriad ways.   875
And so we are disciplined and expiate
Our bygone sins. Some souls are hung
Spread to the winds; others are cleansed
Under swirling waters or purged by fire.
We each suffer our own ghosts. Then we are sent   880
Through spacious Elysium, and a few enjoy
The Blessed Fields, until the fullness of time
Removes the last trace of stain, leaving only
The pure flame of ethereal spirit.
                                    All these,
When they have rolled the wheel of time   885
Through a thousand years, will be called by God
In a great assembly to the river Lethe,
So that they return to the vaulted world
With no memory and may begin again
To desire rebirth in a human body."   890

Anchises paused, and he led his son,
Along with the Sibyl, into the heart
Of the murmuring crowd. He chose a mound
From which he could scan all their faces
As they passed by in long procession.   895

"Now I will set forth the glory that awaits
The Trojan race, the illustrious souls
Of the Italian heirs to our name.
I will teach you your destiny.

That youth you see leaning on an untipped spear   900
Is first in line to be reborn, first in the upper air
From Italian blood mingled with ours,
Silvius, an Alban name, your last child,
Born in your twilight years and reared by your wife,
Lavinia, in a sylvan home,   905
To be a king and father of kings.
We shall rule through him in Alba Longa.

Next comes Procas, pride of our race,
Then Capys and Numitor, and then
Your avatar, Aeneas Sylvius,   910
Equal to you in piety and arms,

If ever he succeeds to Alba's throne.
Look at these young men, their strength,
Their brows shaded with civic oak!
They will build for you Nomentum, Gabii,   915
And the town of Fidena. They will crown
Collatia's hills with towers and will found
Pometii and Inuus, Bola and Cora,
Famous names someday, now places without names.
Then a son of Mars will support his grandsire—   920
Romulus, born to Ilia from the line of Assaracus.
Do you see the double plumes on his head,
And how the Father of Gods honors him
As one of his own? Under his auspices,
My son, Rome will extend her renowned empire   925
To earth's horizons, her glory to the stars.
She will enclose seven hills within the wall
Of one city, blessed with a brood of heroes

> *As the Berecynthian Mother*
> *Is blessed with a brood divine, riding*   930
> *In her chariot through Phrygian towns,*
> *Wearing her turreted diadem, and embracing*
> *A hundred grandsons, all of them gods,*
> *All of them with homes in high heaven.*

Now turn your gaze here and let it rest upon   935
Your family of Romans. Here is Caesar,
And here are all of the descendants of Iülus
Destined to come under heaven's great dome.
And here is the man promised to you,
Augustus Caesar, born of the gods,   940
Who will establish again a Golden Age
In the fields of Latium once ruled by Saturn
And will expand his dominion
Beyond the Indus and the Garamantes,
Beyond our familiar stars, beyond the yearly   945
Path of the sun, to the land where Atlas
Turns the star-studded sphere on his shoulders.

Even now the Caspian Sea trembles
At the oracles that foretell his coming,
As does Persia, and the seven-mouthed Nile.   950

Not even Hercules ranged so far
Though he shot the bronze-hooved stag, brought calm
To Erymanthus' groves, and made Lerna quake
At his bow. Nor did Bacchus, though he drove
Tigers yoked with vine shoots from Nysa's heights.   955
And still we shrink from extending our virtue,
And fear to take our stand in Ausonia?

But who is this in the distance, resplendent
In his olive crown and sacred insignia?
I know that white hair and beard.   960
This is Numa, who will lay a foundation
Of law in our city, sent from a small town
In Sabine country to command a great nation.

Coming up after Numa is Tullus,
Who will shatter his country's leisure   965
And rouse to war men sunk in idleness
And an army unaccustomed to triumphs.

Hard upon Tullus' heels is Ancus,
Flaunting himself, blowing even now
In winds of popular favor.
                         Would you like to see   970
The Tarquin kings, the proud, avenging
Spirit of Brutus, and the rods of office
He will recover? He will be first to receive
The power of consul, and the stern axes.
When his sons stir up rebellious war   975
Their own father will exact punishment
In sweet liberty's name, an unhappy man
However the future might judge his deeds.
Love of country will prevail with him,
And a boundless desire for glory.   980

Look at the Decii and Drusi, still in the distance,
And Torquatus ferocious with his battle-axe,
And Camillus with the legion's standards regained.

But the two you see there, a match for each other
In resplendent armor, harmonious souls   985
While they are buried in night—what wars will they wage

Against each other, what civil slaughter
Should they ever reach the light, the bride's father
Marching down the Alps from Monaco,
His son-in-law drawing up his Oriental troops!   990
Do not inure yourselves to such war, my sons,
Nor rend your country's body with strife.
And you, child of Olympus, should show
Clemency first. Cast down your weapons,
My own flesh and blood. . . .   995

There is Corinth's conqueror, whose chariot
Will ascend the Capitoline Hill in triumph
After the slaughter of his Greek enemies.
And here is the Roman who will uproot Argos
And Agamemnon's Mycenae, and even the blood   1000
Of Aeacus, mighty Achilles' grandsire,
Avenging Troy and Minerva's temple.
Who, great Cato, could leave you unsung,
Or you, Cottus? Or the Gracchi brothers;
Or the two Scipios, twin thunderbolts of war   1005
And bane of Carthage; or Fabricius,
Whose power will be thrift, or you, Serranus,
Who left your plow? And you Fabii,
Where do you draw my weary gaze? Ah,
You are Fabius Maximus, whose strategy   1010
Was delay, and who alone saved our state.

Others will, no doubt, hammer out bronze
That breathes more softly, and draw living faces
Out of stone. They will plead cases better
And chart the rising of every star in the sky.   1015
Your mission, Roman, is to rule the world.
These will be your arts: to establish peace,
To spare the humbled, and to conquer the proud."

Thus Anchises, and as they marvel he adds:

"Look at Marcellus, proud in choice spoils   1020
Torn from the vanquished enemy commander,
Towering triumphant over all the crowd!
When the Roman state is falling in ruin
He will set it upright; he will trample down

The Carthaginians, crush the rebel Gauls,   1025
And offer to Quirinus a third set of arms."

At this, Aeneas, seeing a youth pass by
Beautiful in his gleaming armor
But with downcast eyes and troubled brow,
Asked his father:

        "Who is this,   1030
At the hero's side? His son, or another
In his great line of descendants? What
An impression he makes with his crowd of followers!
But the shadow of death enshrouds his head."

And Anchises, tears welling up in his eyes: 1035

"Son, do not seek your people's great grief.
Fate will permit him on earth a brief while,
But not for long. Gods above, you thought Rome
Would be too powerful had your gift endured.
What lamentation of the brave will hang   1040
Over the Field of Mars. O River Tiber,
What a funeral you will see as you glide past
His new tomb. No boy bred of Troy will ever raise
The hope of his Latin forefathers so high,
Nor the land of Romulus ever be so proud   1045
Of any of its sons. O, lament
His devotion, lament his pristine honor
And his sword arm invincible in war!
No enemy would have faced him unscathed,
Whether he fought on foot or dug his spurs   1050
Into the flanks of a foaming stallion.
If only you could shatter Fate, poor boy.
You will be Marcellus! Let me strew
Armfuls of lilies and scatter purple blossoms,
Hollow rites to honor my descendant's shade."   1055

And so they wandered every region of the wide,
Airy plain, surveying all it contained.
When Anchises had led his son
Through every detail and enflamed his soul
With longing for the glory that was to come,   1060

He told him of the wars he next must wage,
Of the Laurentine people and Latinus' town,
And how to face or flee each waiting peril.

There are two Gates of Sleep. One, they say,
Is horn, and offers easy exit for true shades. 1065
The other is finished with glimmering ivory,
But through it the Spirits send false dreams
To the world above. Anchises escorted his son
As he talked, then sent him with the Sibyl
Through the Gate of Ivory. 1070
Aeneas made his way to the ships,
Rejoined his men, and sailed along the coast
To Caieta's harbor. They cast anchor
From the prow; the sterns faced the shore.

AENEID SEVEN

You too Caieta, nurse of Aeneas,
Have by your death given eternal fame
To our shores. Still your resting place
Is honored, and if bones can lie in glory
So lie yours beneath your name   5
In great Hesperia.

          When the last rites
Were done, and her burial mound heaped up,
Godly Aeneas set sail from the haven
As soon as the high seas had subsided.
Breezes blew on into the night, and the moon   10
Shone white on the tremulous water below,
Lighting their voyage. Hugging the coastline,
They passed the land where Circe,
Daughter of the Sun, lived in opulence.
The woodland rang with her perpetual song,   15
And in her high house she burned fragrant cedar
To illumine the night while she worked the loom,
Combing her shrill shuttle through delicate threads.
And from those shores could also be heard
Lions roaring and snapping at their chains   20
Late into the night, the raging of bristled boars
And caged bears, and huge wolf-shapes howling.
All these were men whom Circe had cruelly drugged
And clad in the hides and faces of beasts.
But Neptune, to save the good Trojans   25
From these monstrous transformations,
Kept them from landing on those deadly shores,
Filling their sails with wind, and bearing them past
The seething shoals and out of danger.

Now the sea was reddening, and Dawn,   30
Saffron in her rosy chariot, shone in the sky,
When the winds fell and every breeze died down.

As the oars struggled in the smooth, marble water,
Aeneas, still far offshore, looked out and saw
A vast forest, and flowing through it   35
The beautiful Tiber, its current swirling
With golden sand as it broke into the sea.
Above and all about, birds of many kinds
That haunted the banks and bed of the river
Flew through the woods, enchanting the air   40
With their trilling.
                    Aeneas ordered his men
To change course and turn their prows landward,
And with joy he drew into the shady river.

And now, Erato, who were the kings
And what was the state of ancient Latium   45
When this foreign army landed in Italy?
Help me, Goddess, your sacred poet,
Recall the prelude to the hostilities,
For I will tell of war's horror, of pitched battle,
Heroes driven by courage to meet their doom,   50
Of Etruscan squadrons, and all Hesperia
Pressed into arms. A higher order of things
Opens before me; a greater work now begins.

King Latinus, old and grey, ruled over lands
And cities through a long twilight of peace.   55
He was born, we are told, from Faunus
And the Laurentine nymph Marica.
Faunus' father was Picus, and Picus
Looked to you, Saturn, as his father:
You were the founder of the royal line.   60
Latinus' son, his sole male heir, was gone,
Torn away by Fate in the springtime of youth.
He had only a daughter to keep his great house,
A daughter ripe for marriage, a bride to be,
Courted by many in broad Latium, by many   65
From all Ausonia, and the handsomest of all
Was Turnus. He was from old blood, powerful,
And Latinus' queen was strangely passionate
To join him to herself as her son in marriage.

But portents from the gods warned otherwise.   70

Book 7

A sacred laurel stood in the inner courtyard
Of the palace, tended in awe for many years.
Latinus himself is said to have found this tree
When he first built the citadel. He dedicated
Its foliage to Phoebus Apollo   75
And from its name called his people
The Laurentines. A thick swarm of bees
Buzzing and humming through the crystal air
Settled in the top of this tree, and—
A sign and a wonder—hung with feet interlaced   80
From the highest branch—a sudden hive.
At once the seer cries:

    "I see an outlander—
Troops arriving from the same direction
As these bees, seeking and mastering the citadel."

And again, while Lavinia at her father's side   85
Kindled the altar with a hallowed torch,
Her long hair, to everyone's horror, caught fire.
Flames crackled in her headdress, her jeweled tiara
Flared with heat, and the princess herself,
Shrouded in glowing yellow smoke,   90
Scattered Vulcan's sparks throughout the palace.
This ghastly miracle was reported widely
And taken to mean that the princess's future was bright,
But that a great war would come upon her people.

The king was troubled by these portents   95
And consulted the oracle of Faunus,
His prophetic father, the vatic grove
Beneath high Albunea, a great forest
That echoes with the sound of a sacred spring
And breathes mephitic vapors from its shadows.   100
The people of Italy and all Oenotria
Come to consult this oracle in time of doubt.
It is here the priest brings his offerings,
And when he has lain down to sleep
Upon the fleeces of slaughtered sheep   105
In the still of the night, he sees many phantoms
Flitting about in strange ways, hears
Many voices, converses with the gods,

And speaks to Acheron in Avernus' depths.
Father Latinus came to consult this oracle.   110
He slaughtered a hundred yearling sheep
In ritual order and lay himself down
Cushioned by their woolly fleece. Suddenly,
A voice came from deep within the grove:

"Seek not, my son, to marry your daughter   115
Into a Latin family. Trust not a wedding
Already prepared. A stranger will come
To be your son-in-law. His blood will exalt
Our name to the stars, and his children's children
Will see the world turn under their feet,   120
And their rule will stretch over all that the Sun
Looks down upon, from sea to shining sea."

Thus the response of father Faunus,
His warning given in the dead of night.
And Latinus did not keep it a secret. Rumor   125
Took flight and had already spread the news
Through all the cities of Ausonia
When the men of Laomedon's Troy
Were mooring their ships to the Tiber's grassy banks.

Aeneas and his captains, and fair Iülus,   130
Reclined in the shade of a towering tree
And spread out a feast on the grass below,
Heaping fruits of the field—Jupiter himself
Gave them this notion—on wheat flatbread
To supplement the meal. When they had eaten   135
Everything else, their appetites drove them
To break the scored, fateful rounds into sections
And sink their teeth into the crusty bread.

"We're so hungry we're even eating our tables!"

Iülus said this in jest and said no more,   140
But Aeneas heard it as the first sign
That their trials were ending. Awestruck,
He seized upon his son's words and cried:

"Hail to the Promised Land and faithful gods
Of Troy! Here is our home, this is our country.   145

My father Anchises foretold this to me—
I remember it now—one of Fate's secrets:
'When you are borne, my son, to shores unknown,
And hunger compels you to eat your tables,
Then in your weariness hope for a home.   *150*
Build your first houses there, roof them well
With your own hands, and bank them with mounds.'
This was that hunger, the final stretch
Of all our misfortunes.
           Come, then, be happy!
With the sun's first light we will explore these lands,   *155*
Find out who lives here, locate their city.
We will fan out from the harbor. For now, though,
Pour libations to Jove, pray to Anchises,
And set the wine again on the tables!"

               Aeneas spoke
And wreathed his temples with leaves.   *160*
Then he prayed to the place's indwelling spirit,
And to Earth, first of the gods, and to nymphs
And rivers yet unknown; then to Night
And Night's wheeling constellations,
To Jove of Ida and the Phrygian Mother,   *165*
And his two parents, one in heaven,
One in Erebus below. And at his prayer
The Father Almighty sent three peals of thunder
From a clear sky, set in the ether
A cloud glowing with shafts of gold,   *170*
And shook the cloud with his own great hand.
Word spread quickly through the Trojan ranks
That the day had come for them to found
Their promised city. They outdo each other
To renew the feast and, cheered by the great omen,   *175*
Fill the bowls with wine to the beaded brims.

*Lines 177–346 are omitted. Aeneas sends envoys to meet Latinus and nego-
tiate an alliance with him. When this embassy has been warmly welcomed
by Latinus, its spokesman asks only for*

    *". . . a safe strip of shore,
    A little land for the gods of our country,*

And water and air that are common to all."
(7.276–78)

Latinus happily grants this request and expresses the hope that Aeneas will prove to be the hero whom, according to prophecy, his daughter Lavinia is destined to marry. The embassy returns to Aeneas bringing an offer of the peaceful outcome he had hoped for.

But now Jupiter's ferocious wife
Was returning from Argos, striding
The level air, when she saw from afar—
All the way from Sicilian Pachynus—   350
Aeneas, his spirits high, with all his people.
They were already building a city,
At home on the land, their ships empty.
She stopped in midair, pierced with grief,
And, shaking her head, poured forth these words: 355

"Ah, hated race, Phrygian fates
At odds with mine! Couldn't they have died
On the Sigean plain? Defeated,
Couldn't they have endured defeat?
Didn't burning Troy cremate these men?   360
No! They found a way through fire and foe.
My divinity must be wearing thin,
Or I have grown content, my wrath appeased.
Not exactly! When they were thrown out
Of their country, I persecuted the outcasts   365
All over the deep blue sea. All the powers
Of sea and sky have been used against them.
But what did the Syrtes get me, or Scylla,
Or gaping Charybdis? They have found shelter
In Tiber's long-sought channel, safe from the sea   370
And safe from me. Mars could destroy
The giant Lapith race; the Father of the Gods
Sacrificed Calydon to Diana's wrath,
But what did the Lapiths or Calydon do
To deserve such punishment? But I,   375
Jove's great consort, who have left nothing
Undared, have tried every trick and turn,
Am bested by Aeneas! But if my powers
Are not great enough, why should I hesitate

To seek help from any source whatever? 380
If I cannot sway Heaven, I will awaken Hell!
I concede Aeneas the rule of Latium,
And Lavinia is his bride by iron fate,
But to draw it out and delay the issue,
That I may do, and destroy both nations. 385
Their people's lives will be the price
For father and son-in-law to form a union.
Trojan and Rutulian blood will be your dowry,
Bride of Aeneas, and Bellona
Your matron of honor! It was not only Hecuba 390
Who conceived a firebrand and gave birth
To nuptial flames. Venus' own child
Is a second Paris, a funeral torch for New Troy."

With these words Juno descended to earth,
A terrifying presence, and called forth Allecto 395
From the home of the Dread Goddesses
And the shadows below, gruesome Allecto
Whose heart is set on war and wrath,
Intrigues and crime. She is hateful
Even to Pluto, who sired her, hateful 400
To her Tartarean sisters: so many shapes
She assumes, so cruel her faces, so vile
The black vipers that sprout from her scalp.
Juno enflamed her with words such as these:

"Daughter of Night, grant me a favor, 405
A special service that will preserve my honor.
Prevent Aeneas from winning over Latinus
Through marriage, or from invading Italy.
You are able to make like-minded brothers
Arm for battle, to overturn homes with hate, 410
To bring lash and funeral torch to the hearth.
You have a thousand names, a thousand ways
To cause harm. Ransack your teeming heart.
Shatter the peace, sow the seeds of war.
Make each man want to grip a weapon, 415
Demand one and seize one all in one breath."

And so Allecto, venomous as any Gorgon,
Makes for Latinus' palace in Latium

And occupies the still threshold
Of Amata. The queen was inside, seething   420
With a woman's fury at the Teucrians' coming
And sick at heart over Turnus' marriage.
The goddess plucks a snake from her dark hair
And throws it on Amata, thrusting it
Deep into her bosom to drive her mad   425
And so bring down the entire house. Gliding
Between her clothes and smooth breasts,
It insinuates itself unseen and unfelt
By the frenzied woman and hisses into her
Its viperous breath. The huge serpent becomes   430
The twisted gold around her neck, becomes
The long band about her brows, entwines itself
Into her hair, and slithers down her limbs.
As the first taint of the poison is absorbed—
Assailing her senses and enflaming her bones   435
But not yet engulfing her soul in fire—
Softly, as mothers do, she murmurs, weeping
Over her daughter's wedlock with Aeneas:

"Will you give Lavinia to Teucrian exiles,
You, her father? Have you no pity left   440
For your daughter or yourself? No pity
For her mother, whom this traitor will desert
With the first North Wind, sailing away
With our girl as plunder? Wasn't this how Paris
Entered Lacedaemon and bore off Helen   445
To Ilium? What of your solemn promise?
What of your old love for your own, what of
Your hand so often pledged to Turnus,
Your kinsman? If it has been decided
That we need a son-in-law of foreign stock,   450
If the words of your father Faunus
Are so important, then I maintain
That every land not under our rule
Is a foreign land, and the gods agree.
Turnus himself, if you trace his lineage,   455
Is descended from Inachus and Acrisius
With roots in Mycenae, the heart of Greece."

Amata's words had no effect on Latinus.

When she saw her husband standing against her,
And when the venom had infected her deeply,   460
Pulsing through her veins, the ill-starred queen
Was swept away by monstrous horrors
And raged in her frenzy all through the city.

    A top kept spinning by a twisted cord,
    As boys, intent on their game, drive it along   465
    In great loops through an empty courtyard,
    Will whip around curve after curve as the throng
    Of entranced children hovers above it,
    Mesmerized by the whirling boxwood toy.

Likewise Amata, driven through the cities   470
Of the fierce Latian peoples and through the forests,
Feigning the spirit of Bacchus, a greater sin,
And reaching new heights of madness.
She hid her daughter in the wooded mountains
To forestall her wedding to the Teucrian,   475
Shrieking:

    "Hail, Bacchus! You alone
Are worthy of her. She waves the thyrsus
For you, worships you in the dance,
Grows her sacred tresses for you, Bacchus!"

Rumor spreads, inflaming the Latian mothers   480
With fury, and they rise as one, abandoning
Their homes, hair streaming in the wind
As they fill the air with their quavering cries,
Dressed in fawnskins and carrying spears
Entwined with vines. The frenzied queen   485
Lifts up a blazing torch of pine and sings
A wedding song for her daughter and Turnus,
Rolling her bloodshot eyes and suddenly
Shouting:

    "Hear me, mothers of Latium,
Wherever you are! If your hearts are still loyal   490
To unhappy Amata, if you still care about her
And a mother's rights—unbind your hair
And celebrate the revels along with me!"

Such was the queen, driven by Allecto
With Bacchic goads through the haunts of wild beasts.   *495*

When the dark goddess thought she had put
A fine enough edge on the first shafts of frenzy
And had undone Latinus and all his house,
She flew on dusky wings to the walls
Of the bold Rutulian's city.   *500*
The story is told that Danaë,
Driven ashore by the strong South Wind,
Built this city with her Acrisian settlers.
Ardea it was called, and the great name remains,
But the place is desolate now.
                              Midnight,   *505*
And Turnus was asleep in his high palace.
Allecto sloughed off her fiend's body
And changed herself into an old woman.
She creased her brow, made her hair white,
And bound it with wool and an olive chaplet.   *510*
She was Calybe now, aged priestess
Of the temple of Juno, and with these words
She offered herself to the young hero's eyes:

"Turnus, will you allow all your work
To be washed away, and the scepter handed   *515*
To these Dardanian settlers? The king
Denies you the bride you won with your blood,
And a stranger is sought as heir to your throne.
Go ahead, face danger unrewarded, you fool,
Smash Tuscan ranks, shield the Latins with peace!   *520*
Saturn's almighty daughter in person
Told me to tell you this while you lay abed
In the still of the night. Up then, smile,
Arm your lads, march them through the gates
Into the fields, and burn the painted Phrygian ships   *525*
Lying at anchor in our beautiful river!
Heaven commands it. And unless King Latinus
Honors his word and gives you your bride,
Let him feel the full force of Turnus as foe."

And Turnus, mocking the seer:

                              "So a fleet   530
Has entered the Tiber's mouth, and you think
I don't know? Don't invent a crisis
For my benefit. Queen Juno does not forget me.
Old age has rotted your mind and deludes
Your prophetic soul with false alarms.   535
See to the gods' temples and statues.
War is the work of the men who wage it."

Allecto's hair spread out in fiery points,
And as Turnus spoke a sudden spasm
Seized his limbs. He stared in horror   540
At the Fury's hissing snakes and the face
That loomed before him. Her eyes rolled in flame
As she pushed him back. Turnus stumbled,
Tried to say more, but the Fury pulled
A pair of snakes from her hair, cracked her whip,   545
And spoke again from her rabid lips:

"Behold me, mind rotted with old age,
Prophetic soul deluded with false alarms.
Look on this! I come from the Dread Sisters,
And in my hand I bear War and Death."   550

And she threw a torch at the young hero,
Sticking it in his chest, where it smoked
With black light. Turnus woke in terror,
Sweat pouring down, drenching him
To the bone. He called madly for arms,   555
Groped wildly in the bed for weapons,
Lusting for steel and the rut of battle,
Rage crowning all.

              A fire crackling
     Under a bronze cauldron heats the water
     Until it seethes and bubbles, unable to contain itself,   560
     And a cloud of dark steam rises into the air.

And so Turnus, peace be damned, ordered his captains
To march on Latinus. His battle cry rang out:

"For Italy! Drive the enemy out!
Turnus is here, a match for Teucrians   565

And Latins alike!"

                    And he called on the gods
To witness his vows. The Rutulians
Outdid each other in the call to arms,
Stirred by Turnus' good looks, his high lineage,
And his prowess in battle, second to none.   570

Lines 571–934 are omitted. Allecto induces Ascanius to shoot a stag that was a pet of local herdsmen. A fight breaks out and Turnus declares war on the Trojans. Latinus withdraws. Juno opens the Gates of War and the troops are mustered.

In the foremost ranks moved Turnus himself,   935
Incomparable, sword in hand, head crowned
With a plumed helmet bearing a Chimaera
That breathed from her jaws Aetnean fire,
Flames all the more fierce the more blood is shed.
On his polished shield Io, horns uplifted,   940
An emblem blazoned in gold—Io,
Covered in bristles, already a heifer,
With Argus her warden and her father, Inachus,
Pouring his stream from a figured urn.
A cloud of foot soldiers followed him,   945
And shielded columns crowded the plain,
Argive troops and Auruncan platoons,
Rutulians and veteran Sicanians,
Lines of Sarcanians and Labicians
With painted shields; tillers of your glades,   950
O Tiber, and the sacred shore of Numicius,
Farmers from the Rutulian hills
And Circe's ridge, whose fields are ruled
By Jupiter Anxur and by Feronia,
Gay in her greenwood, where the black swamp   955
Of Satura lies and the cold Ufens
Winds through valleys and down to the sea.

Last of all rode Camilla the Volscian,
Leading her mounted troops and squadrons
Flowering in bronze. This princess warrior   960

Had not trained her hands to women's work,
Spinning and weaving, but trained to endure
The hardships of war and to outrun the wind.
She could sprint over a field of wheat
And not even bruise the tender ears,   965
Could cruise above the open sea's waves
And never wet the soles of her feet.
All the young men, and their mothers too,
Flocked from their houses and left their fields
To watch her ride by, mouths open in wonder   970
At how the royal purple draped
Her smooth shoulders, how her hair
Was bound in gold, and how she carried
A Lycian quiver and an iron-tipped spear.

AENEID EIGHT

When Turnus raised the flag of war
From Laurentium's high citadel;
When the horns blared, and he whipped
His horses to a fury and clashed his arms,
There was an instant, spirited reaction.   5
All of Latium rose to swear allegiance.
Young men raged to fight. Their leaders,
Messapus and Ufens, with Mezentius,
Who held the gods in contempt, mustered troops
From all over and ransacked the wide fields   10
Of their farmers. They even sent Venulus
To great Diomedes' city to seek aid
And to announce that Trojans were settling
In Latium, that Aeneas had arrived
With his fleet and his vanquished gods,   15
Proclaiming himself king by divine right,
And that many tribes were joining
The Dardan hero as his name spread wide.
All to what end, should Fortune favor him,
Would be clearer to Diomedes himself   20
Than to either Turnus or King Latinus.

Thus Latium. And Aeneas, hero in the line
Of Laomedon, saw it all, and was tossed
On a great sea of troubles. His mind darted
This way and that, turning and shifting.   25

> Sunlight, or the radiant moon, reflected from water
> Trembling in a bronze bowl, will glance and flit
> All over a room—and then flash suddenly
> Onto the coffered ceiling high above.

It was night, and all over earth deep slumber   30
Held weary creatures of the air and field.
Father Aeneas, heart troubled by war,
Lay down on the riverbank under a cold sky

And drifted off at last to sleep. He dreamed
That Tiberinus, the old rivergod himself,   35
Lifted his head amid the poplar leaves
Draped in a fine, grey-linen mantle,
His hair crowned with shady reeds,
And spoke to him, calming his fears:

"Child of the gods, you bring us our Troy   40
Back from the enemy, and you preserve
Pergamum forever. You have been awaited
On Laurentine soil, in Latin fields.
Here your home is sure—do not draw back!—
And sure are your gods. Do not be frightened   45
By threats of war. All the swollen wrath of the gods
Has ebbed away. . . .
To assure you this is no empty dream,
I offer a sign. Lying under oaks
You will find a sow, near a hidden stream,   50
With a litter of thirty, a white mother
Lying on the ground and white young nursing.
Here shall be your city, and surcease from sorrow.
The sign foretells that in thirty circling years
Ascanius will found a city, glorious Alba.   55
My prophecy is sure. As to the present ills,
I will explain in brief how you may emerge
Victorious. On these shores Arcadians,
Descended from Pallas and led by King Evander,
Have built a city in the hills and called it   60
Pallanteum after their forefather Pallas.
They are ever at war with the Latin race.
These Arcadians you must take as allies.
I myself will conduct you straight upstream
So that your oars will overpower the current.   65
Now rise, Goddess-born, and as the stars set
Pray to Juno and prevail upon her
To end her angry threats. And when you win out,
Pay tribute to me. I am he whom you see
Gliding through my banks in full flow   70
And cutting through the rich plowland—
The blue Tiber, river most beloved by Heaven.
Here is my great home, and my headwaters
Flow from high cities."

Thus the River,
And he plunged into a deep pool,   75
Seeking the depths. Night and sleep left Aeneas.
He rose and, looking at the rising sun,
Lifted water from the river with cupped palms
In ritual fashion and prayed aloud:

"Nymphs, Laurentine Nymphs at the source   80
Of all streams, and you, Father Tiber,
With your sacred water—receive Aeneas
And keep him from harm. Whatever spring,
Whatever pool holds you, from whatever soil
You flow forth in all your beauty, pitying   85
My trials, you will be honored forever
With my gifts, O horned Rivergod, lord
Of Hesperian waters. Only be with me now,
And confirm your divine presence."

Thus Aeneas,
And, choosing two galleys from his fleet,   90
He picked out crews and equipped the men.

And then a sudden marvel met his gaze.
Gleaming through the wood and as white
As her milk-white litter, a sow lay outstretched
On the green riverbank. Pious Aeneas   95
Offered her to you, Juno most mighty,
Setting her with her brood before your altar.

All the night long Tiber calmed his current,
Flowing backward until the water stood so still
It might have been a pool or quiet lake   100
Offering no resistance to the dipping oars.
The crews cheered as the ships sped along
And the well-caulked pine glided on the water.
The waves wondered, and the woods too, unused
To such a sight, the shields glittering on the water   105
And the painted hulls floating upriver.
The men rowed night and day, around the long bends
And under changing trees, their oars cutting
Through the green woods on the river's calm surface.
The burning sun had reached heaven's meridian   110

When they sighted walls off in the distance
And a few scattered huts, which Roman might
Has now raised to the sky but at that time
Were King Evander's humble domain.
They turned their prows and drew up to the town.   115

The Arcadian king was making sacrifice
To Hercules that day, and to all the gods,
In a grove outside the city. With him were
His son, Pallas, all the men of rank,
And the humble senate, offering incense   120
As the blood and warm meat smoked on the altar.
When they saw the tall ships gliding up
Between the shady banks, and the crew
Rowing noiselessly, they rose up in alarm
And left the feast. But Pallas kept his nerve,   125
And, ordering them not to break off the rites,
He seized his spear and ran out to meet
The strangers himself. Standing on a mound,
He cried out to them:

                    "Men at arms,
What has forced you to travel routes unknown?   130
Where are you heading? What is your race,
Your home? Do you come in peace or war?"

Then Father Aeneas, holding out a branch
Of peaceful olive, spoke from his high stern:

"You see before you men of Troy, and arms   135
At war with the Latins, who in their arrogance
Have driven us to flight. We seek Evander.
Tell him that Dardanians, men of rank,
Have come to propose an alliance at arms."

Pallas was stunned when he heard the name   140
'Dardanian,' and he said:

                    "Come forward,
Whoever you are, and speak to my father
Face to face, as a guest at our hearth."

And he clasped Aeneas' hand. Together,
They left the river and entered the grove.   145

Then Aeneas addressed the king graciously:

"Noblest of the Greeks, it is my good fortune
To make my prayer to you and offer boughs
Hung with sacral wreaths. I have no cause to fear
Your lineage as a Danaan lord   150
And an Arcadian with ties to Atreus' sons.
My own nobility and heaven's oracles,
Our forefathers' kinship and your fame,
Which has spread throughout the world—all this
Has bound me to you and brought me here,   155
Consenting to Fate.
                    Dardanus, as the Greeks tell it,
Was Ilium's founding father, born of Electra,
Who herself was the daughter of Atlas,
Upon whose shoulders rests the celestial sphere.
Your ancestor is Mercury, whom shining Maia   160
Conceived and bore on Cyllene's cold peak.
Maia herself, if we can trust the tales,
Was the child of Atlas, the same Atlas
Who supports the star-studded sky. And so,
Our bloodlines branch from a common source.   165
Relying on this, I did not approach you
Through ambassadors or artful overtures.
I have come myself and offer you my life,
A suppliant at your door. The same Daunians
Pursue us both in bitter war, thinking that   170
If they drive us out nothing will stop them
From subjugating all Hesperia
And controlling the seas that wash her shores.
Take my pledge and give me yours. Our hearts
Are brave in war, our manhood tested."   175

As Aeneas was speaking Evander
Was watching him, scanning his face and eyes
And entire body. Then he replied briefly:

"Bravest of the Teucrians, how gladly
I receive you—and recognize you!   180

How I recall your father's words, the voice
And the face of great Anchises!
I remember it all—how Priam,
Laomedon's son, on his way to Salamis
Stopped to see his sister Hesione   185
And went on to visit cold Arcadia.
I was young then, my cheeks just bearded,
And I wondered at the Trojan princes,
Wondered at Priam himself, but Anchises
Towered above them all. My heart burned   190
With youthful love. I yearned to meet him,
To clasp his hand, and I did approach him
And led him eagerly to Pheneus' city.
When he left he gave me a beautiful quiver
With Lycian arrows, a cloak woven with gold,   195
And a pair of golden bits that my Pallas now has.
So the hand you seek is now joined with yours,
And when tomorrow's light has dawned
I will send you forth with men and means.
Until then, since you are here as friends,   200
Celebrate with us this annual rite,
Which may not be deferred, and join our feast."

So saying, he ordered the table reset
And arranged his guests on seats in the grass.

Lines 205–421 are omitted. At the feast Evander tells the story of Hercules'
battle with the ogre Cacus. He shows Aeneas around his modest kingdom
(which will be the future site of Rome).

He spoke, led immense Aeneas
Under his low roof, and set him on a couch
Spread with leaves and a Libyan bearskin.
Night fell, enfolding the earth in dusky wings.   425

Venus, her mother's heart troubled
By the very real Laurentine threat,
Spoke to Vulcan in their golden bedroom,
Breathing into her words immortal love:

"While the Argive warlords ravaged Troy   *430*
And her walls doomed to fall in enemy fire,
I asked no aid for the victims, no weapons
Forged by your art. No, dearest husband,
I did not wish to trouble you in vain,
However much I owed to Priam's children,   *435*
And however much I wept for Aeneas
In his distress. Now, by Jupiter's commands,
He stands in Rutulian territory. Now, therefore,
I come, as suppliant to your sacred power,
Begging arms, a mother for her son. Thetis   *440*
Could sway you with tears, and Aurora.
See the nations mustering, the walled cities
Whetting steel to destroy my people!"

Vulcan hesitated, but when the goddess
Wrapped her snowy arms around him   *445*
And fondled him in her soft embrace,
He felt the familiar heat flash though his bones,

>   *Like lightning splitting a thunderhead,*
>   *A crackling flash in the rumbling sky.*

Venus felt it and smiled to herself.   *450*
And Vulcan, chained by eternal love:

"Why reach so far back for reasons?
What happened to your faith in me, Goddess?
If you had been as anxious then,
It would have been right for me to arm the Trojans.   *455*
Neither the Father almighty nor Fate forbade
That Troy stand or Priam live ten years more.
Now, if your mind is set on war,
All the care I can promise in my craft,
All that can be done with iron or electrum,   *460*
All that fire and air can avail—well, stop praying
And just trust your powers!"

                         Saying this,
He gave her the embrace they both wanted
And melted into sleep on his wife's bosom.

Vulcan woke in the middle of the night.   *465*

In the waning darkness, when sleep
Gives way to rest, a housewife who subsists
On spinning and weaving stirs the embers,
Adding night to her workday, and has her women
Toil long hours by lamplight, so she may keep   470
Her husband's bed chaste and rear her sons.

So too the Lord of Fire, no slower at that hour,
Rose from his soft bed and went to his smithy.

There is an island off the Sicilian coast
Hard by Aeolean Lipare. Smoking rocks   475
Rise to a peak, and subterranean vaults
Thunder in its bowels, hollowed out
By Cyclopean forges. Strong hammer strokes
Echo from anvils, smelted lumps of iron
Hiss through caverns, fire pants in the furnace.   480
To this island, called Vulcania from its master's name,
Down came the Fire Lord from heaven's height.

The Cyclopes were forging iron in the vast cave,
Brontes, Steropes, and bare-armed Pyracmon.
They had just shaped a thunderbolt, part polished—   485
Like the many Jupiter hurls down from heaven—
Part still unfinished. They had twisted in three rays
Of pelting hail, three of watery cloud, and added
Three of red fire and winged South Wind.
Now they were blending in terrifying flashes,   490
Noise and fear, wrath with pursuing flames.
Elsewhere they were busy with a flying chariot
For Mars to use when he inflames men and cities.
And they bent over the petrifying aegis of Pallas,
Burnishing it with golden scales of serpents,   495
And polishing the goddess's breastplate,
Which writhed with serpents around the severed head
And rolling eyes of the Gorgon Medusa.

"Stop all work!" he cried. "Cyclopes of Aetna,
Turn your minds now to arms for a hero. I want   500
Strength, fast hands, master craftsmanship—
And no delays!"

That was all they needed to hear.
They divided the work equally and bent down to it.
Bronze and gold flowed in streams of hot metal,
And Chalyb iron, the raw material   505
For so many wounds, was melted down in the furnace.
They formed a great shield, one shield against
All the weapons of the Latins, seven welded layers,
Circle upon circle. Some worked the bellows,
Others tempered the hissing bronze in the lake.   510
The cave groaned with the thud of anvils.
The Cyclopes' great hammers rose and fell
In cadence, and they turned the metal with tongs.

While the Lord of Lemnos was busy
On Vulcania, the gentle light of morning   515
And the songs of swallows beneath the eaves
Roused Evander from his humble home.
The old man put on a tunic and strapped
Tyrrhenian sandals on his feet, buckled on
His Tegean sword, and flung back a leopardskin   520
To hang from his left shoulder. Two hounds,
One trotting ahead and one at his heels,
Accompanied the hero as he left his threshold
And made his way to Aeneas' lodging,
Mindful of the aid he had promised the Trojan.   525
Aeneas was up just as early. With him
Walked Achates, as with Evander walked his son,
Pallas. They clasped hands when they met and sat
In the courtyard, conversing freely at last.
The king began:

                "Trojan commander—   530
For while you live I will never admit
That Troy's realm has been conquered—
Our strength to aid you in war is weak
Compared to our great name. We Arcadians
Are hemmed in on one side by the river,   535
And on the other by Rutulians
Rattling their weapons around our walls.
But I propose to form a coalition,
To link with you an army of royal forces,

A salvation no one could have guessed.   540
The Fates must have called you here.

                              Not far
From where we sit is the city of Agylla,
Built of ancient stone in the Tuscan hills.
The Lydians, a warlike race, settled there
Long ago, and long it prospered,   545
Until an arrogant king, Mezentius,
Came into power and ruled with iron hand.
Why recount the tyrant's acts of butchery?
May it fall on his own head and on his brood!
He would even bind living men to corpses,   550
Hand to hand and mouth to mouth, until
By slow torture the living met their death
In the putrefaction of that ghastly embrace.
At last the weary citizens rose in revolt,
Besieged the unspeakable monster   555
In his palace, cut down his men, and fired the roof.
In the mayhem Mezentius escaped
And found refuge on Rutulian soil
Under the protection of Turnus.
All Etruria has risen in righteous rage.   560
Their terms are extradition of the king
Or immediate war. I will make you
Commander of these thousands, Aeneas.
Their troopships line the shore and clamor
For the standards to advance. However,   565
An old soothsayer holds them in check,
Intoning Fate:

                    'Chosen warriors,
Flower of Maeonia's ancient race,
Just resentment sends you forth to war,
Mezentius inflames your indignant rage.   570
The gods forbid that any Italian
Should be in command of so great a race.
Choose leaders from abroad.'

                    The Etruscans
Are encamped on the plain, in awe of heaven.
Tarchon himself has sent me envoys   575

With the crown and scepter of the realm,
Inviting me to command the army
And succeed to the Etruscan throne.
But my old age, cold and slow, begrudges me
Military command. I am too weak for war.   580
I would urge my son to do it, but his mother
Is Sabine, and so his blood is mixed. But you,
Blessed by Fate in years and race, called by heaven,
Do your duty, lead the Italians and Trojans both.
Further, I will put Pallas at your side, Pallas,   585
Our hope and comfort. Let him learn from you
To endure the work of war. Let him observe
All you do and respect you from his early years.
To Pallas I will give two hundred cavalry,
Arcadia's finest, and he will give you   590
As many more himself."

                    Evander finished.
Aeneas, son of Anchises, and loyal Achates
Would have sat a long time, eyes fixed,
Brooding on troubles of their own,
But Venus gave them a sign. Lightning   595
Flashed with thunder in the open sky,
And everything suddenly seemed to reel.
A Tuscan trumpet pealed through the sky.
They looked up as thunder split the heavens
Again and again. In a clear patch of sky   600
They saw arms gleaming like red fire
Through the pure air and clashing in thunder.
The others gaped with fear, but Aeneas
Knew the sound, and the promise of his mother,
And said:

                    "Ask not what the portents forebode,   605
My dear host; in truth, do not ask. It is I
Who am summoned by heaven. The goddess
Who bore me foretold she would send this sign
If war was near, and that she would aid me,
Bringing through the air arms forged by Vulcan.   610
Ah, the slaughter in store for the poor Laurentines!
What a price you will pay me, Turnus! How many
Shields and helmets and bodies of the brave

Will you, Father Tiber, roll beneath your waves?
Let them call for battle and break their treaty!"   *615*

With this Aeneas rose and rekindled the fire
On Hercules' altar, approaching with joy
The Lar of yesterday and the small household altar.
Evander and the Trojans, side by side,
Sacrificed ewes ritually culled from the herd.   *620*
Then Aeneas went to his ships and handpicked
The best men on board to follow him to war,
Leaving the rest to ride the current downstream
And bring word to Ascanius of his father's fortunes.
The Teucrians bound for Etruscan fields   *625*
Were given horses. Aeneas' spirited mount
Was caparisoned in a lionskin
Tawny and glittering with claws of gold.

Rumor flew through the little town,
Spreading the news that horsemen were storming   *630*
To the shores of the Tyrrhenian king.
Mothers redoubled their vows, their fear
More immediate now, and the image
Of the War God loomed larger.
                              Then Evander,
Clasping the hand of his departing son,   *635*
Clung to him and, weeping beyond measure:

"If only Jupiter could turn back the years
And make me what I was under Praeneste's walls
When I cut down the enemy's foremost ranks
And burned their shields in triumph. This right hand   *640*
Sent King Erulus down to Tartarus.
His mother, Feronia, had given him at birth
Three lives, three changes of armor,
So that he had to be faced three horrifying times
And laid low in death each time. Yet this right hand   *645*
Stripped him of all his lives and of his armor.
If I could be as I was then I would never be torn
From your sweet embrace, nor would Mezentius ever
Have heaped such scorn upon his neighbor's head,
Or put so many to the sword, or widowed the town   *650*
Of so many of her sons.

> You powers above,
And Jupiter, supreme ruler of the gods,
Pity the king of the Arcadians and hear
A father's prayer. If it is your will
To keep my Pallas safe, if it is his destiny,   655
If I will see him and come to him among the living,
Then I pray for life. I can endure any trial.
But if, Fortune, you threaten some dire mischance,
Cut off my cruel life now—now, while fears
Are still unsure and hope uncertain,   660
While you, dear child, my late and only joy,
Are in my arms. Then no ill-omened words
Could wound my ears."

> As Pallas' father
Poured forth these words at their last parting
He fell unconscious, and his servants   665
Lifted him up and bore him into the house.

The horsemen rode out from the open gates,
Led by Aeneas and loyal Achates
And the other foremost Trojans.
Pallas himself rode in the column's center,   670
Conspicuous in his cloak and figured armor,

> *Like the Morning Star, loved by Venus*
> *As no other star, when it rises from Ocean,*
> *A sacred light in the sky melting the dark.*

On the walls mothers stood trembling,   675
Eyes following the cloud of dust
And the gleaming bronze squadrons
Heading off through the brush by the shortest path.
A shout went up, the column tightened,
And the horses thundered across the plain.   680

Near Caere's cold stream stands a vast grove
Steeped in religious awe. It lies in a hollow
Ringed by dark fir trees that march up the hills.
Rumor has it that the old Pelasgians
Who first held Latium in ages past   685
Dedicated the grove and a festal day

To Silvanus, god of fields and flocks.
Not far from this grove Tarchon encamped
With his Tyrrhenians, who pitched their tents
Throughout the fields. Their encampment   690
Could be seen from the hilltops, and Aeneas
Made his way there with his elite troops.
They watered their horses and took their rest.

Venus, a brightness in the air, drew near,
Bearing gifts through the clouds. She saw her son   695
In the hidden valley, standing alone by a cold stream,
And, making herself visible to him, she said:

"Here are the gifts I promised, forged to a wonder
By my husband's skill. Now you need not hesitate,
My son, to challenge the proud Laurentines   700
Or engage Turnus in combat."

                         The Cytherean spoke
And went to receive her son's embrace.
Then she set out before him under an oak tree
The refulgent armor. Aeneas gloried
In the gifts from heaven, in this high honor,   705
And he could not satisfy his eyes as they moved
From one part to another. He was lost in wonder
As he turned each piece over in his hands
And cradled it in his arms: the flaring helmet
With its threatening crest, the lethal sword,   710
The stiff, bronze corselet, as red as blood,
Glowing from within like a cobalt thunderhead
When it catches fire from the rays of the sun;
Then the smooth greaves in electrum and gold,
The spear—and the shield's ineffable design.   715

On it the Fire God had prophetically wrought
The future of Italy, and Roman triumphs
In the coming ages, every generation,
In order, still to be born from the stock
Of Ascanius, and all the wars they would fight.   720

On it he made the she-wolf, lying in Mars' green cave,
With the twin boys playing as they suckled fearlessly

At their mother's breast. Her sculpted head turned back
   To nuzzle each in turn and lick them into shape.

   Close by he put Rome, and the Sabine women   725
Carried off lawlessly from the seated crowds
At the great Circus games.
                    And then sudden war
Between the sons of Romulus and aged Tatius
With his stern Cures.
                    Next, peace between them,
The same kings standing armed before Jupiter's altar,   730
Holding shallow bowls as they made their treaty
Over a sacrificed sow. The roof
   Of Romulus' palace bristled with fresh thatch.

   Not far from there, four-horse chariots
Were driven in opposite directions, and a man   735
Chained between them had been torn apart,
Mettus (you should have kept your word, Alban!).
Tullus was dragging the traitor's entrails
   Through brambles spattered with drops of blood.

   And there was Porsenna, besieging the city   740
To restore by force the exiled Tarquin to Rome.
Aeneas' descendants rushed on the sword
For freedom's sake. You could see Porsenna
Portrayed as scowling, portrayed as threatening,
Because Cocles dared to tear down the bridge,   745
   And Cloelia broke free and swam the river.

   At the top, Manlius, captain of the Tarpeian fort,
Stood before the temple and held the high Capitol.
And here the silver goose was fluttering
Through gilded porticoes, cackling that the Gauls   750
Were at the gate. You could see the Gauls
Lurking in thickets, under cover of darkness
And the shadows of night. Their hair was gold
In the gloom, their cloaks shimmered
With golden stripes, and their milk-white necks   755
Were circled with gold. Each of them wielded
   Two Alpine pikes and a body-length shield.

And here he had forged the leaping Salii,
The naked Luperci, their ritual caps bound with wool,
The shields fallen from heaven, and the solemn procession   760
   Of chaste Roman matrons in cushioned chariots.

Far below he set the hells of Tartarus,
The high gates of Dis, and the wages of sin.
You, Catiline, were hung from the frowning
Face of a cliff and trembled at the Furies   765
   While Cato, set apart, gave laws to the good.

These scenes were lapped by the swelling sea,
Pure gold, yet the water was blue and flecked
With whitecaps. Circling dolphins picked out in silver
   Cut through the waves, and their tails flicked the spume.   770

In the center, bronze ships: the Battle of Actium.
You could see all Leucate seething with War,
   And the waves glistening with golden fire.

On one side, leading Italy into battle,
With the Senate, the People, the city's Penates,   775
And all the great gods, stood Caesar Augustus
On his ship's high stern, a double flame
Licking his temples, and above his head
Shone his father's star.
                       Elsewhere, Agrippa,
Backed by winds and gods, towered over   780
His fleet of ships, and on his brow gleamed
   The beaked Naval Crown, his proud insignia.

On the other side, Antony, Conqueror of the East,
Fresh from the Red Sea, marshaled his armies,
A rich mélange of all the Orient's might   785
From Egypt to Bactria, and in his convoy—
   To his eternal shame—was his Egyptian wife.

The ships all rushed on at once, and the whole sea foamed,
Ripped by the oars and the triple-pronged beaks
As they made for deep water. You would think the Cyclades,   790
Uprooted from the seafloor, were floating there,

Or that high mountains crashed upon mountains,
So massive the assault launched by seamen
From one turreted ship upon another,
Flaming pitch raining down, steel flying,   795
   As Neptune's fields turned crimson with blood.

Among them the Queen, rattling Egyptian timbrels,
Called up her warships, still unaware
Of the twin snakes at her back. Barking Anubis
And monstrous gods of every description   800
Fought against Neptune, Minerva, and Venus.
Chiseled in iron at the eye of the battle
Mars raged, the Furies swooped from the sky,
And exultant Discord, robe torn, strode forward
   Followed by Bellona with her bloody scourge.   805

Apollo looked down on all this from Actium
And was bending his bow. In shock and awe,
Egypt and India, all the Sabaeans and Arabs,
Were in full retreat. The Queen herself
Was calling for wind, spreading her sails,   810
And hurrying to pay out the slackened ropes.
The Fire God had made her pale as death
Amid all the carnage, driven over the waves
By winds from Apulia toward the mourning Nile.
The great rivergod had opened all the folds   815
Of his copious robe and welcomed the vanquished
   Into the sheltering waters of his azure lap.

But Caesar entered Rome in triple triumph
And consecrated his immortal votive offering
To the gods of Italy: three hundred great shrines   820
Throughout the city. The streets rang
With joyful festivities. At every temple
Was a chorus of matrons; there were altars
At every temple, and slaughtered steers
   Blanketed the ground before each altar.   825

Caesar himself, seated at the polished
Marble threshold of Phoebus Apollo,
Reviewed the gifts from the world's nations
And hung them high on the temple's doorposts

While the conquered peoples marched on past   830
In long procession, each as different
In their clothes and gear as in the tongues they spoke.
Here the immortal blacksmith had fashioned
The Nomads, and the loose-robed African people,
The Leleges and Carians and the quivered Scythians.   835
The Euphrates now flowed with a softer current,
The Morini were here from the ends of the earth,
The two-horned Rhine, the indomitable Dahae,
    And the Araxes, vexed at his stream being bridged.

Such was the design of the shield Vulcan made,   840
Venus' gift to her son. Aeneas was moved
To wonder and joy by the images of things
He could not fathom, and he lifted to his shoulder
The destiny of his children's children.

AENEID NINE

Lines 1–211 are omitted. Turnus attacks the Trojan camp and attempts to burn their ships, which are transformed into sea nymphs. Turnus and the Rutulians camp on the plain.

Stationed at one of the gates was Nisus,
Fierce in his bronze. His father
Was Hyrtacus, and the huntress Ida
Had sent him to be Aeneas' companion,   215
Quick as lightning with a javelin or bow.
Next to him was Euryalus. No one
More beautiful followed Aeneas
Or wore Trojan armor. Still a boy,
His face showed the first hint of a beard.   220
One love united them. Side by side
They would charge into battle, and now
They were on watch together at the gate.
Nisus was speaking:

                "Do the gods
Put this fire in our hearts, Euryalus,   225
Or do our passions become our gods?
I've been eager to do battle, or to do
Some great thing. My mind just won't rest.
You see how the Rutulians are getting careless?
Just a few fires winking, the troops flat on their backs,   230
Drunk and half asleep. Dead quiet for miles.
This is what I'm thinking. Everyone,
The elders and the people, is demanding
That scouts be sent to summon Aeneas
And brief him. Well, if they promise   235
What I want for you (the glory will do for me),
I think I can find beneath that mound
A path that leads to the walls of Pallanteum."

136

And Euryalus, struck by a great love
Of praise, said to his ardent friend: *240*

"Are you refusing to let me join you
In this supreme adventure, Nisus?
Am I supposed to send you out alone
Into danger like this? My father, Opheltes,
The old warrior, didn't raise me that way   *245*
During all our struggles with the Greeks,
All the terror at Troy. Nor have I been that way
With you, following great Aeneas
To his utmost destiny. Before you one
Who scorns the light, who believes that honor,   *250*
Which you too strive for, is bought cheaply with life."

And Nisus:

              "I have no doubts about you,
Nor should I. No. And I pray that Jupiter,
Or whichever god might look on this with favor,
Will bring me back to you in triumph. But if,   *255*
As does happen in business like this,
Some god, or just bad luck, takes me down,
I want you to survive me. Someone your age
Is worthier of life, and I'll need someone
To commit me to the earth after my corpse   *260*
Is dragged out of battle, or perhaps ransomed—
Or if circumstance prohibits the usual rites
To perform them in my honor by an empty tomb.
And I would not want to be the cause of grief
For your mother, who alone of many mothers   *265*
Followed her boy and left Acestes' haven."

But Euryalus said:

              "Stop offering excuses.
I'm not going to change my mind. Let's get going."

With that he roused the guards for the next watch.
They took their positions, and Euryalus   *270*
Went with Nisus to find the prince Ascanius.

All creatures throughout the land were asleep,
Their cares forgotten.
                         Not so the Teucrian captains.
They were deep in council, debating what to do
And whom to send to bring word to Aeneas.   275
They were standing in the middle of the camp,
Leaning on their long spears, shields shouldered.
Nisus and Euryalus burst in on them,
Begging to be heard on urgent business.
It was Iülus who came forward and welcomed   280
The nervous pair. He asked Nisus to speak,
And the son of Hyrtacus began:

                         "Please listen to us
With open minds, men of Aeneas, and don't judge
What we have to say by our age. The Rutulians
Have succumbed to sleep and wine. We see   285
A place to ambush them in the fork by the gate
Nearest the sea. The fires have gone out there
And black smoke rises to the sky.
If you let us take this chance you will soon
See us here again with spoils from a great slaughter.   290
Then we can follow the path to Pallanteum
And to Aeneas. On our hunting trips
Down those dark valleys we have sighted
The city's walls, and we know the whole river."

Then Aletes, the grave old counselor, said: 295

"Gods of our fathers and of Troy,
You do not intend after all to blot out our race,
Not if you have brought us youths with such spirit
And steady hearts."

                         Saying this, he held them both
By their shoulders and clasped their hands. Tears   300
Flowed down his cheeks as he said:

                         "What rewards can match
Such glorious deeds? The gods will give you
The most precious rewards, the gods
And your own good character. The rest Aeneas

Will bestow upon you, as will young Ascanius,   305
Forever mindful of service so great."

And taking up his words, "No, I will go further,"
Ascanius said: "My sole safety lies
In my father's return, and so, Nisus,
By the great gods of the house of Troy,   310
By the Lar of Assaracus,
And by the inner sanctum of hoary Vesta,
I implore you both and place in your hands
My hope and my fortune. Call my father
Back into our sight. Our gloom will be gone   315
At his return. As for gifts, I will give you
A pair of silver goblets, richly embossed,
That my father got at the sack of Arisba,
Two matching tripods, two great bars of gold,
And an ancient bowl that he received   320
From Sidonian Dido. And if it is our lot
To take Italy and divide the spoils of war—
You have seen the horse that Turnus rides,
And his armor, all gold—that horse, that shield,
And those crimson plumes I hereby set aside   325
As your reward, Nisus. And besides this
My father will give you twelve chosen matrons,
Beautiful all, and men too, captives of war,
Each with his armor. And on top of this,
Whatever land King Latinus holds.   330
And you, Euryalus, revered in your youth,
Which is close to my own, I welcome you
With all my heart, with open arms,
As my friend and companion in every deed.
No glory will be mine that is not yours,   335
In war and peace, in word and in action
My greatest trust will be placed in you."

And Euryalus answered him with this:

"Never shall a day prove me unfit
For such valor; only let fortune fall   340
In my favor. But more than all you offer
There is one thing I ask. My mother,
Of Priam's ancient line, unhappy woman,

Left Ilium's land and Acestes' city
Rather than leave me. I now leave her   345
Ignorant of whatever peril this may be
And without telling her good-bye, because—
I swear by Night and your own right hand—
I could not bear a mother's tears. So I beg you,
Comfort her in her need and desolation.   350
Let me hope this of you, and I will go
More boldly into danger."

         The Dardanians
Were moved to tears, Iülus most of all.
This picture of a son's devotion
Touched his heart, and he said:

                "Rest assured   355
That all will be worthy of your great endeavor.
Your mother will be mine, lacking only the name
Creüsa. No small gratitude awaits
The woman who bore such a son. Whatever
The outcome of your action, I swear   360
By this head, by which my father once swore,
That what I promise to you on your return
Will be there for your mother and family as well."

And with tears in his eyes he unbuckles his sword,
The gold-crusted wonder forged by Lycaon   365
And fitted by him with an ivory sheath.
Mnestheus gives Nisus a shaggy lionskin,
And loyal Aletes swaps helmets with him.
They head out at once, and the whole company,
Young and old, escort them to the gate with prayers.   370
Iülus, young and beautiful, but mature
Beyond his years, carefully gives them
Messages for his father, but the winds
Would scatter them all to the clouds above.

They leave, cross the trenches, and make their way   375
Through night's shadows to the enemy camp,
Where soon they will be the death of many.
Everywhere they look they see drunken men
Asleep in the grass, chariots tilted upright,

Soldiers sprawled among wheels and reins,   380
Weapons and wine jars lying about.
The son of Hyrtacus was first to speak:

"This is it, Euryalus. Cover our rear
And keep your eyes open. I'll lead,
And I'll make a road of blood you can't miss."   385

Then he closed his mouth and addressed Rhamnes
With his sword. This proud man, propped
On a pile of blankets and snoring loudly,
Was a king himself and served King Turnus well
As his augur, but could not augur his way   390
Out of death. Nisus killed his three attendants first,
And Remus' armor-bearer, and the charioteer,
Finding him at the horses' feet, and then severed
The horses' drooping necks. Then he decapitated
Rhamnes himself and left the trunk spurting blood.   395
The couch and the ground were soaked
With warm black gore. Nisus killed also
Lamyrus, Lamus, and young Serranus,
A handsome boy who had played late that night
But was mastered by Sleep, happy—   400
If only he had played his game until dawn.

>   A lion that has not fed rages through a sheep pen,
>   Mad with hunger. As it mangles the flock,
>   The weak animals stand dumb with fear,
>   And the lion roars from its bloodstained mouth.   405

So too Euryalus, burning with rage,
Fell upon the faceless multitude.
Fadus, Herbesus, and Abaris
Never knew what hit them. Rhoetus, though,
Was awake and saw it all, cowering   410
Behind a large mixing bowl. As he rose
Euryalus buried his sword in his chest
Up to the hilt and then drew the blade out
Drenched in death. Rhoetus belched forth
His purpled life, bringing up wine   415
Mixed with blood as Euryalus pressed on,
Seething in the dark. He was approaching

Messapus' troops and by the fire's dying light
Was watching the tethered horses graze
When Nisus, who felt his friend   420
Was being carried away by blood lust, said:

"Let's get out of here. It's almost light.
We've had our revenge, and we've cut a way
Through the enemy lines."

     They left behind
Whole sets of solid silver armor, bowls too,   425
And beautiful carpets. Euryalus did take
Rhamnes' gear, with his gold-studded sword-belt,
Gifts that long ago wealthy Caedicus sent
To Remulus of Tibur as a pledge of friendship.
As Remulus lay dying he passed them on   430
To his grandson, and then the Rutulians
Took them as spoils of war. This gear Euryalus
Tore away and put on—all for nothing—
And he put on his head Messapus' plumed helmet.
Then the pair left the camp and ran for cover.   435

Meanwhile, a company of horsemen,
Sent ahead from the Latin city
While the rest of the troops halted on the plain,
Rode up with a reply for Turnus—
Three hundred strong, all under shield,   440
With Volcens in command. The walls of the camp
Were just ahead when off in the distance
They saw the pair turning off on a path to the left.
And in the dim shadows the helmet
Euryalus thoughtlessly wore betrayed him.   445
Volcens caught its gleaming reflection
And shouted from the head of the column:

"Halt! Who are you? Why are you armed,
And what mission are you on?"

     They made no response
But hurried into the woods and trusted to night.   450
The horsemen rode to block the crossways
And seal the perimeter of the woods with guards.

It was a wide and dense forest, with thickets
Of dark ilex and brambles everywhere,
And trails that glimmered through open patches.   455
The dark branches and his ponderous spoils
Hampered Euryalus, and the network of trails
Confused and panicked him. Nisus got through
In a blind rush and would have escaped the enemy
And those regions later called Alban   460
(At that time part of Latinus' pasture)
When he stopped and looked back,
To no avail, for his missing friend.

"Poor Euryalus, where did I leave you?
How can I find you?"

                    And Nisus retraced   465
His tangled path through the treacherous forest,
Wandering through the silent thickets
Until he heard the horses and the telltale sounds
Of men in pursuit. A few moments later
A cry reached his ears, and he saw Euryalus.   470
Misled by the terrain, betrayed by the night,
And overpowered in the sudden tumult,
Euryalus struggled desperately
As the band dragged him away.
                    Nisus
Was at a loss. How could he possibly   475
Rescue his friend? With what weapons, what force?
Or should he charge right into their swords
To a swift and beautiful death? Pumping
His spear arm, he looked up to the moon and prayed:

"Be with me now, Goddess, and help me   480
In my need, O daughter of Latona,
Glory of the stars and guardian of groves.
If ever my father brought you offerings
On my behalf, if ever I myself hunted
In your honor, hung sacrifices in your dome,   485
Or fastened them to your temple's roof—
Guide my weapons through the air
And let me break up that party over there."

Nisus spoke, and put all of his weight
Into the throw. The spear split the dark air,   490
Hit a warrior named Sulmo in the back,
And snapped. The splintered shaft
Punched through to his chest, and Sulmo
Spun around, hemorrhaging warm blood
In heaving gasps until he collapsed   495
Into cold death. The Rutulians looked around
In every direction. Breathing more sharply,
Nisus balanced another spear over his shoulder,
And while they hesitated it went hissing
Through both of Tagus' temples   500
And warmed itself deep in his cloven brain.
Volcens seethed with rage but could not see
Who threw the spear or where to unleash his fury.

"All right, then you will pay me with hot blood
For both their deaths."

                As he spoke   505
He went for Euryalus with drawn sword.
This was too much for Nisus. Out of his mind
With terror and no longer able to remain
Hidden in darkness or endure such pain,
He shouted:

              "Me—I did it—turn your swords on me,   510
Rutulians! It was all my idea.
He couldn't have done it, wouldn't have dared,
I swear by the sky and the stars that see all.
He only loved his unlucky friend too much."

Thus Nisus, but the sword, driven home with force,   515
Sliced through the ribs and gashed the white breast.
Euryalus rolled over, dead. Dark blood
Ran over his beautiful limbs, and his head
Sank down onto one shoulder,

    As a purple flower cut by a plow   520
    Droops in death, or as a poppy bows
    Its weary head, heavy with spring rain.

Nisus rushed among them, going only
For Volcens. Volcens alone was his care.
The troops surrounded him, tried to push him back,   525
But he kept on coming, his sword
Flashing like lightning, until he buried the blade
Full in the face of the shrieking Rutulian
And, dying himself, deprived his enemy of life.
Then, pierced and slashed, he threw himself   530
Upon his lifeless friend and there finally
Rested quietly in easeful death.

Happy pair,
If my poetry has any power
Never shall you be blotted from memory,
As long as the house of Aeneas still stands   535
On the Capitol's unmoving rock,
And the Roman Father rules supreme.

*Lines 538–967 are omitted. Turnus and the Rutulians attack the Trojan
camp again. Ascanius kills the boastful Numanus; as a result, Apollo takes
Ascanius out of the war. Turnus, inside the camp, kills many but is hard
pressed by the Trojans. He dives into the Tiber to escape.*

AENEID TEN

Meanwhile, highest Olympus opened,
And the Father of Gods and Men called a council
In the starry halls from which he surveyed
All lands, the Dardan camp, and the Latin peoples.
The gods took their seats, and their lord began: 5

"Why have you gone back on your word,
Divine ones, and fight among yourselves?
I forbade Italy to go to war with Troy.
This quarrel thwarts my will. What fear
Has caused these humans to rush to arms?   10
There shall come a time (do not hasten it)
When wild Carthage will open the Alps
And pour down upon Rome. Then may they fight
And ravage each other. For now, cease your strife
And assent with good will to my covenant."   15

Thus Jupiter, briefly. But golden Venus
Made no brief reply:

"Father Eternal, Power of the Universe—
For what else may we appeal to now?—
Do you see how insolent the Rutulians are,   20
How Turnus, swollen with pride,
Rides his chariot through the crowds,
Rushing into war with Mars at his back?
The Teucrians are no longer protected
By their walls. The fighting has moved   25
Inside the gates, and the trenches flow with blood.
Aeneas, far away, does not know of these dangers.
Will you never allow this siege to be lifted?
A second army threatens the walls
Of an infant Troy, and again there rises   30
From Aetolian Arpi a son of Tydeus.
I feel I myself will be wounded again,

146

I, your child, will stop another mortal spear.
If the Trojans have sought Italy
Without your leave, abandon them   35
And let them pay for their sin. But if
They have followed all the oracles
Given by gods above and shades below,
How can anyone now subvert your will
And establish destiny anew?   40
Why should I even mention the fleet
Burned on the shores of Eryx, or the storms
Stirred up by Aeolus, or Iris
Sent from the clouds? And now Juno
Is mobilizing Hell—a sector   45
Of the universe as yet untried—
And Allecto is turned loose on the upper world
And raves through the cities of Italy.
I no longer care about empire, my hope
While Fortune still smiled. Let those win   50
Whom you want to win. If there is no country
Your hardened wife will allow the Trojans,
Then by the smoking ruins of Troy, I pray,
Let me at least withdraw Ascanius, Father,
Unscathed from war; let my grandson   55
Survive! Aeneas, yes, may be tossed
On unknown seas and follow Fortune's lead,
But let me protect this child and rescue him
From this terrible conflict. Amathus
Is mine, high Paphus and Cythera,   60
A shrine in Idalia. He can live out his life
There, without weapons or glory. Let it be
Your grand decision that Carthage crush Italy.
Nothing then would hinder the Tyrian cities.
But what good has it done him to survive the war,   65
Escape Greek fire, endure endless perils
On land and sea, while his Teucrians sought
To found a new Troy in Latium?
Better to have settled on the dying ashes
Where Troy once stood. You might as well   70
Give them back their Simois and Xanthus
And let them suffer forever Ilium's sorrows!"

Then regal Juno, furious:

"Why do you force me
To break my silence and tell the whole world
My heart's deep sorrow? Did any man or god   75
Compel Aeneas to make war on the Latins?
'He sought Italy at the call of the Fates.'
Yes—driven on by Cassandra's raving.
Did I advise him to leave his camp or entrust
His life to the winds? To put a boy in charge   80
Of their defenses at the height of war?
To tamper with Etruscan loyalties
Or stir up peaceful nations to war? What god,
What cruel power of mine, undid Aeneas?
Where is Juno in all of this, or Iris   85
Sent from the clouds? It is indeed monstrous
That Italians are burning your infant Troy,
And that Turnus has taken a stand
In his native land, Turnus, a mere grandson
Of old Pilumnus and whose mother is only   90
The goddess Venilia! But what about
The Trojans torching the Latin people
And pillaging their fields? Dragging a bride
Away from her betrothed? Offering peace
In one hand and arming ships with the other?   95
You have the power to whisk Aeneas
Away from the Greeks and substitute
Empty mist for the man. You are as well
Perfectly capable of turning their ships
Into so many nymphs. But for us to help   100
The Rutulians is disgraceful? You say,
'Aeneas is far away and doesn't know.'
Let him be utterly ignorant and really far away!
Paphus is yours, Idalium, high Cythera.
Why bother with a city teeming with war   105
Or with savage hearts? Is it because I
Am toppling the tottering Phrygian state?
Is it I? Or is it he who dumped the Trojans
Right in front of the Greeks? What cause was there
That Europe and Asia should rise up in arms   110
And ravage their peace treaties in treachery?
Was it I who led Paris, the Dardan adulterer,
To rape Sparta? Did I arm the man
And goad him on with lust? All this was you!

It was then that you should have been afraid   *115*
For your people. And now you come on late
With your unjust complaints and petty bickering."

Thus Juno's plea, and all the celestials
Murmured various assent,

             a sound like wind
Rising in the forest with whispers and moans   *120*
That tell the sailors a great storm is coming.

Then the Father Almighty, the greatest power
In the universe, begins, and as he speaks
The high house of the gods grows silent,
Earth's foundations tremble, still goes the air,   *125*
The winds are hushed, and the high seas calmed:

"Take my words to heart and keep them there.
Since Ausonians and Teucrians cannot form
An alliance, and your dissension has no end,
I shall make no distinction between the hopes   *130*
And fortunes of either, Trojan or Rutulian,
Whether it be Italy's fortune that holds the camp
Or Troy's tragic error and false prophecies.
Nor do I absolve the Rutulians. The efforts
Of each will bring suffering or success.   *135*
Jupiter rules over all alike. The Fates
Will find their way."

             And he nodded assent
By his brother's Stygian waters, by the banks
That seethe with black and swirling waters.
Then Jupiter rose from his golden throne   *140*
And the gods escorted him to the threshold.

Lines 142–531 are omitted. The battle at the Trojan camp continues.
Aeneas, meanwhile, is sailing back to the camp with his allies. The sea
nymphs who were once the ships of his fleet meet him at sea. Heartened
by the omen Aeneas beaches his ships and leads his troops into battle
against the Rutulians. He and Pallas distinguish themselves in the fighting.

Turnus had a sister, the nymph Juturna,
Who warned him now to bring aid to Lausus.
The hero split the ranks with his swift chariot
And called to his men:

                "Stand down from battle.   535
Pallas is mine, and mine alone.
I only wish his father could watch."

When Turnus said this, his men withdrew,
And Pallas stood there, marveling
At this arrogant command, amazed at Turnus.   540
His eyes took in that giant frame. He scanned
The whole scene with a fierce glare
And made this response to the great Rutulian:

"The praise is mine soon, either for prime spoils
Or a glorious death. My father can live   545
With either fate. Away with your threats."

And he strode out to the middle of the field.
The Arcadians felt their blood turn to ice,
And Turnus vaulted down from his chariot
Ready to fight on foot in hand-to-hand combat.   550

    A lion, poised on a high vantage point,
    Has caught sight of a bull meditating battle
    And charges.

             This was how Turnus charged.
When Pallas thought he was within spear range
He began his own charge, hoping to balance   555
This mismatch in strength with daring and luck,
And he prayed to bright heaven:

               "I beseech you,
Hercules, by the welcome you received
In my father's house, come to me now
And help me in my need. Let Turnus see me   560
Strip the bloody armor from his dying limbs,
Victorious over him as his eyes close in death."

Hercules heard the boy's prayer and stifled

A heavy groan, shedding useless tears. Jupiter
Addressed his son with fatherly words: *565*

"Each has his own day. Brief is the time
And irretrievable the life of every man. Yet,
To lengthen fame by deeds is the task of valor.
Under Troy's high walls fell many sons of gods,
My Sarpedon among them. Fate calls Turnus too,   *570*
And he has reached the end of his allotted years."

Thus Jove,
Who then turned his eyes from the Rutulian fields.

Pallas threw his spear with all his strength,
And his sword flashed from its sheath. The spear   *575*
Flew on and struck the top edge of Turnus' shield,
Forced its way through and nicked his shoulder.
Turnus shrugged and balanced his spear
For what seemed an eternity. When he threw
The iron-tipped oak at Pallas, he said: *580*

"See if my spear goes in farther."

                              No sooner spoken
Than the spearpoint slashed through the center
Of Pallas' shield, with all its layers of iron,
Of bronze, all the folds of oxhide, and then pierced
His corselet and burrowed into his chest.   *585*
Pallas pulled the warm shaft out, but with it came
His blood and his life. He fell onto the wound,
Armor clattering, and his bloody mouth
Struck the hostile earth. He was dying
When Turnus, standing above him, said: *590*

"Remember, Arcadians, to bring my words
To Evander. I send him the Pallas he deserves.
The honor of a tomb, the solace of burial
I freely grant, but he will pay dearly
For welcoming Aeneas."

                              Turnus spoke   *595*
And, bracing his left foot on Pallas' corpse,

He tore away the massive belt engraved
With crime—the sons of Aegyptus murdered
By Danaus' daughters on their nuptial night,
The rooms reeking with blood—the work   *600*
Of Clonus, son of Eurytus, who chased it in gold.
Turnus now exulted in this belt and gloried
In its possession.
               The mind of man
Knows neither fate nor future doom
Nor moderation when elated by fortune.   *605*
The hour will come when Turnus will wish
He had paid handsomely for an unharmed Pallas
And will curse the day he won those spoils.
But now Pallas was surrounded by his friends,
Moaning and weeping as they bore him back   *610*
Lying on his shield. O Pallas, you will go home
To your father a great grief and great glory.
This day brought you to war and took you from it,
Yet you left behind mounds of Rutulians dead.

It was no vague rumor of disaster   *615*
That reached Aeneas but sure intelligence
That his men were inches from death
And that it was time to rescue the Teucrians.
He mowed down everything before him
With his sword, burning a broad path   *620*
Through the enemy, seeking you, Turnus,
Flush with slaughter. Pallas, Evander,
Everything swam in Aeneas' eyes—the table
He came to as a stranger, the right hands pledged.
Four youths, sons of Sulmo, and four of Ufens,   *625*
He took alive, to sacrifice them to the shades
And pour their blood on the funeral flames.
Then he took aim at Magus, who ducked
As the spear trembled through the air above him,
Then he fell in supplication at Aeneas' knees: *630*

"By your father's ghost, and by your hopes
For growing Iülus, spare my life for my own son
And father. Buried deep inside my high house
Lie talents of chased silver, masses of gold
Wrought and unwrought. Troy's victory   *635*

Does not turn on me, one life won't matter!"

He spoke, and Aeneas answered him:

"You can save all that silver and gold
For your sons. Turnus did away with
Such traffic in war when he took Pallas' life.   640
This is the judgment of my father's spirit,
Of great Anchises, and of Iülus my son."

With these words, he grasped Magus' helmet
With his left hand and, bending back
The suppliant's neck, buried the sword   645
Up to its hilt.
                    Close by was Haemonides,
Priest of Phoebus and Trivia, head bound
With a sacred band, shining in white robes
And gleaming armor. Aeneas drove him
Over the plain, and when the priest fell   650
Bestrided the body and slaughtered it
In his own great shadow. Serestus
Gathered up the armor and carried it off,
A trophy for Mars, who walks the lanes of war.

Caeculus, born of Vulcan's race, and Umbro,   655
From the Marsian hills, filled in the ranks.
The Trojan attacked furiously. His sword
Had already severed Anxur's left arm,
Which fell to the ground along with his shield—
Anxur had been talking big and hoped his strength   660
Would match his words, or perhaps he was just
Raising his spirits and had promised himself
A ripe old age—when Tarquitus, strutting
In gleaming arms, crossed paths with Aeneas.
The nymph Dryope had borne this man   665
To Faunus, who haunts the woods. The Trojan
Pinned his heavy shield and corselet together
With a hard spear-cast, and as the boy tried
To get some words of supplication out,
He sent his head whirling to the ground.   670
Then, as he rolled the warm torso over,
He said in a voice without a trace of pity:

"Lie there, you hulk. Your sweet mother will never
Heap earth above you back home in your country.
No, you will be left here for the vultures,   675
Or thrown into the sea, rolled by waves,
And hungry fish will nibble at your wounds."

He caught Lucas and Antaeus next, two
Of Turnus' front-line men, and brave Numa,
And blond Camers, son of noble Volcens,   680
The richest man in all Ausonia
And ruler of silent Amyclae.

> *Aegaeon, men say, had a hundred arms,*
> *A hundred hands, and shot flames from fifty mouths*
> *And chests, when against Jove's thunder he clanged*   685
> *Fifty shields and drew as many swords.*

So Aeneas in triumph savaged the field
Once his blade grew warm. Even the horses
That pulled Niphaeus' chariot, when they saw
The hero advancing in his rage, turned in terror,   690
Spilling their master as they raced for the shore.

Meanwhile, Lucagus and his brother, Liger,
Entered the combat zone in a chariot drawn
By two white horses, Liger handling the reins,
Lucagus swinging a sword. Aeneas   695
Took exception to their ardor for battle
And bore down on the duo, towering above them
As he pumped his spear. Liger spoke:

"These aren't Diomedes' horses you see,
Or Achilles' chariot, or the plains of Troy.   700
Your war and your life now end in this land."

Insane words from Liger, but Aeneas responded
With no words at all. He let his javelin fly,
And as Lucagus leaned forward with his sword,
Stepping into the stroke with his left foot,   705
The point came through the lower rim of his shield
And punctured his left groin. He rolled to the ground,
Dying, while loyal Aeneas offered him bitter words.

"Your horses didn't shy, Lucagus, or run
From a shadow. No, you made a flying leap   *710*
And deserted your team."

                              And he seized the horses
As Lucagus' brother bailed out and stood,
A picture of misery, with outstretched hands:

"By the Trojan hero that you are,
And by the parents who bore such a son,   *715*
Spare this life and have pity on a suppliant."

He had more to say, but Aeneas:

                         "That's not
What you said before. Now die with your brother."

And Aeneas' sword laid bare Liger's soul.

Such were the deaths the Dardanian leader   *720*
Left in his wake, raging like a torrent
Or a black whirlwind over the plain. At long last,
Ascanius and the besieged Trojans
Burst from the camp and left it behind.

*Lines 725–822 are omitted. Juno, fearing for Turnus, creates a phantom
Aeneas and sends it to lure Turnus out of battle and onto a ship that bears
him back to his city.*

Jupiter now prompted fiery Mezentius
To take the battle to the jubilant Trojans.
But it was the Tyrrhenians who responded,   *825*
Focusing all their hatred and all their weapons
On this one man. He took it all,

   *Like a high cliff that juts out
   Into the ocean, exposed to the winds' fury
   And the pounding surf, enduring all the menace*   *830*
   Of sea and sky, but motionless itself.

So too Mezentius, as he laid out on the ground
Hebrus, son of Dolichaon, and with him
Latagus and Palmus, a man fast on his feet.
Latagus he caught full in the face and mouth   835
With a huge slab of granite; Palmus, though,
He hamstrung and left him writhing slowly
While he gave his armor to Lausus, his son,
Along with the plumes to fix on his helmet.
Evanthes was next, the Phrygian, and Mimas,   840
The same age as Paris and his constant shadow
When they were boys. Theano bore him to Amycus
On the very night that Hecuba, pregnant
With a firebrand, gave birth to Paris.
Paris now sleeps in his ancestral city,   845
And Mimas rests in an unmarked grave
On Laurentium's shore.

> When a boar,
> Driven from a mountain by dogs,
> (It has lived for years on piney Vesulus,
> Or has fed on reeds in the Laurentine marsh)   850
> Reaches the hunters' nets, it halts and snorts
> And raises its hackles. No one has the courage
> To come near enough to vent his rage,
> So they throw their javelins and shout at it
> From a safe distance. The boar is undaunted   855
> And turns in all directions, gnashing its teeth
> As it shakes off the javelins stuck in its back.

Just so, none of those who harbored
Righteous rage had courage enough to draw a sword
And face Mezentius, preferring instead   860
To launch spears and insults from a safe distance.

Acron, a Greek, had come from ancient Corythus,
Leaving his home and an unfinished wedding.
Mezentius saw him wrecking battalions,
Helmet's crest shining with his bride's purple.   865

> A lion that has not fed will range
> The deep woods mad with hunger, until
> He spots a timid roe or an antlered stag.

Mouth agape in exultation, mane bristling,
He crouches intently over the warm viscera, 870
And foul gore bathes his cruel jaws.

So too Mezentius,
Charging into the massed enemy ranks.
Acron had no chance. He went down hard,
Hammering the black earth with his heels,
His splintered spear dyed red with his blood. 875
This put Orodes on the run. Mezentius,
Disdaining a cheap shot from the rear,
Caught up with Orodes and faced him man to man,
Besting him not with stealth but superior strength.
Then he planted his foot on the body, and, straining 880
To pull out his spear, he cried to his troops:

"Great Orodes is down, men, no small part of the war!"

Shouting in unison his men raised the victory cry,
But Orodes, breathing his last, said:

"I shall not die
Unavenged, and you, whoever you are, 885
Will not celebrate long. The same fate awaits you.
You too will soon lie dead in these fields."

And Mezentius, with a sneering smile:

"Now die. As for me, the Lord of Gods and Men
Will see to my fate."

And he pulled the spear out. 890
Iron slumber pressed hard on Orodes' eyes,
And their light faded into everlasting night.

Now Caedicus cut down Alcathoüs;
Sarcatur killed Hydaspes; Rapo—Parthenius
And tough Orses; Messapus both Clonius 895
And Lycaon's son Ericetes, the former
As he sprawled on the ground unhorsed, the latter
As he advanced on foot. Agis, a Lycian,
Also advanced on foot but was struck down

By Valerus, who had his ancestors' valor.   *900*
Salius killed Thronius and was killed by Nealces,
A good man with both a spear and a bow.

Stern Mars balanced the suffering and death.
Men on both sides killed and were killed,
Victor and vanquished, and neither side yielded.   *905*
Looking down from the high halls of Jove—
Venus sitting across from Saturnian Juno—
The gods pitied the senseless passion of men
While pale Tisiphone raged among thousands.

Still Mezentius, pumping his huge spear,   *910*
Stormed across the plain.

> *Think of great Orion*
> *Stalking on foot the deeps of Nereus, plowing*
> *Through the water, shoulders above the waves;*
> *Or hefting a mountain ash, his feet treading the earth,*
> *His head shrouded in clouds.*

            So too Mezentius,   *915*
Gigantic in armor. Aeneas, spotting him
In the distance, closed ground quickly.
Mezentius waited for his noble opponent,
Standing unperturbed in his immovable bulk.
His eyes measured the space between them,   *920*
And, when Aeneas was in range, he said:

"May this right hand, which is my god,
And this spear, which I am about to throw,
Come through for me now. Lausus, you yourself,
Clad in the spoils torn from that robber's corpse,   *925*
Will be my trophy over Aeneas."

           He spoke
And let fly. The spear hissed though the air
And, glancing off Aeneas' shield, pierced
Antores under his ribs—noble Antores,
An Argive companion of Hercules   *930*
Who had joined Evander and settled
In an Italian town. Now he lay dying

With a wound meant for another, gazing
At the sky and remembering sweet Argos.
Then Aeneas threw. The hero's spear   935
Punched through the curved shield's triple bronze,
Through the inwoven linen and oxhide layers,
And, losing speed, stuck low in the groin.
Aeneas was glad to see the Tuscan's blood
And, drawing his sword, moved in eagerly   940
On an anxious Mezentius. Lausus, watching,
Groaned deeply for love of his father,
And tears rolled down his face.
                            (Neither your death,
Nor your heroic deeds—if antiquity
Can confer belief in prowess so great—   945
Nor you yourself, noble young man,
So worthy of memory, will I leave in silence.)
Mezentius gave ground, disabled and hobbled,
Aeneas' spear still stuck in his shield.
His son ran into the space between them,   950
Hurling himself into battle, and just as Aeneas
Brought his sword sweeping down,
Lausus parried the blade from below
And held the hero in check. His comrades
Came up from behind with loud cries   955
And held off the enemy with a hail of missiles
Until the father, under the protection
Of the son's shield, could make good his retreat.
Aeneas raged, but took cover.

             When the storm breaks
  And pours down clouds of hail, every plowman   960
  And farmer runs from the fields, and the traveler
  Huddles under a riverbank or rocky ledge
  While the rain falls on the lands. When the sun comes out,
  They go on with the day's work.

                      So too Aeneas,
Overwhelmed by javelins, endured the war cloud   965
Until all its thunder was gone, but all the while
He taunted Lausus and threatened him:

"You're headed for death, Lausus! Why rush it

By daring what's beyond your strength?
Your filial devotion is blinding you."   970

But Lausus was much too wound up to think,
And now the Dardanian leader's rage
Was mounting higher, and the Fates
Gathered up the last threads of Lausus' life.
Aeneas drove his sword straight through   975
The young body he faced and up to the hilt,
The point piercing the shield (far too fragile
To counter this threat) and the tunic
His mother had woven of soft gold threads.
Blood filled his chest; his soul left his body   980
And sighed through the air to the shades below.

When Anchises' son looked on his dying face,
So strangely pale, he groaned in pity
And stretched out his hand. There shone in that face
The image of his own devotion to Anchises.   985

"For all his sense of duty, what now, poor boy,
Can Aeneas give you for such glorious deeds?
What is worthy of so great a heart?
Keep the arms in which you delighted,
And, if it matters to you now, I commit you   990
To the spirits and ashes of your ancestors.
And may this comfort you in death's sadness:
You fell by the hand of the great Aeneas."

Then he scolded Lausus' men for hanging back
And lifted their prince from the ground   995
Where blood was fouling his finely bound hair.

Meanwhile, his father was washing his wound
On the Tiber's bank, leaning back on a tree trunk.
His bronze helmet hung from a branch nearby,
And his heavy arms were at rest on the grass.   1000
His men stood around him as he gasped for breath
And tried to ease his sore neck. His combed beard
Flowed down on his chest. He asked for Lausus
Over and over and sent messengers
To call him back and deliver the commands   1005

Of his despondent father. But Lausus' men
Were bearing him back on his armor, dead,
A great warrior undone by a mighty wound.
They wept as they came, and Mezentius'
Foreboding heart knew their wail from afar. 1010
He defiled his white hair with dust, lifted
His hands to heaven, and, clinging to the corpse:

"Was life so sweet to me, Son, that I let you
Face the enemy in my place—you,
Whom I begot? Am I, your father, saved 1015
By your wounds, alive through your death?
Ah, now at last the bitterness of exile
Comes home to me, the wound is driven deep.
I have stained your good name, my son,
With my guilt—I, driven by resentment 1020
From the throne and scepter of my fathers.
The penalty I owe my native land
And bitter countrymen is overdue.
I should have given up my guilty life
Through any kind of death. Now I still live 1025
And have not yet left the light of day,
But leave I will."

              As he spoke he raised himself
On his injured leg, and though slowed by his wound
He held his head high and called for his horse,
His pride and solace, on which he rode 1030
Victorious from every battle. Now he spoke
To the grieving creature words such as these:

"Rhoebus, we have lived long, if anything
Lasts long for mortals. Today either you will
Bear off Aeneas' head and bloody spoils 1035
And avenge with me the suffering of Lausus
Or, if we cannot find our way through force,
You will die with me. For I do not think,
My brave one, that you would endure
A stranger's orders or a Trojan lord." 1040

He spoke, mounted, and settled into position,
Loading both hands with whetted javelins.

His head glittered with bronze and bristled
With horsehair crests as he galloped off
Into the thick of battle, his heart a seething mass   1045
Of shame, and of grief verging on madness.

Three times his voice boomed out, "Aeneas!"
Aeneas knew that voice and, filled with joy
He prayed:

        "May the Father of the Gods
And Apollo on high make this happen!   1050
It's your move, Mezentius."

                Having said this,
Aeneas moved forward with leveled spear.

But Mezentius:

        "My son's gone,
And you try to frighten me? You murderer.
This was the only way you could destroy me.   1055
We do not fear death, nor do we hold back
For the gods. Break it off. I come to die,
But first I have these gifts for you."

              He spoke,
And let fly with a javelin, then wheeling
In a circle, hit home with another, and another,   1060
But the shield's heavy gold withstood them all.
Three times he rode around a standing Aeneas,
Launching javelins as he circled to the left.
Three times the Trojan pivoted around
With a forest of spears on his shield's bronze skin.   1065
Then, weary of prolonging the fight—
And of plucking out javelins—and feeling the heat
Of this unequal combat, he considered his options
And struck suddenly, hurling his spear
Squarely between the war-horse's temples.   1070
The great stallion reared, pawing the air.
He threw his rider and then, falling himself,
Hit the ground headfirst, disjointing his shoulder
And entangling Mezentius. The Trojans and Latins

Lit up the sky with their cries. Aeneas ran up,   *1075*
Drew his sword, and standing over him cried:

"You're not so tough now, are you, Mezentius?"

The Tuscan lifted his eyes, drank in the bright air,
And, when he had recovered his senses, answered:

"Bitter enemy, why do you taunt me   *1080*
And threaten me with death? Killing me
Is no sin. I did not come into battle
For a truce. My Lausus did not seal such a pact
Between me and you. I ask only one thing,
If the vanquished have any claim to clemency: *1085*
Let my body be covered by earth. I know
My people's hatred surrounds me. Guard me
From their rage; let me join my son in the tomb."

Mezentius said these things and did not flinch
When the sword entered his throat   *1090*
And his life sluiced out in streams of blood.

AENEID ELEVEN

Lines 1–529 are omitted. Aeneas orders his troops to march to Latium. The two sides agree to a truce in order to bury their dead. Pallas' body is brought to Evander for burial. Latinus holds a council in which Turnus, determined to continue the war, prevails.

While the Latins fought among themselves   530
And debated an uncertain future, Aeneas
Was moving his troops from the camp.
A messenger rushed through the general uproar
In Latinus' halls and filled the city
With great alarm: Teucrians and Tuscans   535
Were sweeping down from the Tiber River
In battle formation and covering the plain.
The townspeople were stunned and then,
Bitten by the danger, gave way to panic.
Shaking with fear they called for weapons,   540
The young raged for weapons while their fathers
Wept and moaned, and a great din arose,
A discordant roar that rose to the sky,

> *As when flocks of birds settle in a grove,*
> *Or when by the fish-filled stream of Padusa*   545
> *Raucous swans call out among clamorous pools.*

Turnus seized the moment and cried:

"Right, convene a council, citizens,
And sit there praising peace. The enemy
Is attacking our kingdom!"

                    And he rushed out   550
From the high halls issuing commands:

"Volusus, get the Volscian squadrons armed
And lead out the Rutulians. Coras, you

And your brother, and you, Messapus, deploy
The cavalry on the plain. Post some guards   555
At the city gates and man the towers. The rest
Are going into battle under my command."

The whole city rushed to the walls. Latinus,
Overwhelmed by this grim turn of events,
Quit the council and abandoned his plans.   560
He blamed himself for not warmly welcoming
Dardanian Aeneas and adopting him as a son
For the good of the city. Details set to work
Digging trenches in front of the gates
And hauling stones and stakes. A horn sounded   565
Its bloody signal for battle. Mothers and boys
Ringed the walls: the final struggle
Summoned them all. The queen herself rode
With a throng of women to the temple of Pallas
On the high citadel, bearing gifts,   570
And at her side, eyes lowered modestly,
Was the maiden Lavinia, the cause
Of all this misery. The women went up
And filled the temple with clouds of incense.
Their sad voices drifted down from the threshold: 575

"Mistress of War, Tritonian Maiden,
Break the spear of the Phrygian marauder
And lay him out on the ground before our gates."

Meanwhile, Turnus armed himself for battle,
And every move he made was an act of passion,   580
Strapping on the flashing bronze breastplate,
Sheathing his calves with gold, and, head still bare,
Buckling the sword to his side. He shone
Golden as he ran down from the high citadel,
His exultant mind already engaging the enemy.   585

  A horse has broken his halter and bolted
  Out of his stall, free at last, and now gallops
  Over the plain, making for the mares in pasture
  Or his accustomed swim in the river.
  He holds his head high and whinnies with joy,   590
  Mane streaming like wind on his shoulders.

Camilla, with her army of Volscians,
Rode to meet him, and when she reached the gates
The warrior queen leapt down from her horse.
Following her lead, her troops dismounted   595
And slid to the ground. Then Camilla spoke:

"Turnus, if the brave can trust themselves,
I commit myself to face Aeneas' cavalry
And ride alone against the Tuscan horsemen.
Let me try my hand at the first encounter   600
While you stay on foot to guard the city walls."

And Turnus, eyes fixed on this formidable woman:

"Glory of Italy, how can I ever give you
Sufficient thanks? But since your spirit
Outmatches all I could say or do to repay you—   605
Yes, share the work with me. That dog Aeneas,
As rumor has it and scouts confirm,
Has sent his cavalry ahead to scour the plain.
He himself has crossed the ridge and is now
Marching on the city through the mountain pass.   610
I am concealing units under the canopy
On the forest road to block both ends of the gorge.
Muster the troops and wait for the attack
By the Tuscan cavalry. With you will be
Messapus, a good man, the Latin troops,   615
And Tiburtus' squad. You're in command."

He spoke and with similar words encouraged
Messapus and the other allied captains,
And then he moved out against the enemy.

There is a jagged valley, a perfect place   620
For stratagems of war, both sides walled
With dark forest. It can be reached only
By a narrow path through a deep gorge,
A difficult approach. High above,
Among the mountain peaks, lies a plain   625
Invisible from below, a safe staging area
From which to launch sorties right or left,
Or to take a stand and roll down boulders.

Turnus hurried there by familiar roads
And lay in wait in the treacherous woods.   630

Diana, meanwhile, in the halls above,
Addressed Opis, one of her sacred sisterhood,
With these sorrowful words:

                         "Camilla
Is entering this bloody war, Opis,
And girding herself with our weapons in vain,   635
Camilla, whom I love as no other.
This is no new love for me, no sudden
Sweet infatuation on Diana's part.
        Metabus was driven from his throne
By his subjects' hatred of his tyranny,   640
And as he was fleeing ancient Privernum
In the heat of battle he took with him
His infant daughter to share his exile.
Casmilla, her mother's name,
Was changed by Metabus into Camilla.   645
Holding her to his chest he headed out
To a lonely stretch of mountain forest
With armed Volscians closing in on him
From every side. Blocking his flight
Was the Amasenus, which had flooded its banks   650
After a heavy storm. As the fugitive
Prepared to swim he was held back
By love and fear for his precious burden.
Quickly weighing his options, he settled on this:
He was holding in his hand a huge spear   655
With a hard, burly shaft of seasoned oak,
And to this shaft he fastened his daughter,
Swaddled in the bark of a forest cork tree,
Binding her tightly to the balance point.
Then, cradling the spear in his huge right hand,   660
He cried out to heaven:

                         'Lady of the Woods,
Gracious daughter of Latona, this child
I, her father, vow to your service. Yours
Is the first weapon she grasps as suppliant,
Flying through the air to escape her foe.   665

Accept her as yours, Goddess, I implore you,
As I commit her now to the perilous air.'

He spoke, drew back his arm, and hurled the spear,
Sending poor Camilla flying over the loud
Rushing water on the whistling shaft. Metabus,   670
Hard pressed, entrusted himself to the river
And emerged triumphant to pluck from the turf
The spear and the girl, his gift to Diana.
No cities welcomed him into their walls—
Not that he in his wild state would have accepted.   675
He lived among shepherds in the lonely hills,
And there, amid the woods and rugged lairs of beasts,
He nursed his child on a wild mare's milk,
Pressing the teats into her tender lips.
As soon as the baby could take her first steps,   680
He put into her hands a little sharp spear
And slung on her back a quiver and bow.
Instead of gold for her hair and a trailing robe,
A tigerskin hung from her head and shoulders.
Even then she hurled her childish spears   685
With tender hands and twirled her leather sling
Around her head to bring down snowy swans
And Strymonian cranes. Many a mother
In Tyrrhenian towns prayed for her
To marry her son, but she was always content   690
With Diana alone, inviolate in her love
For her weapons and her chastity. O,
That she had not been swept up in this war
Or tried to challenge the Teucrians!
She would still be my dear companion.   695
But now, since bitter Fate presses her hard,
Glide down from heaven, Nymph, to Latium,
Where battle is joined under an evil star.
Take these, and draw from the quiver
An avenging arrow. With this in his throat   700
May anyone, Italian or Trojan,
Who violates her sacred body with a wound
Pay me an equal penalty in blood.
Then in a hollow cloud I will bear the poor girl,
Body and armor all unspoiled, away to the tomb   705
And lay her to rest in her fatherland."

Diana spoke, and Opis swooped down
Through the light air of heaven,
Shrouding herself in dark, whirling wind.

The Trojans now were approaching the walls   710
With the Etruscan leaders and their squadrons
Of mounted troops. The war-horses neighed
And pranced, swerving all over the plain,
Fighting their reins, and the field was spiked
With lifted iron spearpoints flashing light.   715
Advancing toward them, the swift Latins,
Led by Messapus, by Coras and his brother,
And by Camilla, the warrior princess,
Came into view, pumping their spears.
The sound of horses and men intensified,   720
And then both armies halted, standing
Within a spear-cast of each other. Then,
With a sudden shout, both sides charged,
Spurring on their furious horses. Weapons
Showered down as thick as snowflakes   725
And their shadows darkened the sky.

Tyrrhenus and Aconteus, spears leveled,
Were first to charge each other and first to fall.
Their horses collided chest to chest
With a deafening crash, crippling both.   730
Aconteus was flung off like a thunderbolt
Or a stone shot by a catapult
And scattered his life into the air.

This sent a tremor through the battle-lines,
And the Latins, shields on their backs now,   735
Turned their horses toward the city walls.
The Trojans gave chase, Asilas in the lead.
When the Latins were almost to the gates
They shouted and wheeled their horses around,
Reins pulling their supple necks, and then   740
The Trojans turned and let their horses run.

Picture the sea surging in and ebbing.
A huge swell rushes to shore, breaking
Over the rocks in a foaming arch of water

And drenching the farthest reach of sand,   745
Then seething back over the rolling stones
As the shallows recede and leave the shore dry.

Twice the Tuscans drove the Rutulians
Back to the city, their shields slung behind.
But when they met for the third time, the lines   750
Interlocked, and they fought man to man.
The battle became a welter of bodies, weapons,
The groans of the dying, horses floundering
On their slaughtered riders and dying themselves,
Knee-deep in blood.
                          Orsilochus shot his spear   755
At Remulus' horse, too afraid to confront
The rider himself, and left the steel
Just beneath its ear. The horse reared in agony,
Pawing the air and unseating Remulus,
Who rolled to the ground. Catillus took down   760
Iollas and Herminius, a man of huge stature
And with courage to match. His blond head bare,
Chest and shoulders unarmored, unafraid of wounds,
He was an enormous target. Catillus' spear
Came quivering through his broad torso   765
And doubled him over, transfixed with pain.
Everywhere you looked, blood ran dark
As struggling men killed each other with iron,
Seeking through wounds a glorious death.

And in the center of all this slaughter   770
Camilla raged, an exultant Amazon,
One breast bared for battle, a quiver on her back.
Whipping javelins from her hand, or wielding
A heavy battle-axe for hours on end,
Diana's golden bow clanging on her shoulder.   775
And when she was forced by pressure behind
To withdraw, she turned in her saddle,
Bow in hand, and took aim as she fled.
Around her were her handpicked companions,
Virgin Larina and Tulla, and Tarpeia   780
Slicing the air with her bronze battle-axe,
Daughters of Italy whom godlike Camilla
Chose as her glory in both peace and war.

Think of Amazons in Thrace tramping across
The Thermodon's streams following Hippolyte   *785*
As they go to war with emblazoned weapons;
Or gathered around Penthesilea, daughter
Of Mars, when she returns in her chariot,
An army of women howling in triumph
As they leap exultantly with crescent shields.   *790*

Whom did you strike down first, fierce girl,
Whom last? How many dying bodies
Did you leave on the earth?
                              Euneus was first,
Clytius' son, whose exposed chest
Camilla ripped through with her long pine spear.   *795*
He fell, coughing up blood and chewing
The crimson dust as he writhed on his wound.
Then she brought down Liris, and Pagasus
On top of him. Liris was falling from his horse,
Which had just been hit, clutching at the reins,   *800*
When Pagasus rode up to lend a helping hand;
The pair crashed down headfirst together.
She quickly added Amastrus, son of Hippotas,
And, leaning into long-range spear-casts,
Tereus, Harpalycus, Demophoön, and Chromis,   *805*
Killing a Phrygian with every weapon
That left her hand.
                    The hunter Ornytus,
Wearing strange armor, rode at a distance
On a Iapygian horse. Oxhide protected
The warrior's shoulders; his head was covered   *810*
By the white-fanged jaws of a wolf's gaping mouth,
And he carried a rustic pike in his hands.
He was a full head above the other riders
Clustering around him. Camilla caught him—
Which was no great trouble—pierced him through,   *815*
And cried in a voice without a trace of pity:

"Did you think you were hunting animals,
Tuscan? This is the day all your big talk
Is squelched by a woman's weapons.
But you can boast of this to your ancestral shades,   *820*
That you went down by Camilla's spear."

Next were Butes and Orsilochus, two
Of the biggest bodies in the Trojan army.
Butes she got with a spear from behind
As he sat on his horse, the point going in   825
Where the neck shows between the helmet
And corselet, just above the shield's rim.
She let Orsilochus chase her in a wide circle
And then wheeled into a tighter ring
And pursued the pursuer. Rising in the saddle   830
She hacked away with her battle-axe
Through armor and bone while he begged
Over and over for mercy. His warm brain
Spattered his face.
                         Aunus' warrior son
Then fell in her way, terrified to see her.   835
He was from the Appenines, and not the least
Of the Ligurians while Fate allowed him
His deceitful life. When this man saw
He could not escape combat by outriding
Or outmaneuvering the princess warrior,   840
He resorted to a clever ruse, saying:

"What's so great about a woman who relies
On a strong horse? Why don't you meet me
On a level field and fight me on foot,
Hand to hand? You'll soon find out   845
Who is deceived by windy vanity."

Camilla, furious, burned with indignation.
She handed her horse's reins to a comrade
And, wholly unafraid, confronted the man
On foot, with equal arms, a naked sword   850
And plain light shield. Thinking he had won
By guile, Aunus' son pulled his horse around
And spurred him into a willing gallop.

"You Ligurian fool, your slippery tricks
Aren't going to work this time; cunning   855
Won't get you home safe to lying Aunus."

She spoke, and with feet like lightning
She intercepted the horse, seized the reins,

And took her vengeance in his hated blood.

> *A falcon, sacred to Mars, swoops down*   860
> *From a high rock and overtakes a dove*
> *Flying in a cloud. Clutching her*
> *In his hooked talons he rips her to pieces,*
> *And gore and torn feathers drift from the sky.*

The Father of Gods and Men saw these things   865
With all-seeing eyes as he sat on Olympus.
He roused Tyrrhenian Tarchon to battle,
Inflaming him with spite and rage. And so
Tarchon rode through the murderous lanes of war
Shouting encouragement to his faltering troops,   870
Calling each man by name, and rallied them:

"What are you afraid of, Tyrrhenians?
Where's your sense of shame? Are you just lazy,
Or is this rank cowardice? Letting a woman
Scatter you like this and drive you back!   875
Why do you think we carry these swords?
You're not lazy when it comes to the nightly
Wars of love, when the flute signals
Bacchic dances. You're waiting for the cups
To be set on the table for the feast, aren't you?   880
This is what you like. You can hardly wait
Until the priest announces the sacrifice
And the fattened ox calls you to the deep groves!"

And he spurred his horse into the melee,
Ready to die. He came at Venulus   885
Like a cyclone, tore him from his horse,
And holding him to his chest with one hand
Urged on his horse and carried the man off.
The Latins cheered when they saw this,
And Tarchon bolted over the plain carrying   890
Arms and the man. He snapped off the iron point
Of Venulus' spear and groped around
For an unarmored patch of his captive's skin
Where he could inflict a mortal wound.
Venulus struggled, keeping Tarchon's hand   895
Away from his throat, meeting force with force.

A golden eagle soars on an updraft
Carrying a snake she has caught, her talons
Entwined around it. The wounded serpent,
Writhing sinuously, scales bristling, lifts   900
Its hissing mouth high, but the eagle
Keeps attacking her struggling victim
With her hooked beak, and her wings beat the air.

So Tarchon carried off his prey triumphantly
From the Tiburtine army. His Maeonians   905
Followed their chief's shining example
And ran forward. Arruns, marked by Fate,
Circled Camilla warily, looking for a chance
To use his javelin. Whenever she attacked
In her fury, Arruns crept up from behind,   910
Stalking her silently; whenever, victorious,
She stepped out of battle, Arruns
Stealthily turned his horse in her direction,
Circling, probing, looking for an opening,
And always pumping his unerring spear.   915

It happened that Chloreus, a Trojan
And formerly a priest of Cybele,
Resplendent in his Phrygian armor,
Was charging ahead on his foaming stallion.
This horse was caparisoned in a skin plated   920
With bronze scales and buckled with gold.
Chloreus himself shone in exotic purple
And shot Cretan arrows from a Lycian bow,
Golden the bow, and golden his helmet,
And the rustling folds of his saffron cloak   925
Were clasped with gold. The tunic he wore
And his Asian leggings were finely embroidered.
Camilla wanted either to hang these weapons
As spoils in a temple or to wear the gold herself.
In any case she singled out Chloreus   930
And chased him down like a huntress,
Oblivious to all else and raging recklessly
Through the ranks of men with a woman's passion
For booty and spoils. Arruns saw his chance
And finally sprang into action, spear in hand,   935
As he prayed to heaven in words such as these:

"Lord God Apollo, guardian
Of holy Soracte, where we your votaries
Pass through the fire in our faith
And walk with bare feet over the embers,   940
Grant that this disgrace be effaced by our arms.
O Father Almighty!
I seek no plunder, no spoils,
No trophy for this woman's defeat.
Other feats will bring me fame.   945
If only this dread plague falls beneath my blow,
I will return inglorious to my fatherland."

Apollo heard his prayer, and in his heart
Granted half of it and scattered half to the winds.
Arruns would defeat Camilla, yes, and lay her   950
Low in death, but his high fatherland
Would never see his return. That prayer
The winds bore away to the southern storms.
And so, as the spear flew from his hand
And hissed through the air, all the Volscians   955
Turned their eyes and hearts to their queen,
But she herself noticed neither air nor sound
Nor weapon coming out of the sky
Until the spear transfixed her bared breast,
And drank her virgin blood from deep within.   960
Her comrades hurried around her in alarm
And caught their mistress as she fell. Arruns,
More frightened than any of them, ran away
In mingled joy and fear, unwilling to trust
His own spear or face Camilla's weapons.   965

   Having killed a shepherd, or a great steer,
   A wolf will run before men can come after him
   With their hostile spears. Aware
   That he has done something reckless,
   He loses himself in the trackless mountains,   970
   Tucking his quivering tail beneath his belly.

So too Arruns in his panic wanted only
To be out of sight, and to this end
He plunged into the thick of battle.

Camilla's dying hand pulled at the spear,   *975*
But the iron point was stuck deep in her ribs.
Drained of blood, she sank back; the chill light
Sank in her eyes; and her face, formerly
So radiant, turned pale in death.
As she drew her last breaths she called Acca,   *980*
Who was her own age, loyal to Camilla
Beyond all others and the only one
To share her cares, and said to her:

"I've been strong so far, sister Acca,
But now this bitter wound is finishing me,   *985*
And everything is growing dark
With shadows. Hurry and bring to Turnus
My last command: to take my place in battle
And keep the Trojans from the city.
And now, good-bye."

                     Camilla spoke,   *990*
Dropped the reins, and slipped to the ground
Unwillingly. As her body grew cold
She slowly freed herself from all its bonds,
Relaxing her neck and letting her head fall
Into the grip of Death. Finally,   *995*
She released her weapons, and with a moan
Her soul fled resentfully down to the shades.

The roar that followed broke through the sky
And struck the golden stars. With Camilla down,
The fight intensified, and all forces converged: *1000*
The Teucrian army, the Etruscan captains,
And Evander's Arcadian squadrons.

Opis, Diana's sentinel,
Had been calmly watching the war
A long time from her mountain seat.   *1005*
When she saw, far off in the din of combat,
Camilla pay the penalty of death,
She spoke these words from her heart's deep core:

"Ah, Camilla, you have paid too cruel
A penalty, too cruel, for challenging   *1010*

The Trojans in battle. It has not helped you
That you worshiped Diana alone in the woods,
Or wore our quiver on your shoulder.
But your queen has not left you dishonored
In the hour of death, and your doom   1015
Will be renowned among the nations.
Nor will you be disgraced as one unavenged.
Whoever violated your body with a wound
Will pay with his life."

                    At the foot of the mountain
Stood the great burial mound of Dercennus,   1020
A Laurentine king of old, shaded by ilex.
The beautiful goddess touched down here
And from the high barrow spotted Arruns.
When she saw him swelling with pride
In his gleaming armor, she cried: 1025

"Why are you going off? Turn your steps
This way, come over here to die,
And receive for Camilla your just reward—
Not that you are worthy of Diana's arrows."

Thus the Thracian nymph, and she pulled   1030
From the gilded quiver a feathered arrow
And stretched the bow deliberately
Until its curving tips were almost touching,
Her left hand up against the arrow's metal point,
Right hand and bowstring back against her breast.   1035
Arruns heard the arrow whir through the air
At the same moment that it pierced his chest.
He gasped his life away in the nameless dust,
Forgotten by his comrades, and Opis
Winged her way to high Olympus.   1040

Their commander lost, Camilla's light cavalry
Was the first unit to retreat. The Rutulians
Then withdrew, as did the fighter Atinas.
Scattered captains and abandoned troops,
Seeking safety, wheeled their horses around   1045
And galloped back toward the city walls.
None of them could stop the Trojan onslaught

Or even stand against it. They slung
Their unstrung bows on their sagging shoulders,
And their horses' hooves pounded the crumbling plain.   1050
A dark cloud of dust rolled to the walls,
And in the watchtowers mothers beat their breasts
And raised their cries to the stars.
The first group to race inside the open gates
Was followed so closely by the enemy   1055
That their ranks mingled, and far from escaping
A piteous death they were sliced open
On the very threshold of their native city
And gasped out their lives under the shelter
Of their own homes. Some closed the gates   1060
And did not dare open them for their friends
No matter how much they pleaded.
The slaughter was heartbreaking, citizens
Rushing on the defenders' swords. Shut out
Before the eyes of their weeping parents,   1065
Some were stampeded into the trenches
While others charged blindly at the stout gates
And battered the strongly barred doors.
Even the mothers defended the walls,
Rivaling Camilla out of love of their country,   1070
Hurling missiles from their trembling hands—
Oak poles and seared stakes in place of hard steel.
Each burned to die first defending the walls.

Meanwhile, Acca brought her grim message
To Turnus, still in the forest, and filled his mind   1075
With a picture of immense devastation:
The Volscian ranks destroyed, Camilla fallen,
The enemy advancing relentlessly,
Sweeping everything before them in triumph,
And the panic that had spread to the town.   1080
Raging—and this was the stern will of Zeus—
Turnus abandoned the ambush in the hills
And left the forest. He had just reached the plain
And was out of sight when Father Aeneas
Entered the open pass, scaled the ridge,   1085
And came out from the shadows of the wood.
So both men marched rapidly toward the city
With all their troops, no great distance apart.

Aeneas saw on the plain ahead clouds of dust
Tramped up by the Laurentine army, 1090
And at the same moment Turnus became aware
Of Aeneas' advance, heard the marching feet
And the snorting horses. They would have
Joined battle at once, but the rose-red Sun
Was already bathing his weary team 1095
In the western waters. And so as day ebbed
And night was coming on, one army encamped
Before the city, and the other strengthened its walls.

AENEID TWELVE

Lines 1–528 are omitted. Turnus and Aeneas prepare to meet in single combat to determine the outcome of the war. Juno persuades Turnus' sister Juturna to save her brother, or if she cannot, at least to reignite the hostilities. Juturna, disguised as a nobleman, shames the Rutulians into fighting for their hero and battle is again joined. Aeneas is wounded by a stray arrow but is healed by Iapyx with the help of Venus.

Aeneas was hungry for the fight. Impatient
Of any delay, he clapped golden greaves   *530*
Onto his shins and started handling a spear.
As soon as his breastplate was strapped on
And his shield was fitted to his side,
He put his arms around Ascanius, kissed him
Lightly through his helmet, and said: *535*

"Learn how to be a man from me, my son;
Learn good fortune from others. Today my hand
Will defend you in war and lead you
To great rewards. When you come of age,
See to it that you remember the example   *540*
Of your kinsmen, and that your father, Aeneas,
And your uncle Hector enliven your soul."

Aeneas spoke and then moved through the gates,
Huge himself and brandishing a massive spear.
Close by his side were Antheus and Mnestheus,   *545*
And behind them the entire army poured out,
Emptying the camp. The plain boiled
With blinding dust, and the shocked earth trembled
Under the tramping feet.
                            From the wall opposite
Turnus saw them coming; the Ausonians saw them,   *550*
And a cold shudder ran through their bones.
Before any of the Latins, Juturna
Heard the sound, knew it, and turned and fled.

Aeneas was flying, and his dark line of troops
Was drawn in his wake over the open plains.   555

> When a storm breaks at sea, and the rain cloud
> Moves toward land, pity the farmers,
> Whose prescient hearts know what is coming
> And shudder. Trees will be brought down,
> Crops ruined, everything scattered. The winds   560
> Run before it and their howls carry shoreward.

Just so the Trojan commander brought his troops
Up to the front, and they massed around him.
Thymbraeus landed his sword on Osiris,
Mnestheus killed Arcetius, Achates Epolo,   565
Gyas Ufens. Even Tolumnius fell,
The augur who was first to hurl a spear
In the enemy's face. A shout split the air,
And the routed Rutulians turned around
In a cloud of dust and ran through the fields.   570
Aeneas didn't bother with these fugitives,
Or even with those who opposed him,
On foot or mounted. Turnus alone
He tracked through the thickening gloom,
Turnus alone he called out to combat.   575

Juturna, in her deep distress,
Knocked Turnus' driver, Metiscus,
Out of the chariot and left him behind.
The warrior goddess assumed his form,
His voice and armor, and took the rippling reins.   580

> A black swallow flits through the mansion
> Of a wealthy lord, winging her way
> Through the high halls to scavenge
> Scraps and crumbs for her chirping nestlings,
> Then twittering in and out of the porticoes   585
> And about the courtyard pools.

                            So too Juturna
Guided the horses through the enemy ranks
And flew in the chariot all over the field,
Giving them glimpses of her exultant brother,

Now here, now there, never allowing him   590
To lock up in combat but always flitting away.
Still, Aeneas kept tracking Turnus down
Through the winding maze of war, calling him,
Calling, and when he spotted him, sprinting
To match the horses' speed, only to have   595
Juturna wrench the chariot aside.
What could he do? He was all at sea,
His mind pulled in contrary directions.
Meanwhile, Messapus, treading lightly
And carrying two javelins tipped with steel,   600
Rifled one of them at him with deadly aim.
Aeneas went down to one knee and crouched
Behind his shield as the spearhead sheared
The crest from his helmet. He felt a sudden
Surge of anger at this treacherous attack.   605
He saw Turnus' chariot pulling away.
Calling to witness Jupiter himself
And the altars of the broken treaty,
Aeneas plunged into the general combat
And, with Mars at his back, began to kill   610
Indiscriminately, giving his rage free rein.

What god could now unfold for me
So many bitter deaths, which poet could tell
Of all the captains who met their many dooms
Driven over the plain now by Turnus,   615
Now by the Trojan hero? Did it please you,
Jupiter, that nations destined to live
In everlasting peace should clash so harshly?

Aeneas, in the first combat that halted
The Trojans' onrush, paused only briefly   620
To take out Sucro, driving his steel
Through the rib cage, where death comes most quickly.
Turnus unhorsed Amycus and his brother, Diores,
And then advancing on foot struck down one
With his long spear, the other with his sword;   625
Then hanging their severed heads from his chariot,
He bore them off dripping dewdrops of blood.
Aeneas sent to their deaths Talos, Tanais,
And brave Cethegus, three in one assault,

And then dispatched the shocked Onites,   630
A Theban whose mother was Peridia.
Turnus' next victims were the brothers sent
From Apollo's Lycian fields, and Menoetes,
An Arcadian who hated warfare, in vain.
This man had been a humble fisherman   635
Near the pools of Lerna. He had no patrons,
And his father tilled a rented plot of land.

Like fires set on different sides of a wood,
A dry thicket of crackling laurels;
Or like rivers roaring down a mountainside,   640
Each destroying everything in its path,

So Aeneas and Turnus swept through the battle,
Each of them seething with rage within,
Hearts bursting, neither yielding an inch,
And all their desire was to wound men with steel.   645

Murranus was boasting of his ancient lineage
Stretching back to Latin kings, when Aeneas
Hit him with a huge stone that pitched him
Headfirst over his car, where he was trampled
By horses who did not remember their master.   650
Hyllus was charging forward with insane fury
When Turnus rifled a spear at his golden brow.
The point pierced his helmet and stuck in his brain.
And you, Cretheus, bravest of the Greeks,
Your right hand did not save you from Turnus;   655
Nor did Cupencus' gods protect him
When Aeneas came. He put his chest in the way
Of Aeneas' spear, and the slight reprieve
His bronze shield offered did not help him much.
You also, Aeolus, fell at Laurentum   660
And spread your body out in its fields,
You, whom the Argive army could not lay low,
Nor Achilles, destroyer of Priam's realm.
Here was your end. Your home was in Lyrnesus
Under Mount Ida; in Laurentum is your grave.   665

Now, all up and down the lines, both armies
Engaged—all the Latins and all the Trojans:

Mnestheus and intense Serestus;
Messapus, breaker of horses, and brave Asilas;
Tuscan troops and Evander's Arcadians,   670
Each doing his utmost, each at his limit,
No rest, no respite in the vast, open conflict.

Aeneas' mother now put it in his mind
To advance on the walls, attack the town
With abrupt force, and throw the Latins   675
Into confusion at the sudden slaughter.
Tracking Turnus through the lanes of battle,
He swept his eyes in every direction
And saw the city untouched by the war,
Quiet and at peace. At once a vision   680
Of a greater conflict burned in his mind.
Summoning Mnestheus, Sergestus,
And brave Serestus, he climbed up a mound
To which the rest of the Trojans came at a run,
Still holding their spears and shields. Aeneas,   685
Standing on this height, addressed them:

"I want no delay in carrying out my orders—
Jupiter is on our side—and I don't want anyone
Holding back because the decision is sudden.
That city, the cause of this war, the heart   690
Of Latinus' realm, unless they surrender
And submit to our rule—that city
I will today overthrow and lay its smoking roofs
Level with the ground. Am I supposed to wait
Until Turnus feels like doing battle with me,   695
Until he comes back for more, beaten though he is?
This is the crux of this accursed war, men.
Bring torches and reclaim the treaty with fire!"

They outdid each other in their eagerness,
Formed a wedge, and advanced to the walls en masse.   700
Ladders and torches appeared from nowhere.
One group stormed the gates and cut down the guards,
Others darkened the sky with their javelins.
Aeneas himself stood at the foot of the wall,
Stretched out his hands, and in a great voice   705
Accused Latinus, calling the gods to witness

That he was being forced into battle again,
That the Italians had twice become his foes,
Twice broken a treaty. Inside the walls
Strife arose among the anxious citizens. 710
Some wanted the city gates thrown open
To the Dardanians and called for the king
To be dragged to the walls. Others brought arms
And marched out to defend their city.

A shepherd has followed bees to their hive 715
In tunneled pumice and filled it with smoke.
Anxious for their realm, the bees scurry
This way and that through their wax fortress
And with loud buzzing hone their rage.
The black stench billows through their halls, 720
The hollow rock resounds with a blind hum,
And the smoke comes out into the empty air.

There was more grief for the weary Latins,
And it shook the city to its very foundations.
When the queen saw the enemy coming 725
Into the town, the walls breached, roofs aflame,
And no Rutulians, no troops of Turnus
Opposing them, the poor woman believed
That he had perished in battle. In her distress
She cried out that she was the cause and origin 730
Of all these evils, and said many other things
In her frenzied grief. Determined to die,
She tore her royal robes and from a high beam
Hung a noose for her hideous death.
When the Latin women found her dead, 735
First her daughter Lavinia tore out
Her golden hair and scored her cheeks,
Then all of the people around her raved,
And the house resounded with their laments.
The sad news spread through all the city. 740
Minds and hearts sank. Latinus went about
With rent garments, dazed by his wife's death
And his city's ruin, his white hair grimed with dust.

During all this time, Turnus was pursuing
A handful of stragglers at the edge of the plain, 745

Moving more slowly now, less and less happy
With his horses' brilliance. The wind carried to him
Unseen terrors in the clamor from the town.
Then, as he listened intently, a puzzle of sound
Struck his ears, the murmur of suffering.   750

"What are all these cries coming from the city?
It must be bad if I can hear it from here."

Distracted, he drew in the reins and stopped.
His sister, who still looked like Metiscus
And as such was steering the chariot,   755
Faced him and said:

                    "Let's keep after the Trojans
Out here, where we are already winning.
There are other troops to defend the town.
Aeneas is taking it to the Italians now,
And we should be dealing death to the Teucrians.   760
You'll kill just as many here, with no less honor."

To which Turnus replied:

                    "I knew it was you
Long ago, Sister, when you entered this war
And tricked us into breaking the truce,
And you don't fool me now, Goddess. But why   765
Come down from Olympus and endure all this?
So you can see your brother's miserable death?
What can I do? There are no guarantees.
I saw Murranus before my own eyes,
Calling me as he went down. No one   770
Meant more to me—Murranus,
A mighty man undone by a mighty wound.
Poor Ufens died so he wouldn't have to see
My disgrace. The Trojans have his body and arms.
And now I should allow our homes destroyed   775
(The final touch) and not refute Drances?
Turn tail and let this land see Turnus in flight?
Is it so bad to die? Shades below,
Be good to me, since the will of heaven
Has turned against me. I will go down to you   780

Holy in spirit, innocent of any guilt,
And never unworthy of my great forebears."

He had scarcely finished when Saces,
His face wounded by an arrow, came riding up
On a panting horse through the enemy lines,   785
Calling Turnus by name and imploring him:

"Turnus, you are our last hope. Pity your people.
Aeneas is storming in battle and threatening
To throw down the Italians' topmost towers
And destroy them utterly. Torches are already   790
Flying to the roofs. The Latins are turning
All eyes to you, Turnus. King Latinus himself
Mutters about whom to call his son
And to which alliance he should turn. Moreover,
The queen, who put all her trust in you, is dead   795
By her own hand, gone from the world of light.
Only Messapus and Atinas are holding the gates,
Surrounded by squadrons bristling with steel,
While you wheel your chariot in an empty field."

Turnus was stunned by this changed picture   800
Of his fortunes. He stood rooted in silence,
His great heart roiling with shame, with grief
Verging on madness, with frenzied love
And undeniable courage. When the shadows
Parted, and light returned to his mind,   805
He swept his blazing eyes toward the walls,
Furious, and looked back from his chariot
At the great city.

                    Flames were spiraling skyward
From story to story, about to catch a tower—
A defensive bulwark he himself had built,   810
Set on wheels and hung with high gangways.

"Now, Sister, the Fates triumph at last.
Stop holding me back. We will follow
Where God and cruel Fortune call us.
My mind is made up. I will meet Aeneas   815
And bear death's bitterness. No longer,

Sister, will you see me shamed. But first,
Allow me to rage with furious rage."

Turnus spoke, leapt down from his chariot,
And careened madly through the enemy lines,   820
Leaving his sorrowing sister behind.

    Think of a stone crashing down a mountain,
    Either a storm has washed it free, or time
    In its passing has loosened it, and now
    The shameless mass of rock sweeps down   825
    The steep slopes and bounds over the earth,
    Rolling along with it trees, herds, and men.

So too Turnus scattering the ranks
In his rush to the walls, where the ground
Was most soaked with blood and the air   830
Whined with spears. Turnus lifted his hand,
Had their immediate attention, and spoke:

"Fall back, Rutulians; and you, Latins,
Hold your fire. Whatever fortune is here
Is mine. It is better for your sake   835
That I alone make good the treaty
And settle the issue with steel."

And the troops made room for him in the middle.

When Father Aeneas heard Turnus' name,
He left the walls and left the high fortress,   840
Jettisoned everything he had been doing,
And in great exultation clashed his weapons.
The sound was like thunder, and the hero

    As vast as Mount Athos, vast as Eryx,
    Vast as Father Apennine himself   845
    With his shimmering oaks, when he roars in joy
    And lifts his snowy head toward heaven.

Now every last man turned and stared—
Every Rutulian, Trojan, and Italian soldier,
Both those high on the walls and those below   850

Who were battering the walls—and they all
Took off their armor. Latinus himself
Was lost in wonder that these two great men,
Born in different parts of the world, had met
And now would settle the issue with steel.   855
As soon as the field was cleared out on the plain
They sprinted forward, threw their spears from afar,
Then waded into battle with a clash of bronze.
Earth groaned. Sword struck sword with stroke
After stroke, luck and valor blending into one.   860

   In great Sila, or high on Taburnus,
   Two bulls have locked horns in mortal combat.
   The keepers fall back in fear, and all the cattle
   Stand in silent dread, the heifers musing
   On who will be lord of the entire herd.   865
   The bulls butt heads with tremendous force
   And gore each other, bathing their backs
   And shoulders with blood, and the whole grove
   Resounds with their bellowing groans.

So too the Trojan and Daunian heroes   870
Clashed shield against shield and filled the sky
With crashing thunder. Jupiter himself
Held up his balanced scales and placed on them
The destinies of each man to determine whom
The battle doomed, whose weight sank down to death.   875

Turnus, thinking he could get away with it,
Sprang forward with sword lifted high
And put all of his weight into a sweeping stroke.
A shout went up from both armies, Trojans
And Latins both straining to see, expectant,   880
But the treacherous sword only splintered
In mid-stroke. When Turnus saw
That his right hand held an unfamiliar hilt
He fled, faster than the East Wind.
The story is told that when Turnus   885
First mounted his chariot he neglected,
In his haste, to bring his father's sword,
And snatched up instead the blade of Metiscus,
His charioteer. This served him well enough

When he was chasing down Teucrian stragglers,   890
But when it came up against the divine armor
Forged by Vulcan, the mortal blade
Shattered like brittle ice into fragments
That glittered on the yellow sand.
                                            Turnus
Ran like a madman this way and that   895
Across the plain, weaving in circles.
The Teucrians closed in, confining him
Between the walls and the desolate marsh.
Aeneas, though his knees were slowed
By the arrow wound and he was not at full speed,   900
Nevertheless stayed hot on his heels.

> *A hunting hound has caught a stag*
> *Hemmed in by a stream, or by crimson feathers*
> *That hunters use to hedge in game. The dog*
> *Runs and barks and worries the stag,*   905
> *Who in terror of the snares and the high bank*
> *Runs back and forth in a thousand directions.*
> *But the keen Umbrian hound stays close,*
> *Mouth gaping wide. The hound almost seizes it,*
> *And snaps its jaws shut as if it had seized it,*   910
> *But bites only the empty air.*

                              Another shout arose,
Echoed by the banks and pools, and the sky thundered
With the tumult below. While Turnus ran,
While he was in full flight, he reproached the Rutulians,
Calling them by name, and clamored for his sword.   915
Aeneas, though, promised instant death
For anyone who came near and made them tremble
By threatening to level their town. Wounded,
He pressed on as they ran in loops, circling five times
And doubling back he unwove all their circuits,   920
For they were not running for some trivial prize
At games but for the lifeblood of Turnus.

There was a bitter-leaved wild olive tree,
Sacred to Faunus, out on the plain,
Revered of old by mariners. Onto this tree   925
They would attach their offerings

To the Laurentine god and in its branches
Hang their votive garments. But the Teucrians,
With no regard for the tree's sanctity,
Had cut it down so that they could fight   930
On an open field. The spear Aeneas had thrown
Was stuck in the tough roots of this tree,
And the Trojan now stooped to pull it out
So he could take down with this weapon
The man he could not catch on foot.   935
Turnus, out of his mind with fear, cried out:

"Have pity on me, Faunus and Mother Earth.
Hold fast the spear, if ever I have honored you,
Whom the men of Aeneas now profane in war."

He spoke, and the gods heard his prayer.   940
Aeneas struggled long with the pliant root
But could not with all his strength force open
Its stubborn grip. And while he struggled,
Juturna, transformed again into Metiscus,
Ran up and handed her brother his sword.   945
Venus, outraged at the nymph's audacity,
Came and plucked the spear out from the root.
The two heroes, weapons and spirits restored,
One trusting his sword, the other towering
With his spear, both panting for breath,   950
Stood face to face in the arena of War.

Meanwhile, the Lord of Olympus
Addressed Juno as she watched the fighting
From a golden cloud:

                         "Juno, my wife,
How will it end? What remains at the last?   955
You yourself know, and you admit that you know,
That Aeneas, the hero of his country,
Is destined to be exalted to the stars.
What are you preparing? With what hope
Do you cling to the chill clouds? Was it right   960
That a god be profaned by a mortal's wound?
That the sword be returned—Juturna could never
Have done it without you—which Turnus had lost,

Or that strength increase in the vanquished?
Desist, and yield at last to my prayers,   *965*
Lest your great grief consume you in silence,
Lest your bitter woes return to me often
From your sweet lips. We have come to the end.
You have had the power to pursue the Trojans
Over land and sea, to kindle a terrible war,   *970*
To disfigure a home and blend bridals with grief.
I forbid you to attempt more."

           ·   Thus Jupiter;
And thus Saturn's daughter, with downcast eyes:

"It was because I knew that this was your will,
My mighty lord, that with great reluctance   *975*
I left the earth and left Turnus. Otherwise,
You would not see me sitting here alone
On my airy throne enduring all, right or wrong.
No, I would be standing cinctured in flame
In the front lines of battle, dragging the Trojans   *980*
Into mortal combat. As for Juturna,
Yes, I persuaded her to help her brother,
And for his life's sake I sanctioned daring deeds
But not to shoot the arrow, not to bend the bow.
I swear to this by the implacable water of Styx,   *985*
The one inviolable oath for the gods above.
And now I yield, and quit this loathsome war.
I have one solemn request of you, something
Not prohibited by Fate, for Latium's sake
And for your people's majesty. When soon   *990*
(Let it be) they make peace with happy weddings,
And form alliances with laws and treaties,
Do not command the native Latins
To change their ancient name, nor become
Trojans and be called Teucrians, nor to change   *995*
In language or in dress. Let Latium be,
Let Alban kings rule through the ages,
And let the Roman stock be strong
In Italian manhood. Troy has fallen.
Let the name of Troy be fallen too."   *1000*

Smiling at her, the world's Creator said:

"You are Jove's true sister, and Saturn's child.
The waves of wrath that roll deep in your breast!
Come, dismiss the fury that was aroused in vain.
I grant your request, and I willingly relent.   *1005*
The Ausonians will keep their native tongue
And ancestral ways; as their name is now,
So shall it be. The Teucrians shall be absorbed
In the body at large. I will establish
Their sacred rites and laws and make them all   *1010*
Latins, with a single tongue. From them shall rise
A race blended with Ausonian blood
That you shall see surpass both gods and men
In faith and loyalty. And no nation
Shall be more zealous in Juno's worship."   *1015*

The goddess nodded, happy to assent,
Then left the cloud and departed from the sky.

This done, the Father pondered how
To withdraw Juturna from her brother's side.

There are twin fiends, whom men call Dirae,   *1020*
Born to the Night Goddess in the same litter
As hellish Megaera. Their mother wreathed
The heads of all three with coiling snakes
And gave them wings to ride the winds.
These two Dirae attend the throne of Jupiter   *1025*
And whet the fears of feeble mortals
When the grim monarch visits them
With disease and death, or terrorizes
Guilty cities with war. Jove sent one of them
Down from high heaven with instructions   *1030*
To appear as an omen before Juturna.
The fiend flew down to earth in whirling wind,

> *Like an arrow speeding from a bowstring*
> *Into a cloud bank, a poisoned arrow*
> *Shot by a Parthian archer, a Parthian*   *1035*
> *Or a Cydonian, an incurable shaft*
> *Whining unseen through the flitting shadows.*

Thus the child of Night, speeding to earth.

When she came in sight of the Trojan ranks
And the troops of Turnus, she suddenly shrank   1040
Into the shape of an owl, the small bird
That often perches at night on tombs
And deserted rooftops, singing its late,
Unwelcome song through the shadows.
So transformed, the fiend flits and screams   1045
Before the face of Turnus, her dark wings
Beating his shield. A strange, numbing dread
Washed through Turnus' body; his hair
Bristled with fear; his voice stuck in his throat.

His sister, Juturna, recognized from afar   1050
The harsh whisper of the Dread One's wings.
She tore out her unbound hair, her nails
Clawed her face, and she pounded her breast
With her fists. Then she cried out to her brother:

"How can your sister help you now, Turnus,   1055
And what is left for my own hard life? Nothing
I can do will prolong the light for you.
Can I oppose this terrible portent?
Now at last I quit the field. Don't try to scare me,
You ill-omened vultures! I am already afraid.   1060
I know the beating of your wings,
The sound of death, and I do not mistake
The haughty commands of Jupiter.
Is this how he compensated me
For my lost virginity? Why did he give me   1065
Life everlasting? If I could only die
I could end this sorrow, go through the shadows
At my poor brother's side. I, immortal!
Nothing can be sweet without you, Brother.
What ground can gape deep enough   1070
To send a goddess to the deepest shades?"

So saying, Juturna covered her head
With a sea-grey veil, and moaning profusely
The goddess plunged into the river's depths.

Aeneas kept the pressure on, rocking   1075
His tree of a spear, and cried savagely:

"What's the delay now, Turnus? Why are you still
Holding back? This isn't a footrace, you know;
It's hand-to-hand combat with cold steel.
Go ahead, change yourself into all sorts of shapes,   1080
Collect all your courage and skill, fly away
High on wings if you want, up to the stars,
Or sink into the hollow earth—I'll get you still."

And Turnus, shaking his head:

                    "You don't scare me,
Big-mouth. The gods scare me, and having Jupiter   1085
As my enemy."

           Turnus said no more.
Looking around he saw a huge stone
Lying on the plain, a stone ancient and huge
Set in place to settle boundary disputes.
Twelve chosen men could scarcely lift it   1090
Onto their shoulders, as men are now,
But the hero scooped it up quickly, rose
To his full height, and with a burst of speed
Hurled it at his adversary. But as he ran
He did not know himself, did not know who he was   1095
As he moved toward the immense stone, lifted it,
And sent it flying. His knees buckled,
His blood was like ice. The stone itself,
Rolling through empty air, fell short
And did not deliver its blow.

                In dreams,   1100
  When night's weariness weighs on our eyes,
  We are desperate to run farther and farther
  But collapse weakly in the middle of our efforts.
  Our tongue doesn't work, our usual strength
  Fails our body, and words will not come.   1105

So too Turnus. However bravely he tried
The Dread One would not let him win through.
Shifting images spun through his mind.
He looked at the Rutulians, and the town,
Frozen with fear. He saw death closing in   1110

And trembled, nowhere to escape, no way
To attack his enemy. He could not see
His chariot, or his sister, the charioteer.

While Turnus faltered Aeneas' fatal spear
Quivered in the light. Seeing his chance   1115
He put all his weight behind a long-range throw,
And his weapon flew with deadly force,
Faster than a stone hurled by a catapult
And with a sound louder than thunder.
Roaring through the air like a black tornado   1120
It tore through Turnus' seven-ply shield,
Ripped open his corselet, and with a hiss
Sliced through his thigh. Huge Turnus
Sank down on one knee. The Rutulians
Leapt up with a shout, and the woods and hills   1125
Echoed their groans. Humbled, Turnus
Lifted his eyes to Aeneas
And stretched forth his hand in supplication:

"Go ahead, use your chance. I deserve it.
I will not ask anything for myself,   1130
But if a parent's grief can still touch you,
Remember your own father, Anchises,
And take pity on Daunus' old age,
I beg you. Give me, or if you prefer,
Give my dead body back to my people.   1135
You've beaten me, and the Ausonians
Have seen me, beaten, stretch out my hand to you.
Lavinia is yours. Let your hatred stop here."

Aeneas stood there, lethal in his bronze.
His eyes searched the distance, and his hand   1140
Paused on the hilt of his sword. Turnus' words
Were winning him over, but then his gaze shifted
To the fateful baldric on his enemy's shoulder,
And the belt glittered with its familiar metalwork—
The belt of young Pallas, whom Turnus had killed   1145
And whose insignia he now wore as a trophy.
Aeneas' eyes drank in this memorial
Of his own savage grief, and then, burning
With fury and terrible in his wrath, he said:

"Do you think you can get away from me   1150
While wearing the spoils of one of my men?
                                        Pallas
Sacrifices you with this stroke—Pallas—
And makes you pay with your guilty blood."

Saying this, and seething with rage, Aeneas
Buried his sword in Turnus' chest. The man's limbs   1155
Went limp and cold, and with a moan
His soul fled resentfully down to the shades.

Glossary of Names

Acestes (A-kes´-teez): A Trojan who became a king in Sicily.

Achaeans (A-kee´-unz): General name for the Greeks.

Achates (A-ka´-teez): Companion of Aeneas.

Acheron (A´-ker-on): River in the Underworld.

Achilles (A-kil´-eez): A central character in Homer's *Iliad*. Son of Peleus and Thetis; killer of Hector.

Actium (Ak´-tee-um): A promontory in northwestern Greece near which Octavian defeated Antony and Cleopatra in 31 B.C.E.

Aeneas (Ee-nee´-as): Principal character in the *Aeneid;* Trojan warrior in Homer's *Iliad*. Son of Venus and Anchises; leader of the Trojans after the fall of Troy.

Aeneas Silvius (Ee-nee´-as Sil´-vee-us): Descendant of Aeneas; a future king of Alba Longa.

Aeolus (Ee´-oh-lus): God of the winds.

Agamemnon (A-ga-mem´-non): King of Mycenae; leader of the Greek army during the Trojan War. He was killed by his wife, Clytemnestra, when he returned home.

Agenor (A-gen´-or): Ancient king of Tyre; ancestor of Dido.

Agrippa (Ag-rip´-a): Marcus Vipsanius Agrippa; son-in-law of Augustus and commander under Augustus.

Ajax (Ay´-jax): Son of Oïleus; a Greek warrior in Homer's *Iliad*. He attacked Cassandra during the fall of Troy and was later punished for sacrilege toward the temple of Pallas.

Alba Longa (Al´-ba Lon´-ga): City founded by Ascanius in the Alban hills of Italy.

Allecto (A-lek´-toh): One of the Furies; bringer of war and wrath.

Amata (A-ma´-ta): Queen in Italy; the wife of Latinus and mother of Lavinia.

Amazons (A´-ma-zonz): Women warriors. They were allies of the Trojans.

Anchises (An-keye´-seez): Son of Capys; father of Aeneas by Venus. He escaped Troy on the shoulders of Aeneas.

Andromache (An-dra´-ma-kee): Wife of Hector.

Anna (An´-a): Sister of Dido.

Antenor (An-tee´-nor): Trojan prince who founded Patavium.

Antony (An´-toh-nee): Marc Antony; rival of Octavian. He was defeated at the battle of Actium in 31 B.C.E.

Apollo (A-pol´-oh): Son of Jupiter and Latona; brother of Diana. Patron god of music and prophecy; associated with the lyre and archery.

Arcadia (Ar-kay´-dee-a): Region in the Peloponnesus of Greece known for pastoral practices.

Arethusa (Ar-a-thoo´-za): Nymph who was transformed into a fountain at Syracuse in Sicily.

Argos (Ar´-gos): City or district in the northeastern Peloponnesus of Greece. The name "Argives" is derived from this city and refers to the Greeks.

Argus (Ar´-gus): Hundred-eyed monster charged by Juno with the task of watching over the cow Io. Killed by Mercury.

Ascanius (As-kay´-nee-us): Son of Aeneas and Creüsa; also called Iülus. He eventually founds Alba Longa.

Assaracus (As-ar´-ak-us): A king of Troy; son of Tros; great-grandfather of Aeneas.

Astyanax (As-teye´-a-nax): Son of Hector and Andromache. Killed during the fall of Troy.

Atlas (At´-las): Titan who holds up the sky; son of Iapetos.

Augustus (A-gus´-tus): Gaius Julius Caesar Octavianus Augustus; adopted by Julius Caesar. First Roman emperor; ruled from 27 B.C.E. to 14 C.E. He assumed the name Augustus in 27 B.C.E.

Ausonia (Ow-soh´-nee-a): Italy.

Avernus (A-ver´-nus): Lake near Cumae in Italy near which was said to be an entrance to the Underworld.

Bacchus (Bak´-us): God of wine; son of Jupiter and Semele. Also Liber in Latin. Greek Dionysus.

Baiae (Beye´-eye): Seaside town near Naples.

Belus (Bel´-us): A king of Tyre; father of Dido.

Briareus (Bree´-ar-ee-us): Hundred-handed giant; also known as Aegaeon.

Brutus (Broo´-tus): Lucius Junius Brutus; expelled the last Tarquin king from Rome in 510 B.C.E.

Cacus (Ka´-kus): Son of Vulcan. A giant who was killed by Hercules.

Caesar (Seez´-ar): Gaius Julius Caesar; a Roman statesman and general who adopted Octavian. Killed in 44 B.C.E.

Camilla (Ka-mil´-a): Warrior woman allied with Turnus. She was the leader of the Volscians.

Capitol (Kap´-it-ol): Top of the Capitoline Hill in Rome on which stood the temple to Jupiter Optimus Maximus.

Carthage (Kar´-thaj): City on the northwest coast of Africa; historically a rival of Rome. According to legend it was founded by Queen Dido after she fled her brother's violence.

Cassandra (Ka-san´-dra): Daughter of Priam and Hecuba. A prophetess whom no one believed.

Catiline (Kat´-a-lin): Lucius Sergius Catilina; a Roman conspirator who was exposed by Cicero in 63 B.C.E.

Cato (Kay´-toh): Marcus Porcius Cato; a conservative Roman statesman who strongly urged the destruction of Carthage.

Celaeno (Sel-eye´-noh): Chief of the Harpies.

Centaur (Sen´-tar): Half-man, half-horse mythological creature belonging to a race fathered by Ixion.

Cerberus (Ker´-ber-us): Three-headed dog that guards the gates of the Underworld.

Ceres (Seer´-eez): Goddess of crops and the harvest. Greek Demeter.

Charon (Kay´-ron): Ferryman who transports the dead across the river Styx in the Underworld.

Charybdis (Ka-rib´-dis): Whirlpool near Scylla in the straits of Messina.

Circe (Sir´-see): Sorceress whom Ulysses encountered in Homer's *Odyssey*. She changes Ulysses' men into swine.

Cocytus (Ko-kee´-tus): River in the Underworld.

Corinth (Kor´-inth): City in the northwest Peloponnesus of Greece; captured by the Romans in 146 B.C.E.

Crete (Kreet): Island in the Aegean Sea south of Greece. Aeneas landed here when searching for his destined land.

Creüsa (Kree-oos´-a): Daughter of Priam; first wife of Aeneas; mother of Ascanius. She was separated from Aeneas and lost during the fall of Troy.

Cupid (Kyoo´-pid): God of love; son of Venus.

Cybele (Kee´-bel- ee): (1) Phrygian mother-goddess of Asia Minor. (2) The mountain with which she is associated.

Cyclops (Seye´-klops): (1) Race of giants living in Sicily who have only one eye each. (2) The workers of Vulcan.

Cyprus (Seye´-prus): Eastern Mediterranean island; associated with Venus.

Cythera (Si-thee´-ra): Island southeast of Greece near which Venus was born, hence Venus' name Cytherean.

Daedalus (Deye´-dal-us): Craftsman who built the labyrinth for the purpose of containing the Minotaur on the island of Crete. He escaped Crete by fashioning wings of feathers and wax and using them to fly to Cumae in Italy.

Danaans (Da-nay´-unz): A general name referring to the Greeks.

Danaë (Dan´-ay-ee): Daughter of Acrisius, a king of Argos. She was set adrift in a chest by her father; she reached Italy and founded Ardea, the city of Turnus.

Dardanus (Dar´-dan-us): Ancestor of the Trojans and mythological founder of Troy. From his name the Trojans are called Dardanians.

Delos (Dee´-los): Island in the Aegean Sea; birthplace of Apollo and Diana.

Diana (Deye-an´-a): Daughter of Jupiter and Latona; sister of Apollo; goddess of the hunt and the moon. Greek Artemis.

Dido (Deye´-doh): Queen of Carthage in North Africa. She founded Carthage when she fled from her brother's violence. She killed herself after Aeneas left Carthage. Also called Elissa.

Diomedes (Deye-oh-mee´-deez): Son of Tydeus and Deïpyle. A commander and a foremost warrior in Homer's *Iliad*. He founded the city of Arpi in Italy after the Trojan War.

Drances (Dran´-seez): A Rutulian hostile to Turnus.

Elissa (A-lis´-a): A name of Dido.

Elysium (Ee-lees´-ee-um): Pleasant region of the Underworld reserved for those who led a good life.

Entellus (En-tel´-us): A boxer who defeated Dares.

Erebus (Er´-ab-us): Name of the Underworld.

Eryx (Er´-ix): (1) Son of Venus, and so a half-brother of Aeneas; a king at Sicily known for boxing. (2) The name of a mountain.

Etruria (Ee-tru´-ree-a): Region in Italy north of Rome.

Etruscans (Ee-trus´-cans): People who inhabit Etruria.

Eumenides (Yoo-men´-id-eez): Kind name for the Furies; avengers of crimes committed within a family.

Eurus (Yoo´-rus): Southeast Wind.

Euryalus (Yoo-ree´-a-lus): Trojan, son of Opheltes, beloved of Nisus.

Evander (Ee-van´-der): Son of Mercury; king of Pallanteum. His son, Pallas, fought as an ally of Aeneas.

Fates: Three goddesses who spin the fate of human lives. Also called the Parcae.

Faunus (Faw´-nus): Italian god of woodlands and a deified king.

Furies (Fyur´-eez): Avengers of crimes committed within a family; also called the Eumenides.

Ganymede (Gan´-ee-meed): Son of the Trojan Tros. Snatched up by the eagle of Jupiter, he became Jupiter's cupbearer.

Geryon (Ger´-ee-on): Giant with three bodies; killed by Hercules.

Gorgon (Gore´-gon): One of three sisters with snakes in their hair and the ability to turn anyone who looked at them into stone.

Medusa, one of the Gorgons, was decapitated, and her head was attached to Minerva's aegis.

Gracchi (Grak´-eye): Prominent Roman family whence came two brothers, Tiberius and Gaius, who attempted to reform the Roman state.

Harpies (Har´-peez): Monsters with a bird's body and a woman's head.

Hecate (Hek´-at-ee): Goddess of the Underworld and witchcraft; associated with the moon and Diana.

Hector (Hek´-tor): Eldest son of Priam and Hecuba; husband of Andromache. Leader of the Trojan army at Troy in Homer's *Iliad*; killed by Achilles.

Hecuba (He´-kew-ba): Queen of Troy and wife of Priam; mother of Hector, Paris, Cassandra, and other children of Priam.

Helen (He´-len): Daughter of Leda and Jupiter; wife of Menelaus. The most beautiful woman in the world. Her abduction by Paris was believed to cause the Trojan War.

Helicon (He´-li-kon): Mountain in Greece that the Muses frequent.

Hercules (Her´-kyoo-leez): Son of Jupiter and Alcmene; a hero famed for his twelve labors.

Hesperia (Hes-per´-ee-a): A land in the west; a name for Italy.

Hesperides (Hes-per´-id-eez): Daughters of Hesperus. Keepers of a garden in the far west that contained a tree bearing golden apples.

Hippolytus (Hip-all´-ee-tos): Son of Theseus and Hippolyte. His stepmother, Phaedra, fell in love with him, and when her love was not returned she engineered his death.

Hydra (Heye´-dra): Monster with many heads; killed by Hercules.

Icarus (I´-ka-rus): Son of Daedalus. He escaped Crete with his father by means of wings assembled with feathers and wax; he flew too close to the sun, the wax melted, and he fell into the sea.

Ida (Eye´-da): (1) Mountain near Troy. (2) Mountain in Crete. (3) Mother of Nisus.

Ilia (Il´-ee-a): Mother of Romulus and Remus by Mars.

Ilium (Il´-ee-um): A name for Troy.

Ilus (Ee'-lus): (1) A name for Ascanius, the son of Aeneas. (2) A founder of Troy. (3) A Rutulian allied with Turnus.

Io (I'-oh): Daughter of Inachus. Jupiter fell in love with her; she was changed into a cow and was tormented by Juno.

Iris (Eye'-ris): Goddess of the rainbow; messenger for Juno.

Iülus (Ee-oo'-los): A name for Ascanius, the son of Aeneas.

Jove (Johv): Name of Jupiter.

Juno (Joon'-oh): Daughter of Saturn; wife and sister of Jupiter. She is hostile toward the Trojans. Greek Hera.

Jupiter (Joo'-pit-er): Son of Saturn; husband of Juno; ruler of the gods. Greek Zeus.

Juturna (Joo-turn'-a): A nymph; sister of Turnus.

Laertes (Lay-er'-teez): Son of Arcesius; husband of Anticleia; father of Ulysses.

Laocoön (Lay-ak'-oh-on): A Trojan priest of Neptune. He was devoured by serpents for warning the Trojans about the Trojan Horse.

Laomedon (Lay-om'-ee-don): A king of Troy; father of Priam. He refused to repay Neptune and Apollo for building the walls of Troy.

Lar (Lar): A tutelary deity of the Roman household, associated especially with the hearth.

Latinus (La-tine'-us): Son of Faunus; father of Lavinia; King of Laurentium in Latium.

Latium (Lay'-she-um): Region in west-central Italy; ruled by King Latinus.

Latona (La-tone'-a): Mother of Apollo and Diana.

Lausus (Lau'-sus): Son of Mezentius; ally of Turnus.

Lavinia (La-vin'-ee-a): Daughter of Latinus and Amata. She was courted by Turnus but was destined to be the wife of Aeneas.

Leda (Lee'-da): Mother of Helen. Jupiter impregnated her while he assumed the form of a swan.

Lethe (Lee'-thee): River of forgetfulness in the Underworld. Whoever drank of this river lost memories.

Libya (Lib´-ee-a): Region of North Africa.

Lycurgus (Lie-kur´-jus): A Thracian king.

Manlius (Man´-lee-us): Marcus Manlius Torquatus Capitolinus; Roman general who successfully defended the citadel at Rome from the Gauls in 390 B.C.E.

Marcellus (Mar-sel´-us): (1) Marcus Claudius Marcellus; Roman general during the Second Punic War. (2) Nephew and son-in-law of Augustus: he died at a young age.

Mars: Son of Jupiter and Juno; the god of war. Greek Ares.

Memnon (Mem´-non): Son of Aurora and Tithonus; a king in Ethiopia; ally of the Trojans.

Menelaus (Me-ne-lay´-us): Son of Atreus and Aerope; brother of Agamemnon; husband of Helen; ruler of Sparta.

Mercury (Mer´-kyoor-ee): Son of Jupiter and Maia; the messenger god and guide of souls of the dead. Greek Hermes.

Messapus (Mes-ap´-us): Son of Neptune; ally of Turnus.

Mezentius (Mez-en´-tee-us): Father of Lausus. An exiled king who was an ally of Turnus.

Minerva (Min-er´-va): Daughter of Jupiter; said to have been born from his head; goddess of wisdom, crafts, and battle. Greek Athena.

Minos (Meye´-nos): King of Crete; husband of Pasiphaë. After his death he was a judge of souls in the Underworld.

Mnestheus (Men-es´-thee-us): A comrade of Aeneas.

Mycenae (Meye-see´-nee): City in the Peloponnesus of Greece ruled by Agamemnon.

Myrmidons (Meer´-mi-donz): People from Thessaly; the troops who follow Achilles.

Neoptolemus (Nee-op-tal´-a-mus): A name of Pyrrhus, son of Achilles, that means "young warrior."

Neptune (Nep´-tune): Son of Saturn and Rhea; brother of Jupiter; god of the sea. Greek Poseidon.

Nisus (Neye´-sus): Trojan son of Hyrtacus, lover of Euryalus.

Ocean: Son of Uranus and Earth; thought to be the river that encircled the earth.

Olympus (O-lim´-pus): Mountain in Thessaly thought to be the home of the gods.

Opis (O´-pis): A nymph; follower of Diana.

Orcus (Oar´-kus): Name of Pluto, the god of the Underworld. Or used to refer to the Underworld.

Orestes (O-res´-teez): Son of Agamemnon and Clytemnestra. He killed his mother and her lover in order to avenge the murder of his father.

Orion (O-reye´-on): Mythical hunter who, after his death, was transformed into a constellation. The setting of the constellation signaled stormy weather.

Orpheus (Oar´-fee-us): Mythical poet and singer who attempted to bring his wife, Eurydice, back from the Underworld after she died from a snakebite.

Ortygia (Oar-tij´-ee-a): (1) A name for the island of Delos. (2) A region of Syracuse in Sicily.

Palinurus (Pal-ee-noor´-us): The pilot of Aeneas' fleet.

Pallas (Pal´-as): (1) Name of Minerva. (2) An ancestor of Evander. (3) The son of Evander.

Pan: God of forests and shepherds; half-man, half-goat.

Pandarus (Pan´-dar-us): (1) A Trojan warrior with Aeneas. (2) A Trojan warrior at the battle of Troy who broke the truce between the two armies.

Parcae (Par´-keye): Three goddesses who spin the fate of human lives. Also called the Fates.

Paris (Pa´-ris): Son of Priam and Hecuba; brother of Hector. He took Helen from Menelaus at Sparta.

Pasiphaë (Pas-if´-a-ee): Wife of Minos; queen of Crete. She mated with a bull and produced the Minotaur.

Pentheus (Pen´-thee-us): A king of Thebes. He denied the worship of Bacchus and was killed by maenads, among whom was his mother.

Phaedra (Fay´-dra): Wife of Theseus. She fell in love with Hippolytus, her stepson; when he refused to return her love, she engineered his death and then committed suicide.

Phlegethon (Fleg´-a-thon): Fiery river in the Underworld.

Phoebus (Fee´-bus): Name of Apollo meaning "bright."

Pluto (Ploo´-toh): God of the Underworld. Greek Hades.

Portunus (Por-toon´-us): God of harbors.

Praeneste (Preye-nes´-tee): City in Latium.

Priam (Preye´-am): King of Troy; husband of Hecuba. He was killed during the fall of Troy.

Proserpina (Pros-er´-peen-a): Daughter of Ceres; wife of Pluto. Greek Persephone.

Pygmalion (Pig-mail´-ee-on): Brother of Dido. He killed Dido's husband.

Pyrrhus (Peer´-us): Son of Achilles; a Greek warrior in the Trojan War.

Quirinus (Kweer-in´-us): Italian god. This became the name of Romulus when he was deified.

Remus (Ree´-mus): (1) Son of Ilia; brother of Romulus. He was killed by Romulus. (2) A Rutulian.

Rhadamanthus (Rad-a-man´-thus): Brother of Minos. He became a judge in the Underworld after his death.

Romulus (Rom´-you-lus): Son of Ilia; brother of Remus. Legendary founder of Rome and descendant of Aeneas.

Rutulians (Roo-tul´-ee-anz): People in Italy ruled by Turnus.

Sarpedon (Sar-pee´-don): Son of Jupiter; leader of the Lycians in the Trojan War. Killed by Patroclus.

Saturn (Sat´-urn): Father of Jupiter and Juno. He was driven from Olympus by Jupiter. Greek Cronus.

Scylla (Sil´-a): Sea monster that devoured the passengers of passing ships.

Serestus (Ser-es´-tus): Comrade of Aeneas.

Sergestus (Ser-ges´-tus): Comrade of Aeneas.

Sibyl (Sib´-il): Prophetess at Cumae in Italy. Aeneas consulted her about entering the Underworld.

Sparta (Spar´-ta): City in the Peloponnesus of Greece; ruled by Menelaus.

Styx (Stix): River in the Underworld. The gods swore oaths to this river and could not break the oaths.

Sychaeus (See-keye´-us): Dido's husband who was murdered by her brother, Pygmalion.

Syrtes (Sir´-teez): Sandbanks off the northern shore of Africa that were dangerous for ships.

Tarchon (Tar´-kon): An Etruscan leader; ally to Aeneas.

Tarquin (Tar´-kwin): The name of two kings of Rome. The second of the two, Tarquin the Proud, was driven out of Rome by Lucius Junius Brutus.

Tartarus (Tar´-tar-us): Region of the Underworld in which sinners were punished.

Tatius (Tay´-tee-us): Titus Tatius; a king of the Sabines who fought against the Romans but later made peace with them and joined Romulus as an ally.

Teucer (Too´-ser): (1) A king of Troy from Crete. From his name the Trojans are called Teucrians. (2) A Greek who fought in the Trojan War and later founded Salamis in Cyprus.

Theseus (Thee´-see-us): Son of Aegeas; a king of Athens. Killed the Minotaur. Attempted to help his comrade Pirithöus carry Proserpina from the Underworld.

Tiber (Teye´-ber): River in Italy near which Rome was founded.

Tibur (Teye´-bur): City in Latium.

Tithonus (Tith-oh´-nus): Son of Laomedon; husband of Aurora. He was granted eternal life but did not ask for eternal youth.

Triton (Treye´-ton): Son of Neptune; a sea-god.

Trivia (Triv´-ee-a): Name referring to Hecate and Diana as goddesses of crossroads.

Troy: City in northwestern Asia Minor ruled by Priam. It was the area of focus in Homer's *Iliad* and the city from which Aeneas fled when it was destroyed.

Turnus (Turn´-us): Son of Daunus and Venilia; king of the Rutulians. He was Aeneas' rival for Lavinia and led the armies opposing Aeneas in Italy.

Ulysses (Yoo-lis´-eez): A Greek leader in Homer's *Iliad* and the central character in Homer's *Odyssey*. Greek Odysseus.

Venus (Vee´-nus): Daughter of Jupiter and Dione; goddess of love and beauty. Mother of Aeneas by Anchises. Greek Aphrodite.

Vesta (Ves´-ta): Goddess of the hearth.

Vulcan (Vul´-can): Son of Juno; god of the forge and fire. He made armor for Aeneas. Greek Hephaestus.

Xanthus (Zan´-thus): River near Troy.

Zephyrus (Zef´-eer-us): The West Wind.

Suggestions for Further Reading

Fairclough, H. R. *Virgil*. 2 vols. Loeb Classical Library. Harvard University Press. Cambridge, Mass., 1978.

Mynors, R. A. B. *P. Vergili Maronis Opera*. Claredon Press. Oxford, 1972.

Page, T. E. *Aeneid*. 2 vols. Macmillan. London, 1900.

Williams, R. D. *The Aeneid of Virgil*. 2 vols. Macmillan. London, 1973.

Maffeo Vegio: Short Epics. Edited and translated by Michael Putnam. Harvard University Press (The I Tatti Renaissance Library). Cambridge, Mass., 2004.

Boyle, A. J., ed. *Roman Epic*. Routledge. London, 1993.

Broch, Hermann. *The Death of Virgil*. Translated by Jean Starr Untermeyer. Vintage Books. New York, 1995.

Cairns, Francis. *Virgil's Augustan Epic*. Cambridge University Press. New York, 1989.

Clausen, Wendell. *Virgil's Aeneid and the Tradition of Hellenistic Poetry*. University of California Press. Berkeley, 1987.

Commager, Steele, ed. *Virgil: A Collection of Critical Essays*. Prentice-Hall. Englewood Cliffs, N.J., 1966.

Dyson, Julia T. *King of the Wood: The Sacrificial Victor in Virgil's Aeneid*. University of Oklahoma Press. Norman, 2001.

Farrell, Joseph. "Which *Aeneid* in Whose Nineties." *Vergilius* 36 (1990): 74–80.

Feeney, D. C. *The Gods in Epic: Poets and Critics of the Classical Tradition*. Oxford University Press. New York, 1991.

Gransden, K. W. *Virgil's Iliad: An Essay on Epic Narrative*. Cambridge University Press. New York, 1984.

Gurval, Robert Alan. *Actium and Augustus: The Politics and Emotions of Civil War*. University of Michigan Press. Ann Arbor, 1995.

Hardie, Philip R. *Virgil's Aeneid: Cosmos and Imperium*. Clarendon Press. Oxford, 1986.

———, ed. *Virgil. Critical Assessments of Classical Authors*. Routledge. London, 1999.

Harrison, S. J. *Oxford Readings in Vergil's Aeneid*. Oxford University Press. New York, 1990.

Heinze, Richard. *Virgil's Epic Technique*. Translated by Hazel Harvey, David Harvey, and Fred Robertson. University of California Press. Berkeley, 1993.

Hinds, Stephen. *Allusion and Intertext: Dynamics of Appropriation in Roman Poetry.* Cambridge University Press. New York, 1998.

Horsfall, N. M. *A Companion to the Study of Vergil.* E. J. Brill. Leiden, 1995.

Jenkyns, R. *Virgil's Experience: Nature and History, Times, Names, and Places.* Oxford University Press. New York, 1998.

Johnson, W. R. *Darkness Visible: A Study of Vergil's Aeneid.* University of California Press. Berkeley, 1976.

Keith, A. M. *Engendering Rome: Women in Latin Epic.* Cambridge University Press. Cambridge, 2000.

Lyne, R. O. A. M. *Words and the Poet: Characteristic Techniques of Style in Vergil's "Aeneid."* Oxford University Press. New York, 1989.

Mackie, C. J. *The Characterisation of Aeneas.* Scottish Academic. Edinburgh, 1988.

Martindale, Charles, ed. *The Cambridge Companion to Virgil.* Cambridge University Press. New York, 1997.

McKay, Alexander G. *Vergil's Italy.* Adams and Dart. Bath, 1971.

Monti, Richard C. *The Dido Episode and the Aeneid: Roman Social and Political Values in the Epic.* E. J. Brill. Leiden, 1981.

Most, Glenn W., and Sarah Spence, eds. *Re-presenting Virgil: Materiali e discussioni No. 52: Special Issue in Honor of Michael C. J. Putnam.* Istituti editoriali e poligrafici internazionali. Pisa, 2004.

Nelis, D. *Vergil's Aeneid and the Argonautica of Apollonius Rhodius.* Francis Cairns. Leeds, 2001.

O'Hara, James J. *Death and the Optimistic Prophecy in Vergil's "Aeneid."* Princeton University Press. Princeton, N.J., 1990.

———. *True Names: Vergil and the Alexandrian Tradition of Etymological Wordplay.* University of Michigan Press. Ann Arbor, 1996.

Otis, Brooks. *Virgil: A Study in Civilized Poetry.* Clarendon Press. Oxford, 1963.

Perkell, Christine, ed. *Reading Vergil's Aeneid: An Interpretive Guide.* University of Oklahoma Press. Norman, 1999.

Pöschl, Viktor. *The Art of Vergil: Image and Symbol in the Aeneid.* Translated by Gerda Seligson. University of Michigan Press. Ann Arbor, 1962.

Putnam, Michael C. J. *The Poetry of the Aeneid: Four Studies in Imaginative Unity and Design.* Harvard University Press. Cambridge, Mass., 1965.

———. *Virgil's Aeneid: Interpretation and Influence.* University of North Carolina Press. Chapel Hill, 1995.

————. *Virgil's Epic Designs: Ekphrasis in the Aeneid.* Yale University Press. New Haven, 1998.

Quinn, Stephanie, ed. *Why Vergil? A Collection of Interpretations.* Bolchazy-Carducci. Wauconda, Ill., 2000.

Schmidt, Ernst A. "The Meaning of Vergil's *Aeneid:* American and German Approaches." *Classical World* 94.2, 145–71. Classical Association of the Atlantic States. New York, 2001.

Segal, C. P. "*Aeternum per saecula nomen,* The Golden Bough and the Tragedy of History," Part I, *Arion* 4 (1965): 615–57; Part II, *Arion* 5 (1966): 34–72.

Spence, Sarah, ed. *Poets and Critics Read Vergil.* Yale University Press. New Haven, 2001.

Stahl, Hans-Peter, ed. *Virgil's Aeneid: Augustan Epic and Political Context.* Duckworth. London, 1998.

Thomas, Richard F. *Reading Virgil and His Texts*: Studies in Intertextuality. University of Michigan Press. Ann Arbor, 1999.

————. *Virgil and the Augustan Reception.* Cambridge University Press. Cambridge, 2001.

Wigodsky, Michael. *Vergil and Early Latin Poetry.* F. Steiner. Wiesbaden, 1972.

Wilhelm, Robert M., and Howard Jones, eds. *The Two Worlds of the Poet: New Perspectives on Vergil.* Wayne State University Press. Detroit, 1992.

Williams, Gordon. *Technique and Ideas in the Aeneid.* Yale University Press. New Haven, 1983.

Wiltshire, Susan Ford. *Public and Private in Vergil's Aeneid.* University of Massachusetts Press. Amherst, 1989.

Ziolkowski, Theodore. *Virgil and the Moderns.* Princeton University Press. Princeton, N.J., 1993.